THE NEW
INTERNATIONAL
WEBSTER'S
POCKET
THESAURUS
OF THE ENGLISH LANGUAGE

TRIDENT
PRESS
INTERNATIONAL

Published by

Trident Press International

1997 EDITION

ISBN 1-888-777-16-8 Deluxe Edition
ISBN1-888-777-26-5 Hardcover Edition
ISBN1-888-777-34-6 Paperback Edition

Printed in the United States of America

aback *adv.* **BACKWARD:** back, behind, rearward; **UNEXPECTED:** suddenly, unawares, unexpectedly

abandon *n.* **ENTHUSIASM:** impetuosity, spontaneity; **IMMORALITY:** shamelessness, wantonness

abandon *v.* **GIVE UP:** forgo, forswear, quit, relinquish; **DESERT:** forsake, leave, resign, vacate

abandonment *n.* abdication, renunciation, repudiation, resignation, surrender

abase *v.* debase, degrade, disgrace, dishonor, humble, humiliate

abased *adj.* degraded, disgraced, dishonored, humbled, humiliated, lowered

abasement *n.* degradation, deterioration, disgrace, dishonor, groveling, humiliation, lowering, shame

abash *v.* confound, confuse, disconcert, embarrass, humble, humiliate, mortify, shame

abashed *adj.* ashamed, chagrined, confused

abasing *adj.* abusive, insulting, offensive

abate *v.* **LESSEN:** decline, decrease diminish, ease, ebb, fade, lower, moderate, slacken, relieve, slow; **DISCOUNT:** allow, deduct, rebate, remit, subtract

abatement *n.* **LESSENING:** alleviation, decrease, mitigation, slackening, subsidence; **ENDING:** cessation, remission, suppression, termination

abbreviate *v.* abridge, condense, contract, cut, reduce, shorten, truncate

abbreviation *n.* abridgement, brief, compendium, condensation, shortening, truncation

abdicate *v.* abandon, cede, disavow, disclaim, disown, relinquish, renounce, resign, secede

abdomen *n.* belly, breadbasket, gut, midsection, paunch, potbelly, stomach, tummy

abduct *v.* capture, kidnap, seize, shanghai

abecedarian *n.* beginner, novice

abed *adj.* asleep, resting

aberrant *adj.* DEVIATING: divergent, errant, irregular, straying; ODD: abnormal, peculiar, queer, strange, unnatural, unusual, weird

aberrational *adj.* curious, odd, peculiar, strange

abet *v.* advance, aid, assist, back, condone, favor, further, help, promote, sanction, second, support

abettor *n.* accessory, accomplice, ally, associate, cohort, confederate, conspirator

abeyance *n.* cessation, deferral, discontinuance, hiatus, moratorium, suspension

abhor *v.* despise, detest, disgust, hate, loathe

abhorrence *n.* aversion, disgust, dislike, distaste, hatred, loathing, horror, repugnance

abhorrent *adj.* abominable, despicable, detestable, disgusting, loathsome, offensive, nauseating, odious, repugnant, repulsive, revolting, shocking, vile

abidance *n.* compliance, continuance

abide *v.* DWELL: inhabit, live, reside, stay; WAIT: attend, await, remain, stay, tarry; ENDURE: allow, bear, remain, stand, suffer

abiding *adj.* enduring, lasting, permanent, steadfast

ability *n.* aptitude, bent, capability, capacity, competence, dexterity, expertise, facility, faculty, knack, proficiency, qualification, skill, skillfulness, talent

abject *adj.* base, contemptible, degrading, despicable, disheartening, ignominious, miserable, poor, sorry

abjection, abjectness *n.* churlishness, degradation, humiliation, meanness, nastiness

abjuration *n.* abnegation, denial, disavowal, rejection, renouncement, renunciation

abjure *v.* forswear, recant, recall, renounce, retract, withdraw

ablaze *adj.* **BURNING:** aflame, blazing, fiery, flaming; **FERVENT:** ardent, eager, excited, exhilarated, intense

able *adj.* **CAPABLE:** adequate, apt, competent, efficient, fit, qualified; **SKILLFUL:** accomplished, adroit, dexterous, expert, gifted, ingenious, proficient, talented

able–bodied *adj.* fit, healthy, robust, strong

abloom *adj.* blossoming, flowering, sprouting

ablution *n.* cleansing, purification, purging, washing

abnegation *n.* abjuration, denial, disavowal, rejection, renouncement, renunciation, self–denial

abnormal *adj.* aberrant, anomalous, curious, deviant, irregular, odd, peculiar, unnatural

abnormality *n.* anomaly, curiosity, irregularity, malformation, nonconformity, peculiarity, perversion

abode *n.* domicile, dwelling, habitat, house, residence

abolish *v.* abrogate, annul, cancel, eliminate, end, eradicate, erase, extinguish, nullify, obliterate

abolishment *n.* annulment, cancellation, elimination, eradication, nullification

abolition *n.* annulment, cancellation, dissolution, elimination, eradication, repeal, revocation

abominable *adj.* abhorrent, contemptible, despicable, detestable, disgusting, hateful, horrible, loathsome, offensive, repugnant

abominate *v.* abhor, despise, detest, hate, loathe

abomination *n.* **HORROR:** loathing, revulsion; **WICKEDNESS:** amorality, depravity, evil, immorality

aboriginal *adj.* domestic, indigenous, local, native, original, primitive

abort *v.* annul, cancel, destroy, fail, interrupt, miscarry, nullify, scrap, stop, terminate

abortion *n.* CESSATION: cancellation, interruption, termination; MONSTROSITY: abnormality

abortive *adj.* fruitless, futile, ineffectual, unavailing

abound *v.* overflow, pour, swarm, swell, teem

abounding *adj.* abundant, lavish, luxuriant, plentiful

about *adv.* CONCERNING: referencing, regarding; APPROXIMATELY: almost, around, close, near, nigh

above *adv.* HIGHER: atop, beyond, over, overhead; GREATER: preeminent, superior, surpassing

aboveboard *adj.* candid, frank, guileless, honest, open, overt, sincere, straightforward

abradant *adj.* annoying, harsh, nasty, offensive

abrade *v.* WEAR: chafe, corrode, erode, grind, rub, scrape; IRRITATE : anger, annoy, bother, gall, irk

abrading *n.* abrasion, attrition, erosion

abrasion *n.* blemish, bruise, cut, scrape, scratch

abrasive *adj.* annoying, exasperating, grating, harsh, jarring, nasty, offensive, rasping, shrill, strident

abreast *adj., adv.* BESIDE: against, aligned; INFORMED: apprised, familiar

abridge *v.* abstract, compress, condense, curtail, cut, decrease, diminish, lessen, reduce, restrict, shorten

abrogate *v.* abolish, annul, cancel, invalidate, nullify, repeal, rescind, revoke, void

abrupt *adj.* SUDDEN: quick, sharp, unexpected; CURT: blunt, boorish, brusque, discourteous, hasty, impatient, rude; STEEP: craggy, hilly, precipitous, sheer

abruptness *n.* brevity, curtness, shortness, terseness

abscessed *adj.* inflamed, painful, ulcerated

abscission *n.* deletion, eradication, excision, removal

abscond *v.* bolt, depart, escape, flee

absconder *n.* charlatan, cheat, rogue, swindler

absence *n.* **LACK:** dearth, default, defect, deficiency, need, want; **AWAY:** nonattendance, truancy

absentee *n.* defector, delinquent, deserter, fugitive, escapee, runaway, truant

absent-minded *adj.* forgetful, oblivious, preoccupied, unmindful

absolute *adj.* **PERFECT:** certain, definite, faultless, ideal, sure, unconditional, unquestionable, utter, whole; **AUTHORITARIAN:** autocratic, despotic, dictatorial, imperious, peremptory, strict, tyrannical

absolution *n.* acquittal, clearance, exoneration, vindication

absolvable *adj.* excusable, forgivable, inconsequential, justifiable, minor, pardonable, permissible, venial

absolve *v.* acquit, clear, discharge, excuse, exonerate, forgive, free, justify, liberate, pardon, release

absorb *v.* **INCORPORATE:** amalgamate, assimilate, consume, devour, engulf; **ENGROSS:** engage, employ, occupy; **UNDERSTAND:** assimilate, grasp, learn, sense

absorbed *adj.* **INCORPORATED:** assimilated, digested, dissolved, permeated; **ENGROSSED:** enthralled, immersed, intent, involved, preoccupied, rapt

absorbent *adj.* permeable, penetrable, porous, spongy

absorbing *adj.* engaging, enthralling, exciting, fascinating, interesting

absorption *n.* absent-mindedness, preoccupation, reflection, reverie

abstain *v.* avoid, decline, eschew, forgo, refrain, shun

abstinence *n.* avoidance, forbearance, moderation, self-denial, sobriety, temperance

abstinent *adj.* abstemious, continent, moderate

abstract *adj.* THEORETICAL: conceptual, ideal, hypothetical; ISOLATED: apart, separate, special, unrelated; COMPLEX: complicated, deep, difficult, obscure

abstract *n.* abridgment, brief, compendium, condensation, digest, distillation, outline, summary

abstract *v.* REMOVE: disjoin, dissociate, isolate, separate, withdraw; CONDENSE: abbreviate, abridge, digest, distill, edit, outline, summarize

abstruse *adj.* complex, difficult, intricate, involved

absurd *adj.* asinine, foolish, inane, irrational, ludicrous, preposterous, ridiculous, silly

abundance *n.* bounty, extravagance, fullness, profusion, prosperity, wealth

abundant *adj.* abounding, copious, flowing, fruitful, opulent, plentiful, prodigal, profuse, prolific, teeming

abuse *n.* misuse, defilement, desecration, mistreatment, profanation, subversion, violation

abuse *v.* MISUSE: attack, desecrate, harm, hurt, injure, maltreat, mistreat, wrong; BERATE: assail, denounce, disparage, insult, malign, reproach, revile, scold

abusive *adj.* AGONIZING: insufferable, intolerable, painful, unbearable, unendurable; DISCOURTEOUS: rude, sarcastic, slanderous, truculent, vituperative

abut *v.* adjoin, border, touch, verge

abysmal *adj.* bottomless, deep, immeasurable, profound, unfathomable

abyss *n.* chasm, gorge, gulf, hole, perdition

academic *adj.* SCHOLARLY: collegiate, erudite, learned, lettered, literary, scholastic, schooled; TRADITIONAL: conventional, conservative, established, formalistic; THEORETICAL: conjectural, speculative, suppositional

academician *n.* intellectual, egghead, scholar

academics *n.* courses, studies

academy *n.* college, conservatory, school

accede *v.* acquiesce, agree, allow, assent, comply, consent, grant, permit, sanction

accelerate *v.* hasten, expedite, quicken, throttle

acceleration *n.* dispatch, hastening, quickening

accent *n.* **MODULATION:** beat, inflection, emphasis, rhythm; **SIGNIFICANCE:** importance, prominence

accent, accentuate *v.* emphasize, stress, underscore

accept *v.* **RECEIVE:** embrace, take, welcome; **ACQUIESCE:** accede, acknowledge, allow, assent, concede, concur, grant; **BELIEVE:** affirm, hold, maintain, trust; **UNDERSTAND:** appreciate, conclude, construe

acceptable *adj.* adequate, agreeable, permissible, pleasant, pleasing, satisfactory, sufficient

acceptance *n.* acknowledgement, agreement, assent, capitulation, concurrence, consent, recognition

accepted *adj.* **ACCREDITED:** accustomed, acknowledged, allowed, recognized; **SETTLED:** admitted, affirmed, endorsed

accessible *adj.* approachable, attainable, available, convenient, obtainable, reachable

accessory *adj.* added, contributing, extra

accessory *n.* abettor, accomplice

accident *n.* **MISHAP:** casualty, misadventure, misfortune, pileup, wreck; **CHANCE:** coincidence, fortune

accidental *adj.* **UNEXPECTED:** casual, chance, fortuitous, odd, random, unintentional, unplanned; **INCIDENTAL:** insignificant, minor, nonessential, secondary, subsidiary

acclaim *n.* applause, approval, enthusiasm, fame,

plaudits, praise, recognition

acclaim *v.* applaud, celebrate, commend, laud, praise

acclamation *n.* acclaim, accolades, applause, approval, jubilation, plaudits, praise

acclimate *v.* accommodate, adapt, adjust, conform

acclimation *n.* adaptation, adjustment, conformity

acclimatize *v.* acclimate, adapt, adjust, conform

acclivity *n.* ascent, incline, slope, upgrade

accolade *n.* acknowledgement, esteem, praise, tribute

accommodate *v.* **AID:** abet, assist, oblige, provide, serve, supply; **ENTERTAIN:** board, house, lodge, quarter; **ADJUST:** adapt, conform, fit, harmonize, reconcile, temper; **RECEIVE:** contain, have, hold

accommodating *adj.* kind, gracious, helpful, neighborly, obliging

accompaniment *n.* addition, accessory, adjunct, appendage, appurtenance

accompany *v.* **ATTEND:** chaperon, convey, escort, follow, join, see, show, usher; **APPEND:** augment, complement, complete, enhance, supplement

accomplice *n.* accessory, affiliate, associate, confederate, conspirator, partner

accomplish *v.* achieve, attain, complete, do, effect, execute, fulfill, make, manage, perform, realize

accomplished *adj.* skillful, able, cultivated, cultured, expert, proficient, refined, talented

accomplishment *n.* achievement, attainment, exploit, feat, fulfillment, success

accord *n.* agreement, conformity, consent, harmony, peace, unanimity

accord *v.* **AGREE:** accommodate, adapt, affirm, assent, coincide, concur, correspond, harmonize, reconcile;

BESTOW: allow, deign, grant, concede, yield

accordance *n.* accord, agreement, coincidence, concordance, conformity, harmony

accost *v.* address, approach, confront, face, greet, halt, meet, proposition, solicit, waylay

account *n.* **NARRATIVE:** anecdote, chronicle, description, explanation, exposé, journal, narration, recital, report, story, tale; **REASON:** consideration, excuse, grounds, motive; **WORTH:** advantage, benefit, consideration, estimation, importance, profit, reputation

account *v.* **EXPLAIN:** describe, justify, rationalize; **REGARD:** consider, count, credit, deem, estimate, hold, judge, reckon, think

accountable *adj.* answerable, culpable, liable, responsible

accredit *v.* certify, endorse, pass, ratify, recognize, sanction, support, uphold, validate, warrant

accrual, accruement *n.* accumulation, expansion, growth, increase, recovery, return, yield

accumulate *v.* accrue, amass, collect, cumulate, gather, heap, garner, increase, stockpile, store

accuracy *n.* exactness, precision, sureness

accurate *n.* careful, correct, exact, factual, faithful, flawless, precise, proper, right, true, unerring

accursed *adj.* doomed, bewitched, condemned, damned, haunted, ill–fated

accusation *n.* allegation, charge, complaint, denunciation, indictment, insinuation, slur, smear

accuse *v.* arraign, arrest, blame, charge, denounce, implicate, impute, incriminate, indict, involve

accustom *v.* familiarize, habituate, inure, season

ace *n.* champion, expert, master, specialist

acerbate *n.* heighten, increase, intensify, worsen

acerbic *adj.* bitter, harsh, rough, sharp, sour

ache *n.* agony, pain, pang, spasm, twinge

ache *v.* hurt, pain, suffer, throb

achievable *adj.* attainable, feasible, obtainable

achieve *v.* accomplish, effect, fulfill, finish, reach, attain, gain, get, realize, secure

achy *adj.* aching, bruised, painful

acid *adj.* biting, cutting, sarcastic, sardonic, satirical, scornful, sharp, vitriolic

acknowledge *v.* admit, agree, allow, appreciate, approve, avow, concede, confess, confirm, declare, endorse, grant, ratify, recognize, reply, respond

acknowledgment *n.* **ACCEPTANCE:** affirmation, corroboration, recognition; **RESPONSE:** answer, call, greeting, letter, nod, note, reaction, reply, thanks

acme *n.* apex, peak, summit, top, zenith

acolyte *n.* aide, assistant, helper, subordinate

acquaint *v.* inform, accustom, advise, familiarize, reconnoiter, introduce, present

acquaintance *n.* friend, associate, colleague, companion, crony, pal

acquainted *adj.* conversant, familiar, introduced

acquiesce *v.* assent, accede, accept, agree, bend, comply, concur, consent, rest, submit, yield

acquire *v.* appropriate, attain, earn, gain, get, obtain, procure, secure

acquisitive *adj.* avaricious, grasping, greedy

acquisitiveness *n.* covetousness, greed

acquit *v.* absolve, exonerate, pardon, release

acquittal *n.* absolution, amnesty, deliverance, discharge, dismissal, exoneration, pardon, vindication

acreage *n.* grounds, land, property, spread, terrain

acrid *adj.* astringent, biting, bitter, caustic, harsh

acrimonious *adj.* acerbic, caustic, irascible, testy

acropolis *n.* bastion, citadel, blockhouse, fort, fortification, redoubt, stronghold

across *adv.* athwart, crosswise, over, transversely

act *n.* **EXPLOIT:** accomplishment, deed, feat, performance; **DECREE:** edict, law, order, resolution, statute, writ; **PERFORMANCE:** routine, sketch, stint, turn

act *v.* **DO:** accomplish, conduct, operate; **SUBSTITUTE:** represent, officiate, serve; **PERFORM:** appear, dramatize, impersonate, pretend, play, simulate

acting *adj.* deputy, officiating, surrogate, temporary

acting *n.* depiction, performance, role impersonation

action *n.* **MOTION:** activity, maneuver, movement, performance; **FEAT:** accomplishment, exercise, transaction; **BEHAVIOR:** conduct, response; **MACHINE:** apparatus, contrivance, mechanism; **CONFLICT:** battle, contest, encounter, engagement, skirmish; **LAWSUIT:** case, claim, litigation, proceeding, process, suit

activate *v.* animate, begin, initiate, stimulate

active *adj.* animated, busy, dynamic, energetic, functioning, industrious, lively, living, mobile, moving, operative, spirited, tireless, working

actively *adv.* energetically, spryly, vigorously

activist *n.* agitator, firebrand, malcontent, radical, reformer, revolutionary

activity *n.* action, motion, movement, pastime

actor *n.* artist, entertainer, impersonator, mime, performer, player, thespian, trouper

actual *adj.* **FACTUAL:** certain, definite, genuine, sure, true; **EXISTING:** concrete, material, real, tangible

actually *adv.* indeed, really, truly

actuate *v.* drive, impel, move, propel, push

acuity *n.* discernment, discrimination, insight, perception, perspicacity, sharpness, shrewdness

acumen *n.* cleverness, discernment, insight, intelligence, keenness, sagacity, shrewdness

acute *adj.* **POINTED:** keen, sharp; **IMPORTANT:** critical, crucial, intense, serious; **PERCEPTIVE:** astute, clever, discerning, ingenious, intelligent, keen, penetrating

adage *n.* cliché, maxim, motto, proverb, saying, slogan

adamant *adj.* firm, fixed, insistent, obstinate, resolute, set, steadfast, stubborn, unbending, unyielding

adapt *v.* acclimatize, accustom, adjust, conform, fashion, fit, modify, reconcile, shape, tailor, temper

adaptable *adj.* docile, flexible, pliable, pliant, tractable, versatile

adaptation *n.* **ACCLIMATIZATION:** acculturation, conversion, revising; **DEVICE:** apparatus, appliance, contraption, contrivance, gadget, mechanism

add *v.* **AFFIX:** annex, append, attach, augment, connect, supplement, unite: **CALCULATE:** compute, figure, increase, sum, tally, total

addendum *n.* addition, adjunct, annexation, appendix, attachment, augmentation, codicil, rider

addict *n.* buff, devotee, fan, hound, junkie, lover

addicted *adj.* chronic, dependent, fanatical, fixated, habituated, hooked, inclined, obsessed

addictive *adj.* compelling, irresistible, overpowering

additional *adj.* added, auxiliary, collateral, extra

addle *v.* cloud, confound, confuse, obfuscate

addled *adj.* befuddled, bewildered, confounded, confused, dazed, disconcerted, flustered, muddled

add–on *n.* improvement, modernization, supplement

address *n.* **SPEECH:** discourse, lecture, oration, sermon; **LOCATION:** dwelling, house, lodging, residence

adept *adj.* able, capable, competent, expert, proficient, skilled

adequacy *n.* acceptability, plenty, sufficiency

adequate *adj.* ample, enough, satisfactory, suitable

adhere *v.* **STICK:** attach, cleave, cling, fasten, hold; **CONFORM:** comply, follow, heed, obey

adherent *n.* advocate, devotee, disciple, fan, follower

adhesive *n.* cement, epoxy, glue, mucilage, tape

adjacent *adj.* abutting, adjoining, bordering, close, contiguous, near, nearby, neighboring, touching

adjoin *v.* abut, append, border, butt, meet, neighbor, touch, verge

adjourn *v.* defer, discontinue, dissolve, recess, interrupt, postpone, suspend

adjournment *n.* break, continuance, deferment, intermission, pause, postponement, recess

adjudicate *v.* arbitrate, decide, mediate, settle

adjudication *n.* determination, judgment, finding, ruling, verdict, sentence

adjudicator *n.* arbiter, judge, mediator, referee

adjunct *n.* accessory, addition, attachment

adjure *v.* ask, appeal, beg, beseech, entreat, implore, petition, plead, request, supplicate, urge

adjust *v.* adapt, alter, calibrate, correct, modify, regulate, tune, temper, true

adjustable *adj.* flexible, malleable, tractable, variable

adjustment *n.* **ALTERATION:** calibration, modification, setting; **COMPENSATION:** allotment, compromise, reconciliation, redress, remuneration, settlement

adjutant *n.* aide, assistant, attaché, deputy, helper

ad–lib *adj.* improvised, spontaneous, unrehearsed

administer *v.* **MANAGE:** control, direct, execute, oversee, supervise; **DISPENSE:** distribute, give, parcel

administrative *adj.* bureaucratic, executive, governmental, jurisdictional, official, managerial

admirable *adj.* commendable, excellent, meritorious, noble, praiseworthy, splendid, superb, worthy

admiration *n.* affection, approbation, awe, esteem, fondness, regard, respect, veneration, wonder

admire *v.* celebrate, esteem, honor, regard, respect, revere, venerate

admirer *n.* **FAN:** devotee, enthusiast, follower, patron, supporter; **BEAU:** adorer, suitor, sweetheart, wooer

admissible *adj.* allowable, lawful, legal, legitimate

admission *n.* **ACCESS:** admittance, entrée, entrance, entry, pass, ticket; **AFFIRMATION:** acknowledgment, confession, confirmation, disclosure, divulgence

admit *v.* **ACCOMMODATE:** allow, grant, permit; **AFFIRM:** concede, confess, disclose, divulge, expose, reveal

admittance *n.* access, admission, entrance

admonish *v.* caution, counsel, exhort, reprove, warn

admonition *n.* **COUNSEL:** advice, caution, warning; **REBUKE:** censure, reprimand, reproach, scolding

ado *n.* bother, bustle, commotion, fuss, stir

adolescence *n.* puberty, pubescence, teens, youth

adolescent *adj.* childish, immature, juvenile, youthful

adolescent *n.* minor, teen, teenager, youth

adopt *v.* **APPROPRIATE:** assume, borrow, espouse, utilize; **RATIFY:** approve, confirm, endorse, sanction

adorable *adj.* charming, cute, darling, delightful, enchanting, lovable, precious, sweet

adoration *n.* devotion, idolatry, veneration, worship

adore *v.* cherish, esteem, idolize, love, revere, venerate, worship

adorer *n.* admirer, beau, suitor, sweetheart, wooer

adorn *v.* beautify, bedeck, decorate, embellish, garnish, festoon, ornament, trim

adroit *adj.* adept, dexterous, expert, handy, quick, resourceful, skillful

adulation *n.* adoration, glorification, laudation, praise, worship

adult *adj.* developed, grown, mature, ripe

adulteration *n.* contamination, pollution, taint

adulterer *n.* debaucher, lecher, libertine, philanderer, rake, reprobate

adulterous *adj.* dissolute, immoral, licentious, lustful

adultery *n.* cuckoldry, fornication, infidelity

adulthood *n.* majority, maturity

advance *v.* **PROGRESS:** go, move, proceed, update, upgrade; **BROACH:** introduce, propose, present, suggest; **PROMOTE:** encourage, foster, propound; **OFFER:** lend

advanced *adj.* aged, elderly, futuristic, precocious, radical, seasoned, unconventional

advancement *n.* betterment, elevation, preference, progression, promotion

advantage *n.* benefit, edge, gain, leverage, profit

adventure *n.* undertaking, experience, exploit

advantageous *adj.* beneficial, expedient, favorable, lucrative, profitable, worthwhile

advent *n.* appearance, arrival, coming

adventure *n.* escapade, experience, exploit, feat, happening, quest, undertaking, venture

adventuresome, adventurous *adj.* bold, courageous,

daring, enterprising, gallant

adversarial *adj.* antagonistic, hostile, unfriendly

adversary *n.* antagonist, enemy, foe, opponent

adverse *adj.* antagonistic, conflicting, contrary, detrimental, hostile, negative, unfavorable, unfriendly

adversity *n.* affliction, distress, hardship, misery, misfortune, sorrow, trouble

advertise *v.* broadcast, communicate, divulge, exhibit, expose, proclaim, promote, publicize, show

advertisement, advertising *n.* blurb, broadside, endorsement, handbill, pitch, poster, plug

advice *n.* counsel, guidance, lesson, suggestion

advisable *adj.* advantageous, desirable, expedient, politic, prudent, sensible, sound

advise *v.* admonish, caution, counsel, consult, forewarn, inform, notify, recommend

advised *adj.* cautious, circumspect, deliberate

adviser, advisor *n.* attorney, consultant, counsel, counselor, elder, expert, guide, instructor, lawyer, mentor, patriarch, teacher, tutor

advocacy *n.* adoption, belief, espousal, promotion

advocate *v.* advance, bolster, champion, further, promote, recommend, support

aesthete *n.* collector, connoisseur, dilettante

aesthetic, aesthetical *adj.* artistic, discriminating, elegant, pleasing, polished, refined, tasteful

afar *adj.* abroad, distant, remote

affable *adj.* agreeable, amiable, civil, cordial, courteous, friendly, gracious, obliging, pleasant, sociable

affair *n.* CONCERN: business, circumstance, pursuit; ROMANCE: liaison, relationship, rendezvous, tryst; GATHERING: event, function, party

affect *v.* **INFLUENCE:** alter, change, modify, sway, stir, transform; **PRETEND:** assume, dissemble, fake, feign

affectation *n.* artificiality, pose, pretense, show

affection *n.* devotion, fondness, friendship, liking, love, regard, respect, tenderness, warmth

affectionate *adj.* attentive, devoted, loving, tender

affianced *adj.* betrothed, pledged, plighted

affidavit *n.* affirmation, deposition, oath, testimony

affiliate *n.* agent, associate, colleague, partner

affiliation *n.* alliance, association, coalition, confederation, connection, federation, pact, union

affinity *n.* **ATTRACTION:** affection, closeness, fondness; **SIMILARITY:** correspondence, likeness, resemblance

affirm *v.* **DECLARE:** assert, claim, maintain, state, swear, testify; **CONFIRM:** approve, endorse, ratify

affirmative *adj.* concurring, confirming, endorsing, supporting

affix *v.* add, append, attach, bind, connect, fasten

afflict *v.* ail, beset, distress, hurt, torment

affliction *n.* distress, hardship, misfortune, suffering

affluence *n.* abundance, prosperity, wealth

afford *v.* allow, grant, permit, provide, sustain

affront *v.* insult, abuse, offend, provoke, slight

aficionado *n.* buff, devotee, fan, hound, lover

afield *adv.* amiss, astray, awry

afoot *adj.* **WALKING:** hiking, marching; **FORTHCOMING:** brewing, happening, hatching, progressing

aforementioned *adj.* earlier, former, preceding, prior

afraid *adj.* anxious, apprehensive, disquieted, fearful, frightened, scared, shocked, terrified

after *adj., adv.* afterward, following, later, subsequent

aftereffect *n.* consequence, outcome, result

afterthought *n.* addendum, addition, appendix

agape *adj.* **ASTONISHED:** aghast appalled confounded dismayed horrified shocked; **AJAR:** open

age *n.* **PERIOD:** eon, epoch, era, generation, time; **STAGE:** adolescence, adulthood, childhood, infancy

age *v.* decline, deteriorate, develop, mature, mellow, ripen, season

ageless *adj.* classic, timeless, traditional

agenda *n.* aims, goals, program, calendar, list, plan

agent *n.* **REPRESENTATIVE:** ambassador, attorney, broker, factor, intermediary, proxy, surrogate; **MEDIUM:** agency, cause, instrument, means, method, vehicle

agglomerate *adj.* clustered, collected, jumbled

agglomerate *v.* amass, concentrate, consolidate

aggrandize *v.* **ENLARGE:** amplify, expand, extend, increase; **ACCLAIM:** boast, exaggerate, extol, praise

aggravate *v.* **WORSEN:** deepen, exacerbate, heighten, increase, intensify; **PROVOKE:** anger, annoy, exasperate, irritate

aggravating *adj.* bothersome, disquieting, disturbing

aggravation *n.* **AFFLICTION :** annoyance, exasperation, irritation; **WORSENING:** deepening, heightening

aggregate *adj.* combined, complete, entire, total

aggressive *adj.* **HOSTILE:** belligerent, combative, contentious, pugnacious; **ASSERTIVE:** determined, dynamic, energetic, enterprising, forward, pushy

aggressor *n.* attacker, intruder, invader, trespasser

aggrieve *v.* disturb, harass, irritate, trouble, worry

aggrieved *adj.* harmed, hurt, injured

aghast *adj.* appalled, astonished, horrified, shocked

agile *adj.* **QUICK:** brisk, deft, lithe, lively, nimble, sprightly, vigorous; **BRIGHT:** clever, keen, smart

agility *n.* dexterity, liveliness, nimbleness

agitate *v.* **STIR:** churn, mix, toss, tumble; **DISTURB:** discomfit, disquiet, fluster, perturb, ruffle, trouble, unsettle, upset; **DEBATE:** argue, dispute

agitator *n.* activist, firebrand, rabble–rouser, radical

agnostic *n.* doubter, non–believer, skeptic, unbeliever

agog *adj.* anxious, breathless, eager, enthusiastic

agonize *v.* struggle, suffer, writhe, toss

agony *n.* anguish, distress, misery, pain, suffering, torment, torture

agree *v.* **CONSENT:** accede, acquiesce, allow, assent, concede; **COINCIDE:** correspond, equal, harmonize, match, suit; **COMPROMISE:** contract, resolve, settle

agreeable *adj.* **PLEASING:** amiable, congenial, gracious, pleasant, polite; **SUITABLE:** acceptable, satisfactory

agreement *n.* **COVENANT:** bargain, compact, contract, deal, pact, settlement, understanding; **ACCORD:** compromise, harmony, peace, unity

ahead *adj., adv.* before, earlier, leading, preceding

aid *n.* **ASSISTANCE:** backing, charity, help, relief, support; **HELPER:** aide, assistant, colleague, supporter

aid *v.* assist, facilitate, help, serve, support, sustain

ailment *n.* illness, affliction, infirmity, sickness

air *n.* atmosphere, breeze; tune; affectation, manner

air *v.* ventilate; announce

alarm *v.* warn; frighten

alert *adj.* ready, aware, attentive, intelligent, wary

alert *v.* caution, inform, warn

alien *adj.* different, foreign, strange, unfamiliar

alienation *n.* animosity, disaffection

allay *v.* calm, alleviate

allegation *n.* accusation, assertion, claim

allege *v.* assert, attest, declare
alleviate *v.* abate, ease, relieve, lessen, soften
alley *n.* byway, lane, street, passageway
alliance *n.* union, treaty, marriage
allocate *v.* allot, designate
allow *v.* approve, grant, let, permit, sanction
allure *v.* tempt, attract
ally *n.* associate, backer, confederate
alms *n.* charity, dole, donation
aloof *adj.* cool, detached, distant, reserved
alter *v.* change, modify, adjust
altercate *v.* contend, oppose, quarrel, bicker
alternate *n.* replacement, substitute
alternative *n.* choice, option
altruism *n.* benevolence, charity, kindness
amateur *n.* beginner, neophyte, novice
amaze *v.* astonish, dumfound, stupefy, surprise
amazement *n.* awe, shock, surprise
ambassador *n.* diplomat, emissary, envoy, minister
ambiguous *adj.* indistinct, puzzling, unclear, vague
ambitious *adj.* determined, industrious, intent
ambivalent *adj.* uncertain, wavering
ameliorate *v.* alleviate, improve, rectify
amenable *adj.* agreeable, docile, pliable, responsive
amend *v.* improve, change, correct
amenity *n.* courtesy, consideration, pleasantness
amiable, amicable *adj.* friendly, affable, agreeable,
  congenial, kindly, genial, sweet, peaceful
amiss *adj.* wrong, faulty, erroneous, imperfect, awry
amity *n.* goodwill, regard, friendliness, affection
amnesty *n.* pardon, liberation, acquittal, reprieve
among *prep.* amid, amongst, amidst

amount n. TOTAL: sum, product; PRICE: expense, output, outlay; QUANTITY: bulk, mass, number

ample adj. sufficient, plenty, adequate, enough

amplify v. increase, augment, magnify

amulet n. charm, talisman

amuse v. entertain, divert, cheer, enliven

amusement n. entertainment, recreation, pastime

analyze v. dissect, examine, investigate

anarchy n. disorder, turmoil, chaos

ancestor n. forebear, progenitor, forefather

ancestry n. lineage, heritage, parentage, family

anchor n. stay, tie, mooring, support

ancient adj. old, antiquated, antique, aged

anecdote n. story, tale, incident, episode

anger n. ire, wrath, rage, fury, exasperation, irritation

anger v. infuriate, annoy, irritate enrage

angle n. PLAN: plot, scheme, maneuver; VIEWPOINT: standpoint, outlook, perspective; INTERSECTION: notch, crotch, elbow, fork

angry adj. enraged, furious, infuriated, irate, raging, cross, annoyed, displeased, riled, hostile

anguish n. pain, wretchedness, agony

angular adj. intersecting, crossing, crotched, forked

animate v. activate, vitalize, arouse, energize

animosity n. hatred, dislike, enmity, displeasure

annex v. add, incorporate, append, attach, affix.

annihilate v. destroy, demolish, exterminate

annotate v. comment, explain, interpret

announcement n. declaration, publication, statement, bulletin, notice, communiqué, release

annoy v. bother, irritate, pester, trouble

annoyance n. irritation, pique, displeasure, nuisance,

discontent, dissatisfaction, impatience,
annul *v.* invalidate, repeal, revoke, cancel
anoint *v.* sprinkle, consecrate
anonymous *adj.* unsigned, nameless, unknown
answer *v.* **REPLY:** respond, retort, acknowledge, refute, react, rebut; **EXPLAIN:** solve, elucidate, clarify
answerable *adj.* responsible, liable
antagonism *n.* hatred, enmity, hostility, opposition
antic *n.* prank, joke, trick, frolic, caper
anticipate *v.* expect, forecast, predict, assume, await
antipathy *n.* aversion, dislike, hatred, repulsion
antiquated, antique *adj.* old, outmoded, out-of-date
antiseptic *adj.* clean, germ-free, sterilized, pure
antithesis *n.* contrasting, reverse
antitoxin *n.* vaccine, antibody, serum
anxiety, anxiousness *n.* concern, trouble, misgiving
anxious *adj.* **APPREHENSIVE:** concerned, dreading troubled; **EAGER:** desirous, fervent, zealous
apathetic *adj.* unemotional, unconcerned, indifferent.
ape *v.* imitate, mimic, copy, impersonate.
aperture *n.* opening, hole, slot
aphorism *n.* motto, proverb, saying
apologetic *adj.* regretful, contrite, remorseful, sorry
appall *v.* horrify, amaze, dismay, shock
apparatus *n.* equipment, appliance, machinery
apparel *n.* clothes, attire, suit, dress
apparent *adj.* open, visible, clear, manifest, obvious
apparition *n.* ghost, manifestation, phantom, spirit
appeal *n.* **PLEA:** request, petition, entreaty, prayer, supplication; **ATTRACTIVENESS:** charm, glamour
appeal *v.* **REQUEST:** beg, urge, petition; **FASCINATE:** attract, interest, engage, tempt

appear *v.* emerge, rise, loom, arrive, recur, materialize, show; seem, resemble

appearance *n.* bearing, demeanor, features

appease *v.* satisfy, do, serve

appeasement *n.* settlement, amends, reparation

append *v.* add, affix, attach, supplement

appendix *n.* supplement, attachment, index, addition

appetite *n.* hunger, thirst, craving, longing, desire

appetizing *adj.* savory, tasty, delectable, delicious

applaud *v.* approve, cheer, clap, acclaim, praise

applicable *adj.* suitable, appropriate, usable, fit

applicant *n.* petitioner, claimant, candidate.

application *n.* **USE:** employment, utilization; **ATTENTION:** devotion, zeal, diligence; **PETITION:** entreaty, appeal; **INSTRUMENT:** petition, form, requisition

apply *v.* **REQUEST:** petition, beg; **UTILIZE:** employ, practice, exploit; **PERTAIN:** involve, affect

appoint *v.* name, select, designate, delegate

appointment *n.* **DESIGNATION:** selection, nomination, choice; **ENGAGEMENT:** meeting, rendezvous, date

apportion *v.* distribute, share

appraise *v.* assess, price, assay, rate

appreciable *adj.* considerable, sizable, tangible, large

appreciate *v.* **THANK:** acknowledge; **ESTEEM:** honor, praise, admire

appreciative *adj.* grateful, obliged, satisfied, thankful

apprehend *v.* **COMPREHEND:** understand, perceive, grasp; **ARREST:** detain, seize

apprehension *n.* **FOREBODING:** trepidation, dread, misgiving, fear; **UNDERSTANDING:** comprehension; **ARREST:** capture, seizure, detention

apprentice *n.* beginner, student, learner

apprise *v.* notify, teach, warn

approach *n.* **ACCESS:** avenue, path, entrance, gate, way; **PLAN:** method, program, procedure

approbation *n.* approval, regard

appropriate *adj.* suitable proper, suited, fitting, fit

appropriate *v.* **SEIZE:** secure, usurp, take; **SET APART:** allocate, assign, reserve, apportion, budget, allot

appropriation *n.* stipend, grant, fund, allotment, allowance, allocation, contribution, support

approval *n.* **REGARD:** esteem, favor, admiration; **SANCTION:** endorsement, consent, permission

approve *v.* authorize, endorse, ratify, confirm, sanction, legalize, accredit, allow, advocate, pass

approximate *adj.* inexact, imprecise, close

appurtenance *n.* adjunct, accessory

apropos *adj.* applicable, appropriate, befitting

apt *adj.* **APPROPRIATE:** apropos, suitable, fitting; **INCLINED:** probable, prone, liable, likely; **QUICK:** adept, clever, bright, intelligent, talented

aptitude *n.* ability, capability, competence, capacity

arbitrary *adj.* **OPTIONAL:** discretionary, unscientific; **WHIMSICAL:** capricious, fanciful, inconsistent, irrational; **AUTOCRATIC:** willful, tyrannical,

arbitrate *v.* settle, adjust, reconcile, negotiate

arch *n.* arc, curve, vault, bend, arching, archway

archaic *adj.* antiquated, old, obsolete

architect *n.* planner, designer, draftsman, artist

archive *n.* repository, vault, museum, storage

ardent *adj.* fervent, impassioned, zealous, passionate, enthusiastic

arduous *adj.* hard, laborious, difficult, strenuous

argue *v.* dispute, contend, wrangle, bicker, debate

argumentative *adj.* hostile, contentious, factious
arid *adj.* parched, desert, dried, dry, barren
arise *v.* **GET UP:** rise, stand, awaken; **ASCEND:** mount, climb, rise
aristocracy *n.* nobility, elite, gentry, patricians
aristocratic *adj.* noble, refined, well–bred
arm *n.* limb, member, appendage, projection, branch
armistice *n.* treaty, cease–fire, truce
aroma *n.* smell, fragrance, perfume, odor
arouse *v.* awaken, stir, excite, move, stimulate
arraign *v.* accuse, summon
arrange *v.* order, regulate, systematize, organize
arrest *v.* apprehend, capture, imprison, incarcerate
arrival *n.* **ENTRANCE:** appearance, landing, debarkation; **NEWCOMER:** visitor, guest, traveler
arrive *v.* land, disembark, reach, appear, attain
arrogance *n.* insolence, audacity, haughtiness, pride
art *n.* representation, illustration, abstraction, portrayal, design, painting, creation
artery *n.* **BLOOD VESSEL:** aorta, capillary, vein; **MAIN CHANNEL:** highway, line, route, canal, roadway
artful *adj.* crafty, cunning, clever, adroit, ingenious
article *n.* **WRITING:** essay, editorial, commentary; **ITEM:** object, substance, commodity, thing
articulate *v.* **SPEAK:** enunciate, pronounce, verbalize; **JOIN:** combine, connect, link
artifact *n.* antique, heirloom, relic
artifice *n.* ruse, scheme, trick
artificial *adj.* synthetic, counterfeit, false, imitation
artistic *adj.* imaginative, creative, accomplished, cultured, sensitive, elegant, harmonious
artistry *n.* workmanship, skill, proficiency

artless *adj.* innocent, rough, unskilled
arty *adj.* affected, ostentatious
ascend *v.* soar, rise
askance *adv.* suspiciously, disapprovingly
aspect *n.* **APPEARANCE:** looks, countenance, face, features; **VIEW:** perspective, regard, slant, viewpoint
asperity *n.* roughness, harshness
aspiration *n.* desire, yearning, inclination, ambition
assail *v.* assault, attack
assailant *n.* antagonist, foe, enemy, opponent
assassin *n.* murderer, slayer, butcher, killer
assassinate *v.* **MURDER:** kill, slay, slaughter; **SLANDER:** defame, denigrate, libel
assault *n.* **ATTACK:** charge, advance, onslaught
assay *v.* test, analyze
assemble *v.* **CONVOKE:** convene, mobilize, gather, collect; **CONSTRUCT:** erect, join, unite, mold
assent *n.* approval, consent, permission, agreement
assert *v.* state, say, affirm, declare
assertion *n.* affirmation, statement, declaration
assess *v.* **TAX:** charge, exact; **ESTIMATE:** appraise, judge, reckon, guess
asset *n.* property, holdings, possessions, capital
assiduous *adj.* painstaking, diligent
assign *v.* **ALLOCATE:** allot, earmark; **APPOINT:** commission, name, select, deputize, charge, elect
assimilate *v.* **UNDERSTAND:** grasp, learn, sense; **ABSORB:** digest, osmose
assist *v.* aid, support, serve, help
assistance *n.* comfort, support, compensation, help
assistant *n.* aid, deputy, lieutenant, helper, flunky
associate *n.* comrade, peer, colleague, friend, ally,

henchman, confederate, collaborator, teammate

associate *v.* relate, link, connect, join, compare

association *n.* **RELATIONSHIP:** friendship, camaraderie, membership, community; **RECOLLECTION:** impression, remembrance; **ORGANIZATION:** union, club

assortment *n.* variety, combination, group, collection

assuage *v.* alleviate, calm, satisfy

assume *v.* suppose, theorize, presuppose, postulate, hypothesize, guess, conjecture, deem, imagine, surmise, opine, estimate, speculate, deduce, infer

assurance *n.* **GUARANTY:** support, pledge, promise; **CONFIDENCE:** conviction, trust, certainty, faith

assure *v.* **GUARANTEE:** aver, attest; **CONVINCE:** prove, persuade, induce

astonish *v.* shock, amaze, astound, surprise, stun

astonishment *n.* amazement, bewilderment, wonder

astute *adj.* perceptive, shrewd

asunder *adv.* apart, divided, separated, disjoined

athletic *adj.* hardy, robust, vigorous, powerful

atmosphere *n.* sense, impression, taste, character

atone *v.* compensate, pay

atrocious *adj.* cruel, offensive

atrocity *n.* **BRUTALITY:** inhumanity, wickedness, barbarity, cruelty; **OFFENSE:** outrage, horror, crime

attach *v.* **ADHERE:** join, connect, append, add; **ATTRIBUTE:** associate, impute, ascribe, give

attachment *n.* **AFFECTION:** fondness, liking, devotion; **ACCESSORY:** adjunct, annex, addition

attack *n.* **ASSAULT:** raid, onslaught, offensive, siege, invasion, incursion; **LIBEL:** slander, denunciation, blame, **ILLNESS:** seizure, breakdown, relapse

attacker *n.* aggressor, assailant, antagonist, invader

attain *v.* achieve, accomplish, arrive, reach, gain

attempt *v.* endeavor, strike, venture, try

attend *v.* heed; minister; frequent, visit, revisit, haunt

attention *n.* regard, vigilance, heed, alertness, diligence, thoroughness, recognition

attentive *adj.* considerate, thoughtful

attest *v.* testify, certify

attitude *n.* **BEARING:** air, demeanor; **DISPOSITION:** inclination, nature, temperament, mood, viewpoint

attorney *n.* lawyer, barrister, counsel

attract *v.* **DRAW:** pull, drag, bring; **ALLURE:** entice, lure, charm, fascinate

attraction *n.* **ALLUREMENT:** magnetism, enticement, appeal; **EVENT:** spectacle, display, demonstration

attractive *adj.* engaging, beautiful, handsome

attribute *n.* peculiarity, quality, characteristic, trait

attribute *v.* ascribe, impute, give

audacious *adj.* bold, daring, shameless

audible *adj.* perceptible, discernible, distinct

audience *n.* interview; spectators, witness, patrons

audit *n.* checking, scrutiny, inspection, examination

auditorium *n.* hall, theater, playhouse, amphitheater

augment *v.* increase, enlarge, expand, magnify

auspices *n. pl.* protection, aegis, patronage, omen

austere *adj.* stern, harsh, hard, ascetic, severe, plain

authentic *adj.* genuine, real, true, actual

authenticate *v.* verify, confirm, validate, prove

author *n.* writer, journalist, columnist, playwright, poet, novelist, essayist

authority *n.* **COMMAND:** jurisdiction, power; **SPECIALIST:** expert, veteran, professional

authorization *n.* sanction, signature, permission

authorize *v.* **ALLOW:** permit, tolerate, suffer; **APPROVE:** sanction, ratify, affirm, endorse

autocratic *adj.* domineering, aggressive, absolute

autograph *n.* signature, handwriting

automatic *adj.* **MECHANIZED:** computerized, self-regulating, automated; **INVOLUNTARY:** instinctive, spontaneous, intuitive

autonomous *adj.* self-governing, independent, free

auxiliary *adj.* **SUBSIDIARY:** secondary, subordinate; **SUPPLEMENTARY:** reserve, supplemental, spare, extra

available *adj.* accessible, convenient, handy, obtainable, practicable, feasible, possible, realizable

avarice *n.* acquisitiveness, greed

aver *v.* assert, claim, declare, swear

average *adj.* ordinary, medium, mediocre, common

averse *adj.* disinclined, opposed

aversion *n.* abhorrence, disgust, dislike, loathing

avocation *n.* hobby, sideline

avoid *v.* evade, shun, elude, dodge, withdraw,

avow *v.* affirm, assert, declare, swear

awake *adj.* alert, attentive, vigilant; conscious

awake, awaken *v.* stir, arise, waken, arouse

award *n.* citation, honor, scholarship, prize, judgment

award *v.* grant, confer, bestow, give

aware *adj.* conscious, knowledgeable, cognizant

awareness *n.* discernment, alertness, keenness, attentiveness, perception, apprehension, appreciation

awe *n.* fright, wonder, reverence

awesome *adj.* striking, moving, exalted, grand

awkward *adj.* clumsy, bungling, gawky, floundering, ungainly, unwieldy, inept, amateurish

axiom *n.* adage, maxim, proverb, saying

babble *n.* chatter jabber, twaddle, nonsense.
babel *n.* bedlam, clamor, commotion
baby *adj.* juvenile, childish, small
baby *v.* pamper, coddle, spoil, caress, nurse, indulge
backlash *n.* repercussion, reaction, recoil
backlog *n.* queue, reserve
badge *n.* marker, symbol, emblem, pin, medal, insignia, shield, medallion, button, crest
baffle *v.* perplex, confuse, puzzle, bewilder
baggage *n.* luggage, gear, trunk, valise, suitcase,
bail *v.* dip, scoop, empty, drain
bait *v.* LURE: entice, attract, draw, fascinate; TEASE: provoke, torment, anger, nag, bother
balance *n.* REMAINS: excess, surplus, residue, remainder; EQUILIBRIUM: symmetry, equivalence, parity
balance *v.* equalize, even, compensate, adjust, coordinate, equate, match, harmonize
balcony *n.* gallery, verandah, terrace
baleful *adj.* noxious, harmful
balk *v.* refuse, demur, desist
balky *adj.* contrary, obstinate, perverse, stubborn
ball *n.* SPHERE: globe, spheroid, orb, globule, pellet, pill; DANCE: promenade, reception, party
ballad *n.* carol, chant, song
ballot *n.* tally, ticket, poll, vote
balm *n.* OINTMENT: salve, lotion, dressing, medicine; SOLACE: comfort, relief, refreshment, remedy
ban *n.* taboo, prohibition, limitation, refusal
ban *v.* forbid, prohibit, outlaw, prevent
banal *adj.* dull, trite, hackneyed, prosaic, trite
bandage *n.* compress, cast, gauze, dressing
bandage *v.* tie, swathe, truss, bind, fasten.

bandit *n.* highwayman, thief, brigand, robber

bang *n.* **REPORT:** blast, detonation; **BLOW:** hit, cuff, whack; **THRILL:** enjoyment, kick, excitement

banish *v.* exile, deport, expel, expatriate, ostracize, outlaw, extradite, isolate

bank *n.* shore, ledge, embankment, edge

bankrupt *adj.* failed, broke, ruined, insolvent

banner *n.* flag, colors, pennant, emblem; headline

banquet *n.* feast, repast, festivity, dinner

bar *n.* **STICK:** boom, crosspiece, rod; **OBSTRUCTION:** hindrance, obstacle, hurdle, barrier; **SALOON:** tavern, lounge, cabaret, dive, pub; **LAWYERS:** counselors, barristers, solicitors, jurists, attorneys, advocates; **STRIP:** stripe, ribbon, band

bar *v.* **OBSTRUCT:** barricade, blockade, impede; **REFUSE:** ban, forbid, prevent, stop; **CLOSE:** shut, lock, seal

barbarian *n.* savage, brute, beast

barbaric *adj.* inhuman, brutal, fierce, cruel

bare *adj.* **UNCOVERED:** bald, naked; **PLAIN:** unadorned, simple, modest; **EMPTY:** barren, void, unfurnished

bare *v.* divulge, reveal, uncover, expose

bargain *n.* **UNDERSTANDING:** agreement, pact, compact, contract, deal; **DISCOUNT:** reduction, steal, giveaway

bargain *v.* barter, buy, sell, negotiate

barrel *n.* cask, keg, vat, receptacle, container, vessel

barren *adj.* childless, fallow, unproductive, fruitless

barricade *n.* obstacle, obstruction, barrier, blockade

barrier *n.* obstruction, hindrance, obstacle, hurdle, restriction, restraint, impediment, barricade

barrister *n.* advocate, attorney, lawyer, solicitor

barter *v.* trade, bargain, swap, buy, sell

base *n.* **BOTTOM:** footing, foundation; **BASIS:** principle;

HEADQUARTERS: terminal, harbor, station
bashful *adj.* retiring, reserved, timid, modest, shy
basic *adj.* fundamental, essential, central, primary
basin *n.* bowl, pan, tub, container
basis *n.* foundation, justification, reason, explanation, background, source, authority, principle, grounds
bask *v.* relax, enjoy, wallow
basket *n.* container, bushel, crate, bin
baste *v.* **SEW:** stitch, tack; **MOISTEN:** grease, season
bathe *v.* soap, scour, scrub, wash.
batter *n.* dough, mix, paste
battery *n.* beating, assault, attack, mugging
bauble *n.* ornament, trifle, trinket
bazaar *n.* market, fair
beach *n.* shore, seaside, sand, coast
beached *v.* stranded, marooned, aground, abandoned
beacon *n.* signal, flare, beam
beam *n.* timber, brace, rafter, stringer, stud, joist, girder, support, trestle, post, column, pillar, shaft
beam *v.* **TRANSMIT:** broadcast, send; **SHINE:** radiate, glitter, glare; **SMILE:** grin, laugh, smirk
bear *v.* **TOLERATE:** undergo, endure; **SUPPORT:** sustain
bearable *adj.* endurable, tolerable, sufferable
beard *n.* whiskers, goatee, sideburns
beastly *adj.* brutal, savage, coarse, depraved, loathsome, vile, foul, base, disgusting, vulgar
beat *adj.* weary, fatigued, tired, exhausted
beat *v.* **HIT:** whip, flog, spank, scourge, buffet, bash; **PULSATE:** pound, thump, pulse, throb; **MIX:** whip, knead; **WORST:** overcome, conquer, defeat
beautiful *adj.* lovely, attractive, appealing, charming, enticing, elegant, gorgeous, exquisite, alluring

beckon *v.* summon, signal, motion

becoming *adj.* attractive, handsome, comely, fair

bedlam *n.* pandemonium, clamor, confusion, noise

befall *v.* occur, happen

beg *v.* entreat, implore, beseech, supplicate, solicit, plead, petition, request, ask

beggar *n.* panhandler, moocher, bum

begin *v.* initiate, start, inaugurate, launch, mount, create, institute, introduce, originate, found, establish, commence, arise

beguile *v.* charm, deceive

behavior *n.* conduct, performance

behold *v.* observe, regard, view

belie *v.* deceive, mislead, misrepresent

belief *n.* opinion, feeling, conviction

believable *adj.* trustworthy, creditable, convincing

believe *v.* trust, accept, think

believer *n.* convert, devotee, adherent, apostle, disciple, prophet, follower

bellicose *adj.* hostile, aggressive

belligerent *adj.* warlike, pugnacious, hostile

bellow *v.* howl, call, shout, cry, yell

beloved *adj.* cherished, loved, adored, worshipped, idolized, precious, prized, treasured, favored

beloved *n.* fiancé, sweetheart, lover

below *prep.* BENEATH: underneath, under; INFERIOR: subject, subordinate; IN HELL: damned, condemned

bend *v.* turn, twist, contort, coil, curl, loop, curve

beneficial *adj.* advantageous, helpful, useful

benefit *v.* help, aid, serve, profit

benevolence *n.* altruism, charity, kindness

bent *adj.* curved, warped, crooked, contorted, twisted

bent *n.* leaning, tendency, propensity, inclination

bequeath *v.* grant, give

beseech *v.* ask, implore

best *adj., adv.* first, greatest, finest, incomparable, unrivaled, unequaled, inimitable, foremost

best *v.* overcome, defeat, worst

bestow *v.* bequeath, present, offer, give, endow

betray *v.* **DOUBLE–CROSS:** delude, trick, deceive; **REVEAL:** divulge, disclose

betrayal *n.* treason, treachery, disloyalty, deception

bevy *n.* group, herd, pack, swarm

bewail *v.* complain, gripe, grumble, lament

bewilder *v.* confound, disconcert, puzzle, confuse.

bewildered *adj.* confused, muddled, dazed, puzzled, baffled, disconcerted, adrift, stupefied, befuddled, stunned, electrified, confounded, flabbergasted

bewitch *v.* charm, enchant, fascinate, captivate

bias *n.* prejudice, partiality, preference, inclination

bicker *v.* wrangle, squabble, dispute, argue, quarrel

bid *n.* proposal, proposition, declaration, suggestion

bigoted *adj.* biased, dogmatic, opinionated, prejudiced

bill *v.* dun, solicit, invoice

billow *v.* surge, swell

bind *n.* dilemma, quandary, predicament

bind *v.* **SECURE:** attach, adhere, fasten; **OBLIGATE:** oblige, compel, force; **CONTAIN:** shackle, fetter, leash, restrict, hitch, yoke, tether; **BANDAGE:** dress, treat; **JOIN:** unite, connect

biography *n.* memoir, journal, autobiography, life

bit *n.* **FRAGMENT:** piece, crumb, particle, morsel, speck, flake, scrap; **TRIFLE:** iota, mite, whisker, hair

bite *n.* **MOUTHFUL:** taste, morsel, nibble; **WOUND:** sting, laceration; **QUICK MEAL:** snack

biting *adj.* **TANGY:** sharp, keen, sour; **SARCASTIC:** caustic, acrimonious, bitter

bitter *adj.* **ACRID:** astringent, acid; **INTENSE:** harsh, severe; **SARCASTIC:** acrimonious, caustic, biting

bizarre *adj.* unusual, unexpected, fantastic, grotesque

blackmail *n.* extortion, tribute, protection, bribe

blackout *v.* **DELETE:** eradicate, erase; **FAINT:** swoon; **DARKEN:** batten, shade

blade *n.* **LEAF:** frond, spear, shoot; **INSTRUMENT:** edge, sword, knife

blame *v.* charge, condemn, denounce, disparage

bland *adj.* insipid, flat, dull, tasteless

blanket *n.* quilt, robe, comforter, featherbed, throw, cloak, covering

blanket *v.* cover, envelop, conceal, bury

blast *v.* explode, dynamite, detonate; denounce

blatant *adj.* clear, obvious, plain

blaze *n.* conflagration, combustion, burning, fire

bleak *adj.* dreary, desolate, bare, cheerless, barren

bleary *adj.* blurred, fuzzy

bleed *v.* hemorrhage, gush, spurt, flow

blemish *n.* flaw, defect, stain, imperfection, dent

blemish *v.* damage, deface, mar

blend *n.* mixture, combination, compound, amalgam

blight *n.* disease, withering, mildew, decay

blind *adj.* **OBTUSE:** unseeing, unaware; **CLOSED:** obstructed, blocked; **RANDOM:** accidental, unplanned, aimless

blindly *adv.* wildly, frantically, heedlessly, carelessly, recklessly, aimlessly, indiscriminately

bliss *n.* joy, rapture, ecstasy, happiness

blithe *adj.* gay, lighthearted, vivacious
blizzard *n.* snowstorm, tempest, blast, gale
block *n.* **CHUNK:** slab, cake, clod, hunk; **BARRIER:** obstruction, hindrance, bar, obstacle
block *v.* **IMPEDE:** prevent, hinder, restrict; **TACKLE:** check, stop
blockade *n.* barrier, barricade, bar, barrier
bloom *n.* **FLOWER:** blossom, floweret; **GLOW:** blush, flush
blossom *n.* flower, bloom, floweret, bud
blot *n.* flaw, spot, stain, smudge, blemish
blotch *n.* stain, blemish
blow *n.* hit, strike, bump, wallop, rap, knock, clout
blow *v.* **PUFF:** blast, fan; **FLUTTER:** waft, whisk, flap, wave, buffet; **PLAY:** pipe, toot, tootle; **SPEND:** waste, squander; **FAIL:** miss, flounder, miscarry
blubber *v.* bawl, cry, sob, weep
blue *adj., n.* despondent, depressed, melancholy, sad
bluff *n.* **BANK:** hill, cliff, precipice, steep, mountain; **DECEPTION:** trick, ruse, delusion
bluff *v.* fool, mislead, trick, deceive
blunder *n.* mistake, lapse, oversight, error
blunt *adj.* **DULL:** unsharpened, unpointed, round; **ABRUPT:** brusque, curt, bluff, rude
bluster *v.* brag, swagger, strut, boast
board *n.* **PLANK:** lath, strip, lumber; **MEALS:** food, fare, provisions; **REGULATORS:** council, cabinet, committee
boast *n.* brag, pretension, self–satisfaction, bravado
boast *v.* gloat, swagger, swell, brag, strut, flaunt
boastful *adj.* bragging, pretentious, bombastic
body *n.* **CHASSIS:** fuselage, hull, skeleton; **GROUP:** society, organization; **COLLECTION:** reservoir, supply,

variety; **HUMAN:** anatomy, physique, figure, trunk, build; **CORPSE:** cadaver, carcass, mummy; remains
bog *n.* marsh, swamp
boil *v.* cook, steep, seethe, stew, simmer
boisterous *adj.* rowdy, uproarious, noisy, loud, rude
bold *adj.* **DARING:** courageous, intrepid, fearless; **IMPERTINENT:** brazen, audacious, presumptuous, rude; **PROMINENT:** strong, clear, plain, definite
boldness *n.* audacity, self-reliance, courage
bolster *v.* reinforce, sustain, support
bombastic *adj.* high-sounding, pompous
bond *n.* **LINK:** attachment, connection, affiliation, friendship, marriage; **DEBENTURE:** security, warranty, certificate; **BAIL:** surety, guaranty, warrant
bonus *n.* reward, compensation, payment, incentive
book *n.* volume, manual, handbook, reference
boom *n.* **SOUND:** roar, blast, blare, noise; **ACTIVITY:** rush, growth, inflation
boor *n.* yokel, lout, clown, bumpkin, churl, oaf, boob
boost *n.* **ASSISTANCE:** aid, help; **INCREASE:** addition, advance, hike
boost *v.* **PUSH UPWARD:** raise, hoist; **INCREASE:** raise, heighten, expand; **SUPPORT:** promote, encourage
booth *n.* stall, counter, nook, corner, stand
bootleg *adj.* illegal, illicit, unlawful
border *n.* **EDGE:** hem, end, trim, decoration, fringe, margin; **BOUNDARY:** frontier, outpost, perimeter
bore *v.* **DRILL:** ream, perforate; **WEARY:** fatigue, tire
boredom *n.* apathy, doldrums, listlessness, monotony, tedium, indifference
borrow *v.* take, sponge, bum, beg, chisel, mooch
botch *v.* bungle, blunder, mishandle, muddle

bottom *n.* underside, base, foot; depths, bed, floor
bough *n.* limb, arm, fork, branch
boulder *n.* stone, slab, crag, rock
boulevard *n.* street, avenue, highway, road
bounce *v.* rebound, ricochet, recoil
bound *adj.* determined, compelled, driven, pressed
bound *v.* **LEAP:** spring, vault, jump; **BOUNCE:** ricochet, recoil; **LIMIT:** restrict, confine, circumscribe
boundary *n.* border, rim, bounds, extremity, perimeter, extent, periphery, limit
boundless *adj.* limitless, endless, unlimited, infinite
bounteous *adj.* abundant, lavish, plentiful
bounty *n.* bonus, inducement, reward; profusion
bouquet *n.* fragrance, aroma, scent, smell
bow *v.* **CURTSEY:** stoop, dip; **YIELD:** submit, surrender, acquiesce, capitulate
bowl *n.* dish, vessel, tureen, pot, saucer, crock
boycott *v.* ostracize, avoid, strike
brace *v.* support, prop, bolster, hold up, steady
brackish *adj.* salty, disagreeable, tainted
brag *v.* boast, swagger, exult, gloat, boast
braggart *n.* blowhard, windbag, swaggerer, strutter
braid *v.* interweave, plait, twine
brain *n.* **INTELLECT:** genius, mentality; **SCHOLAR:** egghead, intellectual
brake *v.* check, dampen, slow, stop
branch *n.* **DIVISION:** office, bureau, extension; **SHOOT:** bough, limb, sprig, twig, arm, fork, growth
brand *n.* mark, scar, welt, earmark, trademark
brand *v.* blaze, stamp, imprint, mark
brandish *v.* wave, flourish, gesture, warn, threaten
brass *n.* boldness, impudence, effrontery, rudeness,

impertinence, audacity

bravado *n.* pretense, bluster

brave *adj.* fearless, daring, dauntless, valiant, intrepid, bold, unafraid, stout, stalwart

brawl *v.* fight, quarrel, squabble

brawn *n.* power, strength

brazen *adj.* bold, brassy, forward, impudent

breach *n.* **BREAK:** opening, rupture; **VIOLATION:** infringement, transgression, crime

breadth *n.* largeness, extent, vastness, size, width

break *n.* **BREACH:** fracture, split, rupture; **PAUSE:** intermission, interim; **LUCK:** accident, opportunity

breakthrough *n.* finding, discovery, invention

breath *n.* inhalation, exhalation, gasp, sigh, wheeze

breathe *v.* respire, inhale, exhale, gasp, pant

breed *n.* strain, variety, kind, race, type

breeze *n.* zephyr, flurry, wind

brevity *n.* conciseness, shortness, terseness

brew *v.* make, concoct, ferment, mull, cook, formulate

bribe *v.* corrupt, influence, entice, tempt

bridge *n.* **STRUCTURE:** viaduct, pontoon, catwalk, trestle; **LINK:** connection, bond, tie, joint

bridle *n.* halter, leash, restraint

brief *adj.* momentary, fleeting, concise, abrupt

brief *n.* abstract, outline, summary

bright *adj.* **QUICK–WITTED:** intelligent, clever, alert; **CLEAR:** sunny, fair; **LIVELY:** cheerful, vivacious; **SHINING:** luminous, lustrous, sparkling, illuminated

brighten *v.* lighten, glow; polish, intensify, shine

brightness *n.* shine, luster, illumination, light

brilliant *adj.* **SPARKLING:** shining, dazzling, gleaming, bright; **TALENTED:** profound, intelligent

brim *n.* rim, margin, border, edge
bring *v.* transport, convey, bear, carry
brink *n.* edge, limit, brim, rim
brisk *adj.* keen, invigorating, stimulating, active
briskly *adv.* energetically, brusquely, nimbly
bristle *n.* hair, fiber, quill, point
brittle *adj.* fragile, crisp, inelastic, weak
broad *adj.* **COSMOPOLITAN:** cultivated, experienced, cultured; **WIDE:** large, extensive, spacious, expansive, roomy; **TOLERANT:** progressive, unbiased, liberal
broadcast *v.* announce, transmit, air, send
broaden *v.* widen, expand, increase, grow
broad-minded *adj.* tolerant, progressive, unprejudiced, liberal
brochure *n.* handout, circular, pamphlet, folder
broil *v.* cook, sear, bake, roast
broiler *n.* oven, grill, barbecue, appliance
broken *adj.* **INOPERABLE:** busted, faulty; **FRACTURED:** shattered, smashed, damaged, cracked; **SPASMODIC:** erratic, intermittent, irregular; **INCOHERENT:** muttered, mumbled
brood *v.* pine, grieve, fret, sulk, mope, muse, deliberate, worry
brook *n.* stream, creek, streamlet, river
broth *n.* soup, consommé, bouillon, stock
browbeat *v.* intimidate, bully, frighten, threaten
browse *v.* skim, peruse, scan, inspect, examine
bruise *v.* wound, damage, beat, injure, hurt
brush *n.* **THICKET:** undergrowth, cover, shrubbery, grove, hedge, fern, scrub; **TOUCH:** rub, tap, stroke
brush *v.* **CLEAN:** sweep, whisk, wipe; **TOUCH LIGHTLY:** stroke, smooth, graze

brusque *adj.* abrupt, blunt, curt, terse
brutal *adj.* pitiless, harsh, unmerciful, cruel
brutalize *v.* degrade, demean
bubble *v.* froth, foam, gurgle, effervesce, percolate
bucket *n.* container, pail, canister, can, pot
buckle *n.* clasp, clamp, harness, fastening, fastener
budge *v.* stir, shift, move
budget *n.* projection, estimate, allocation, plan, funds
buffet *v.* batter, strike, whip
buffoon *n.* clown, jester, fool, jerk
bug *n.* **INSECT:** beetle, pest, gnat; **MICROORGANISM:** bacillus, virus; **DEFECT:** flaw, fault, annoyance
bug *v.* **EAVESDROP:** spy, overhear, wiretap; **ANNOY:** irritate, plague, pester, bother, disturb
build *v.* increase; construct, create, form, erect, make, manufacture, fabricate, fashion, produce, devise
bulb *n.* globe, globule, ball, knob
bulge *n.* swelling, protuberance, bump, prominence
bulk *n.* most, majority
bulk *v.* enlarge, expand
bull *n.* **ANIMAL:** steer, calf, ox, cow; **NONSENSE:** balderdash, rubbish, trash
bulletin *n.* report, newsletter, release, notice
bully *n.* ruffian, rowdy, tough, rascal
bully *v.* intimidate, tease, domineer, harass, threaten
bum *n.* derelict, loafer, hobo, tramp, vagrant, beggar
bump *n.* **COLLISION:** knock, jounce, jar, nudge; **BULGE:** swelling, projection, protuberance, knob, lump
bump *v.* **COLLIDE:** strike, crash, hit; **SOUND:** thud, whack, sock
bumper *n.* guard, absorber, cover, protector, fender
bun *n.* roll, muffin, scone, bread, roll, pastry

bunch *n.* cluster, clump, group, sheaf, tuft, shock, bundle, knot, collection

bungalow *n.* cottage, house, lodge

bungle *v.* botch, blunder, fumble, mishandle, fail

bungler *n.* muddler, numskull, dolt, dunce, clod

bunk *n.* **BED:** berth, cot, pallet; **MEANINGLESS INFORMATION:** rubbish, rot, hogwash, nonsense

burden *v.* hinder, encumber, hamper, strain, load, tax, try, trouble, oppress

burglar *n.* thief, housebreaker, robber, criminal

burglary *n.* crime, stealing, robbery, theft

burial *n.* interment, funeral

burlesque *v.* imitate, mock, satirize

burly *adj.* strong, muscular

burn *v.* ignite, kindle, incinerate, blaze, scorch

burnish *v.* polish, shine, smooth

burnt *adj.* scorched, singed, charred, burned

burrow *n.* hole, shelter

burrow *v.* dig, hide

burst *v.* **EXPLODE:** erupt, rupture, disintegrate; **BREAK:** crack, split, fracture, destroy

bury *v.* **INTER:** entomb, enshrine, embalm; **HIDE:** cover, conceal, secrete; **DEFEAT:** overcome, conquer

bush *n.* bramble, thicket, hedge, shrubbery, plant

bushy *adj.* fuzzy, shaggy, tufted, woolly, bristly

bushed *adj.* tired, fatigued

busy *adj.* active, occupied, diligent, employed, working

butcher *v.* **MASSACRE:** slaughter, slay, kill; **RUIN:** mutilate, spoil, botch, destroy

button *n.* knob, catch, disk, fastener

buy *v.* obtain, purchase, get, procure, gain, shop

buzz *v.* hum, drone, whir

cabaret *n.* bar, café, nightclub
cabin *n.* house, cottage, hut, home, shelter
cabinet *n.* advisors, council, bureau, ministry
cable *n.* rope, cord, chain, wire
cacophony *n.* dissonance, noise
cadaver *n.* body, corpse, remains
cadaverous *adj.* pale, gaunt
cadence *n.* rhythm, meter, flow, beat, measure
cadge *v.* beg, freeload
café *n.* coffeehouse, restaurant, cafeteria, lunchroom
cage *n.* coop, jail, crate, enclosure, pen
cagey *adj.* cunning, shrewd, clever
cajole *v.* appeal, wheedle
calamity *n.* tragedy, cataclysm, catastrophe, disaster
calculate *v.* count, measure, reckon, enumerate, determine, forecast, weigh, gauge, compute, cipher
calculating *adj.* scheming, shrewd, crafty
calendar *n.* schedule, journal, diary, daybook, chronology, logbook, register, almanac, agenda, docket
calisthenics *n.* exercise, workout, gymnastics
calling *n.* profession, vocation, occupation, job, trade
callous *adj.* heartless, indifferent, unfeeling, hardened, insensitive
callow *adj.* inexperienced, immature
calm *adj.* tranquil, reserved, cool, composed, collected, impassive, aloof, serene, placid
calm *v.* tranquilize, soothe, pacify, quiet
calumniate *v.* defame, slander, sully, vilify
camouflage *v.* conceal, cover, veil, disguise, hide
campaign *v.* crusade, electioneer, run, contend, contest, lobby, barnstorm, stump
canal *n.* waterway, trench, ditch, channel, duct

cancel *v.* invalidate, rescind, repeal, retract, void
cancerous *adj.* carcinogenic, virulent, mortal, harmful
candid *adj.* sincere, open, frank, honest
candidate *n.* nominee, aspirant, office–seeker
candor *n.* frankness, honesty
canny *adj.* cautious, watchful, shrewd
canon *n.* law, principle, standard, decree, rule
cantankerous *adj.* quarrelsome, disagreeable
canteen *n.* container, jug, flask, bottle
canvas *n.* SAILCLOTH: tarpaulin tenting, awning, duck, tarp; PAINTING: portrait, oil, art
canyon *n.* gorge, gulch, gully, ravine, valley
capability *n.* capacity, skill, aptitude, ability
capable *adj.* proficient, competent, able, intelligent
capacity *n.* limit, size, volume, scope, dimensions
cape *n.* CLOAK: mantilla, mantle, shawl, wrap, poncho; HEADLAND: peninsula, point, promontory, jetty
caper *n.* FROLIC: play, romp; PRANK: trick, escapade
capital *n.* assets, cash, estate, property, wealth
capitalist *n.* entrepreneur, investor, financier
capitulate *v.* submit, surrender, yield
capsize *v.* upend, overturn, invert, tip over, upset
caption *n.* heading, title, inscription, subtitle
captious *adj.* critical, fault–finding
captivate *v.* attract, charm, fascinate, bewitch
captive *adj.* restrained, incarcerated, jailed, bound
captive *n.* prisoner, hostage, convict
capture *v.* take, hold, seize, apprehend, arrest
cardinal *adj.* primary, foremost
care *n.* CONCERN: worry, anxiety, distress; CAUTION: concern, regard, precaution, wariness, vigilance; CUSTODY: keeping, watch

careen *v.* lean, swerve

career *n.* work, occupation, vocation, job, profession

careful *adj.* thorough, deliberate, meticulous, finicky, exacting, wary, vigilant, painstaking, conscientious, cautious, guarded, discreet, thrifty

careless *adj.* loose, lax, incautious, reckless, indiscreet, imprudent, heedless, negligent, casual, rash

carelessness *n.* unconcern, nonchalance, neglect, negligence, disregard, imprudence, indifference

caress *v.* touch, love, embrace, cuddle, pat

cargo *n.* freight, shipload, baggage, lading, load

caricature *v.* mimic, ridicule, satirize

carnage *n.* bloodbath, massacre, slaughter

carnal *adj.* fleshly, worldly, sensuous, lewd

carnival *n.* merrymaking, festival, fair, entertainment

carol *n.* song, hymn, ballad

carouse *v.* drink, imbibe, party, revel

carriage *n.* **BEARING:** presence, look, demeanor, poise, air; **VEHICLE:** buggy, surrey, gig, sulky, hansom

carry *v.* **TRANSPORT:** convey, transfer, cart, take, bring, haul, tote; **TRANSMIT:** transfer, relay; **SUPPORT** bear, sustain, shoulder

cartel *n.* alliance, coalition, federation

carve *v.* fashion, shape, form, chisel, sculpture, cut

cascade *v.* cataract, flow, rapids

casket *n.* box, chest, coffin

cast *n.* **REPRODUCTION:** facsimile, replica, copy; **ACTORS:** players, company, troupe; **APPEARANCE:** aspect, complexion; **TINGE:** hue, shade, tint, color

cast *v.* **THROW:** pitch, fling, hurl; **MOLD:** shape, form

caste *n.* position, status, birth

casual *adj.* **CHANCE:** unplanned, spontaneous;

BLASÉ: apathetic, unconcerned, indifferent
catalog *n.* register, directory, index, classification
catalog *v.* list, organize
catastrophe *n.* disaster, calamity, misadventure, misery, affliction, devastation, tragedy, upheaval
categorize *v.* classify, type, arrange
caucus *n.* conference, faction
cause *n.* **AGENT:** condition, circumstances; **PURPOSE:** goal, motive, foundation, basis, reason; **BELIEF:** principles, conviction, creed, faith
cause *v.* originate, provoke, generate, occasion, begin
caution *n.* discretion, care, heed, prudence, warning
cautious *adj.* circumspect, watchful, wary, careful
cavil *v.* criticize, object
cavity *n.* pit, depression, basin, hole, hollow
cavort *v.* frolic, prance
cease *v.* stop, desist, terminate, discontinue, halt
cede *v.* relinquish, surrender, yield
celebrate *v.* **COMMEMORATE:** observe, consecrate, honor; **INDULGE:** feast, carouse, rejoice, revel
celebrity *n.* notable, dignitary, personage, luminary
celibate *adj.* unmarried, abstaining
cement *n.* adhesive, glue, tar, gum, mortar, paste
cement *v.* join, unite, mortar, plaster, connect, fasten
cemetery *n.* churchyard, necropolis, catacomb, tomb, vault, crypt, sepulcher, graveyard, mortuary
censor *n.* restrict, suppress, withhold, expurgate
censor *v.* review; ban
censorship *n.* restriction, restraint
censure *v.* **BLAME:** criticize, judge, disapprove; **SCOLD:** rebuke, reprove, attack
census *n.* count, enumeration, tabulation, tally

center *n.* MIDDLE: nucleus, core, heart; HUB: metropolis, plaza, mart; ESSENCE: gist, kernel, character

center *v.* focus, concentrate, centralize, converge

central *adj.* middle, midway, equidistant, focal

cerebral *adj.* brainy, intelligent

ceremonial *adj.* ritualistic, stately, solemn, formal

ceremonious *adj.* formal, ritualistic

ceremony *n.* function, commemoration, celebration, rite, observance, ritual, formality, custom, tradition

certain *adj.* CONFIDENT: assured, positive, untroubled, confident; BEYOND DOUBT: conclusive, incontrovertible, irrefutable, true, unmistakable; FIXED: settled, concluded, definite, determined; SPECIFIC: definite, particular, singular, precise, express

certainly *adv.* positively, absolutely, unquestionably

certificate *n.* document, warrant, credentials, certification, document, warranty, guarantee

certify *v.* swear, attest, state, declare, testify

cessation *n.* ending, stopping

chagrin *n.* embarrassment, setback

chain *n.* LINKS: series, string, cable, manacle; SEQUENCE: succession, progression, continuity

chain *v.* connect, secure, fasten hold, bind, restrain

challenge *v.* COMPETE: defy, denounce, invite, dare, threaten; QUESTION: dispute, inquire, ask, doubt

challenging *adj.* difficult, intriguing

champion *n.* conqueror, victor, hero

chance *adj.* accidental, unplanned, unintentional, aimless, incidental, fortuitous

chance *v.* risk, venture, stake, hazard, wager, jeopardize, speculate

change *v.* MAKE DIFFERENT: vary, alter, transform,

turn; **BECOME DIFFERENT:** evolve, transform, adapt, moderate, adjust; **EXCHANGE:** displace, supplant, transpose; **DRESS:** undress, disrobe

changeable *adj.* **FICKLE:** flighty, unreliable, unstable; **VARIABLE:** unsteady, unsettled, uncertain

channel *n.* conduit, duct, gutter, trough, artery

chant *n.* recitation, chorus, incantation

chaos *n.* confusion, disorder, turmoil, discord

character *n.* **SYMBOL:** mark, sign, figure, emblem; **QUALITY:** temperament, nature, attribute, characteristic; **ECCENTRIC:** crank, nut, oddball, weirdo

characteristic *n.* attribute, quality, faculty, peculiarity, aspect, distinction, nature, essence, component

charge *v.* **PRICE:** cost; **ACCUSE:** indict, censure, blame; **ATTACK:** assail, assault, invade

charitable *adj.* generous, philanthropic, forgiving

charlatan *n.* cheat, fake, fraud

charming *adj.* alluring, appealing, captivating, diverting, enchanting, fascinating, lovable, provocative

chart *n.* outline, diagram, plan, map, graph

chary *adj.* cautious, timid, wary

chase *v.* pursue, trail, track, seek, hunt

chasten *n.* correct, punish

chastise *v.* scold, discipline, spank, punish

cheap *adj.* **INEXPENSIVE:** competitive, reasonable, economical; **INFERIOR:** shoddy, poor

cheapen *v.* depreciate, degrade, spoil, demean

cheat *n.* rogue, charlatan, fraud, swindler, chiseler, deceiver, trickster, crook, shill

cheat *v.* defraud, swindle, beguile, deceive

check *v.* **CONTROL:** bridle, repress, inhibit, neutralize, restrain; **EXAMINE:** review, monitor, investigate

cheer *v.* **HEARTEN:** console, brighten, comfort, encourage, help; **APPLAUD:**, shout, salute, support, yell

cheerful *adj.* **HAPPY:** gay, merry, joyful; **BRIGHT:** sunny, sparkling, pleasant

cherish *v.* treasure, value, adore, love, protect

chest *n.* **BREAST:** thorax, bosom, peritoneum, ribs; **BOX:** case, coffer, cabinet, strongbox, crate

chew *v.* munch, masticate, nibble, gnaw, eat

chide *v.* scold, reprimand

chief *adj.* leading, first, foremost, main, principal

chilly *adj.* brisk, fresh, crisp, cold, cool

chivalrous *adj.* courteous, valiant, brave, noble, polite

choice *n.* selection, preference, election, favorite, pick

choke *v.* asphyxiate, strangle; gag, gasp

choose *v.* pick, prefer, appoint, favor, decide

chop *v.* cut, mince, fell, whack

chore *n.* task, routine, errand, job

chronic *adj.* deep–seated, persistent, lingering, protracted, prolonged, recurrent

chronologic, chronological *adj.* arranged, ordered, classified, sequential, consecutive, sequenced

chunk *n.* lump, piece, mass, part

churlish *adj.* crude, vulgar, grouchy, surly

churn *v.* stir, beat, mix, agitate

circle *n.* disk, ring, loop, orbit, hoop, periphery

circle *v.* circumscribe, enclose, circulate, surround

circuitous *adj.* roundabout, devious

circular *adj.* spherical, cyclical, globular, round

circulate *v.* send, report, distribute

circulation *n.* rotation, current, flow

circumference *n.* perimeter, periphery, boundary

circumspect *adj.* cautious, prudent

circumstance *n.* situation, condition, contingency, status, occurrence, episode
circumstantial *adj.* inconclusive, presumptive
circumvent *v.* avoid, bypass, dodge, elude, evade
civic *adj.* civil, urban, municipal, public
civil *adj.* formal, polite, courteous, refined
claim *v.* **DEMAND:** request, own; **STATE:** assert, insist
clamber *v.* climb, scramble
clamor *n.* outcry, din, discord, noise, uproar
clamp *n.* snap, clasp, catch, fastener, lock
clan *n.* family, tribe, group, organization, race
clandestine *adj.* covert, furtive, secret, sly
clarify *v.* interpret, define, elucidate, explain
clash *v.* conflict, mismatch, contrast, differ
clasp *n.* fastener, buckle, pin, clamp
classic *n.* masterwork, masterpiece
classical *adj.* distinguished, superior, well–known
classify *v.* arrange, order, pigeonhole, organize, categorize, label, catalogue, tag, sort, index
clatter *n.* noise, racket, hubbub
clause *n.* provision, condition, codicil, requirement
clean *adj., adv.* **PURE:** unadulterated, undefiled, spotless, cleansed; **DISTINCT:** clear–cut, sharp, readable; **THOROUGH:** complete, entire, total, absolute
clean *v.* cleanse, wash, scrub, disinfect, polish, sterilize, scour
clean–cut *adj.* clear, precise; pleasing
clear *adj., adv.* **OBVIOUS:** explicit, plain, manifest; **TRANSPARENT:** limpid, translucent; **UNCLOUDED:** sunny, bright, fair; **INNOCENT:** exonerated, absolved
clearly *adv.* **OBVIOUSLY:** plainly, unmistakably, apparently, evidently; **ACUTELY:** sharply, audibly

clemency *n.* leniency, mercy
clench *v.* hold, grip, grasp, double up
clever *adj.* SKILLFUL: apt, expert, adroit, able; INTELLIGENT: smart, bright, shrewd
cliché *n.* platitude, slogan, banality, triviality, motto
client *n.* customer, patient, patron, buyer
climax *n.* crisis, peak, culmination, zenith, summit,
climb *v.* scale, ascend, surmount, mount
cling *v.* hold, adhere, attach, clasp, stick
clip *v.* shorten, snip, crop; strike; cheat; fasten
cloak *v.* cover, conceal, camouflage
clog *v.* obstruct, impede, seal, close, hinder
cloister *v.* seclude, protect
close *adj.* nearby; like; confining; restrictive, limited,
close *n.* ending, conclusion
close *v.* END: conclude, finish, terminate; SEAL: shut, clog, block, bar, dam, cork; COME TOGETHER: connect, meet, unite, agree, join; SHUT: slam, fasten, bolt, clench, bar, shutter, lock
closely *adv.* approximately, similarly, nearly, intimately, jointly, almost
clot *v.* thicken, coagulate, set, lump
cloth *n.* fabric, material, stuff, goods
clothe *v.* cover, attire, dress, costume
clothes, clothing *n.* apparel, raiment, garments, garb, vestments, attire, outfit, toggery, togs, duds
clown *n.* fool, buffoon, joker, harlequin
clumsy *adj.* ungainly, gawky, inexpert, awkward
cluster *n.* group, gathering, batch, clump, bunch
clutch *v.* grasp, grab, grip, hold, seize
clutter *n.* disarray, jumble, disorder, confusion
coach *v.* teach, train drill, instruct

coagulate *v.* clot, curdle, congeal, thicken
coalition *n.* union, group, association, faction
coarse *adj.* ROUGH: unrefined, crude; VULGAR: low, common, base, obscene, rude
coast *n.* shore, shoreline, beach, seaboard
coast *v.* glide, float, drift, ride
coax *v.* cajole, wheedle, inveigle, influence, urge
cocky *adj.* overconfident, flamboyant
codicil *n.* addendum, addition, appendix, rider
coerce *v.* force, compel, impel, constrain
cogent *adj.* forceful, compelling
cogitate *v.* consider, ponder, reflect
cognizance *n.* knowledge, awareness
coherent *adj.* comprehensible, intelligible, logical
coincide *v.* correspond, match, agree
coincidence *n.* chance, happening, accident
cold *adj.* WINTRY: crisp, cool, freezing, frosty, frigid, nippy, brisk, numbing, raw; UNFEELING: unfriendly, indifferent, reserved
collaborate *v.* cooperate, conspire
collapse *v.* drop, deflate, fall, fail
collateral *n.* security, guarantee, pledge, insurance
colleague *n.* associate, partner, collaborator
collect *v.* CONSOLIDATE: amass, accumulate, concentrate; CONGREGATE: assemble, flock, gather
collection *n.* assortment, accumulation, assemblage, concentration, mess, lot, heap, bunch
collector *n.* hobbyist, fancier, curator, hoarder
collide *v.* hit, strike, crash; clash, disagree, oppose
collision *n.* impact, contact, encounter, crash
collusion *n.* conspiracy, plot
colorful *adj.* bright, vivid; picturesque, quaint

colossal *adj.* large, huge, enormous, immense

column *n.* **SUPPORT:** pillar, shaft, pylon, post; **COMMENTARY:** article, editorial

coma *n.* unconsciousness, trance, stupor, sleep

combat *n.* conflict, battle, struggle, warfare, fight

combine *v.* link, join, fuse, merge, blend, mix, unite

comedian *n.* comic, jester, entertainer, actor, clown

comedy *n.* farce, satire, burlesque, slapstick

comely *adj.* attractive, pleasing

comfort *n.* contentment, relaxation, repose, ease

comfort *v.* soothe, encourage, reassure, console

comfortable *adj.* **CONTENTED:** relaxed, untroubled, soothed, satisfied; **SATISFACTORY:** snug, cozy, luxurious, rich, restful, pleasant

comic, comical *adj.* funny, silly, humorous, ironic

command *v.* **ORDER:** charge, tell, demand; **CONTROL:** rule, dominate, master

commemorate *v.* honor, solemnize, memorialize

commence *v.* begin, start, originate

commend *v.* praise, laud, support, acclaim, approve

commensurate *adj.* equivalent, comparable

comment *v.* remark, criticize, mention, interject, say

commentary *n.* criticism, analysis, interpretation

commerce *n.* trading, marketing, business

commission *n.* **AUTHORITY:** license, permission; **COMMITTEE:** representatives, board; **PAYMENT:** royalty, fee

commission *v.* delegate, appoint, authorize, charge

commit *v.* **PERPETRATE:** complete, perform; **ENTRUST:** delegate, promise, charge, employ, dispatch

commitment *n.* responsibility, duty, promise

commodious *adj.* comfortable, large, spacious

commodity *n.* goods, merchandise, wares
commotion *n.* disturbance, tumult, uproar
communal *adj.* shared, cooperative, mutual, public
communicate *v.* impart, inform, tell, confer, talk, converse, chat, write
communication *n.* utterance, writing, broadcasting, speaking, interchange
community *n.* public, people; village, colony, hamlet
compact *adj.* small, light, dense
compact *n.* covenant, understanding
compact *v.* pack, compress
companion *n.* comrade, escort, chaperon, bodyguard
companionship *n.* brotherhood, fellowship, friendship
company *n.* **ASSEMBLY:** throng, band, gathering; **BUSINESS:** firm, corporation; **GUEST:** visitor, caller
comparable *adj.* **SIMILAR:** akin, relative, alike, like; **EQUAL:** equivalent, tantamount
compare *v.* **LIKEN:** relate, associate, link, correlate; **EXAMINE:** contrast, weigh, analyze
compassion *n.* concern, sympathy, pity
compatible *adj.* agreeable, congruous, harmonious
compel *v.* force, enforce, constrain, coerce
compelling *adj.* forceful, impressive
compensate *v.* offset, repay, recompense, remunerate
compete *v.* strive, struggle, oppose, clash, encounter
competent *adj.* qualified, suitable, fit, skilled, able
competition *n.* rivalry; contest, meet, game
compile *v.* gather, collect, assemble, accumulate, edit
complacent *adj.* self–satisfied, egotistic, happy, smug
complain *v.* grumble, remonstrate, fret, fuss, gripe
complaint *n.* **OBJECTION:** charge, criticism, reproach, accusation; **ILLNESS:** ailment, disease, infirmity

complete *v.* execute, consummate, perfect, accomplish, realize, perform, achieve, fulfill, conclude
complex *adj.* MULTIPLE: combined, compounded; CONVOLUTED: intricate, complicated, tortuous, knotty
complex *n.* phobia, mania, insanity
complexion *n.* coloration, tinge, cast, pigmentation
compliance *n.* agreement, assent, conformity
complicate *v.* snarl, confound, jumble, tangle
complicated *adj.* intricate, tangled, complex
complicity *n.* collusion, conspiracy, involvement
compliment *v.* congratulate, honor, cheer, salute, hail, toast, applaud, commend, acclaim, glorify
complimentary *adj.* flattering, laudatory, approving
composure *n.* self–control, calmness, poise, aplomb
compound *v.* combine, mix
comprehend *v.* understand, grasp, discern, perceive
comprehensive *adj.* broad, extensive, sweeping
comprise *v.* include, contain, embrace, embody
compromise *v.* settle, agree, conciliate, negotiate
compulsive *adj.* driven, passionate
compulsory *adj.* obligatory, requisite, necessary
compunction *n.* apprehension, qualm, uneasiness,
conceal *v.* cover, screen, secrete, hide
concede *v.* acknowledge, grant, yield, admit, allow
conceit *n.* arrogance, narcissism, vanity
conceivable *adj.* believable, understandable, likely
concept *n.* theory, idea, notion, thought
conceptual *adj.* theoretical, ideal
concern *v.* PERTAIN: relate, influence; BOTHER: worry
conciliate *v.* appease, placate
concise *adj.* succinct, brief, condensed, short
conclave *n.* gathering, meeting, parley

conclude *v.* **CLOSE:** terminate, finish, complete, achieve; **DEDUCE:** presume, reason, gather, assume
concoct *v.* make, devise
concur *v.* correspond, coincide, agree, equal
concurrent *adj.* parallel, coexisting, simultaneous
condemn *v.* doom, sentence, damn, convict, punish
condescending *adj.* patronizing, disdainful, smug
condiment *n.* seasoning, relish
condition *n.* **REQUIREMENT:** stipulation, provision; **FITNESS:** tone, shape; **CIRCUMSTANCE:** situation, position, status; **MODIFIER:** limitation, restriction, qualification, restraint; **ILLNESS:** ailment, infirmity
condone *v.* forgive, disregard, excuse, overlook
conduct *n.* behavior, deportment, demeanor, manner
conduct *v.* **LEAD:** guide, escort, attend, accompany; **MANAGE:** administer, handle
confederacy *n.* alliance, coalition, federation
confer *v.* converse, deliberate, parley, discuss
conference *n.* meeting, discussion, gathering
confess *v.* acknowledge, own, concede, admit
confession *n.* disclosure, acknowledgment
confidant *n.* friend, adherent, companion
confident *adj.* assured, fearless, dauntless, bold
confidential *adj.* secret, classified, intimate, private
confine *v.* restrain, restrict; imprison, incarcerate
confirm *v.* **RATIFY:** affirm, settle, approve, endorse; **PROVE:** validate, verify, authenticate, explain
confiscate *v.* seize, appropriate, impound, usurp
conflict *v.* clash, contrast, contend, fight, oppose
conform *v.* adapt, accommodate, reconcile, agree
conformity *n.* **SIMILARITY:** correspondence, resemblance; **OBEDIENCE:** submission, compliance

confound *v.* confuse, bewilder, puzzle, perplex
confront *v.* brave, defy, repel, dare, face
confrontation *n.* meeting, battle, strife, dispute
confuse *v.* bewilder, befuddle, puzzle, perplex, confound, fluster, embarrass, disconcert, baffle, mystify
congeal *v.* thicken, solidify
congenial *adj.* friendly, compatible, harmonious
congregate *v.* gather, assemble, convene, meet
congruous *adj.* appropriate, suitable, fitting
conjecture *n.* guess, opinion, speculation
connect *v.* join, link, attach, associate, relate
connoisseur *n.* critic, expert, judge
connotation *n.* implication, meaning, insinuation,
conquer *v.* overcome, subdue, crush, defeat
conqueror *n.* vanquisher, champion, hero, winner
conquest *n.* triumph, success, conquering, victory
conscience *n.* duty, morals, shame
conscientious *adj.* thorough, fastidious, meticulous, complete, careful, reliable
conscious *adj.* awake, aware, sentient, cognizant, discerning, knowing, mindful, understanding
consecutive *adj.* ordered, chronological, sequential
consensus *n.* agreement, consent, unison, accord
consent *v.* accede, acquiesce, agree, allow, approve
consequence *n.* **EFFECT:** outgrowth, end, outcome, result; **IMPORTANCE:** moment, value, weight
conservative *adj.* cautious, reserved, conventional
consider *v.* contemplate, regard, think, believe
considerable *adj.* **IMPORTANT:** noteworthy, significant; **SUBSTANTIAL:** abundant, lavish, bountiful, plentiful
considerate *adj.* kind, solicitous, polite, thoughtful
consideration *n.* **THOUGHTFULNESS:** attentiveness,

kindness; **PAYMENT:** remuneration, salary, wage
consistent *adj.* constant, rational, regular
consolation *n.* sympathy, compassion, pity
console *v.* comfort, cheer, gladden, encourage
consolidate *v.* combine, mix, unify, compress, pack
consortium *n.* alliance, union
conspicuous *adj.* obvious, striking, prominent, flagrant, noticeable
conspiracy *n.* plan, intrigue, collusion, connivance
conspirator *n.* betrayer, schemer, cabalist, traitor
constant *adj.* unchanging, steadfast, steady, uniform, unvarying, unbroken, regular
consternation *n.* confusion, distress
constituent *adj.* component, element, ingredient, part
constitute *v.* **FOUND:** develop, create, establish; **MAKE UP:** frame, compound, compose
constraint *n.* **FORCE:** coercion, compulsion, pressure; **SHYNESS:** bashfulness, restraint, humility, reserve; **CONFINEMENT:** captivity, detention, restriction, arrest
constrict *v.* squeeze, contract, cramp, tighten
construct *v.* build, erect, make, fabricate, create
constructive *adj.* helpful, useful, instructive, valuable, effective
consult *v.* confer, parley, conspire, counsel, ask
consume *v.* **USE:** spend, deplete; **EAT:** absorb, devour
consumer *n.* user, customer, shopper, buyer
consummate *v.* complete, perfect
consumption *n.* spending, expense, use, waste,
contact *v.* touch, reach, communicate, talk
contagious *adj.* communicable, infectious, spreading, epidemic, deadly, endemic, catching
contain *v.* hold, keep, limit, stop, restrain

contaminate *v.* pollute, infect, defile, corrupt, dirty
contemplate *v.* study, ponder, consider, muse, think
contemporary *adj.* current, fashionable, modern
contempt *n.* disdain, disrespect, scorn, derision
contend *v.* compete, contest, battle, dispute, fight, argue, claim
content, contented *adj.* satisfied, appeased, gratified
contention *n.* **ARGUMENT:** quarrel, struggle, competition, dispute; **ASSERTION:** charge, declaration
contest *n.* competition, trial, match, challenge, game
contest *v.* dispute, challenge, compete, oppose,
contiguous *adj.* touching, adjacent
contingency *n.* possibility, likelihood, chance
continual *adj.* uninterrupted, unbroken, regular
continuation *n.* extension, supplement, addition
continue *v.* **PERSIST:** endure, persevere, progress; **RESUME:** renew, return, reinstate, reestablish
contort *v.* twist, deform, misshape, distort
contraband *n.* plunder, booty
contract *v.* **AGREE:** pledge, bargain, stipulate, obligate; **REDUCE:** diminish, shrink, recede, condense, compress, decrease; **ACQUIRE:** catch, get, incur
contradiction *n.* incongruity, inconsistency, opposition, difference, opposite
contrary *adj.* **OPPOSED:** antagonistic, hostile, counter; **DISAGREEABLE:** contradictory, unpropitious; **OBSTINATE:** willful, headstrong, stubborn
contrast *v.* compare, differentiate, deviate, differ, vary
contribute *v.* give, endow, bestow, present, confer, bequest, grant, donate, bequeath, subsidize
contrive *v.* create, devise, scheme, improvise, invent
control *v.* **CHECK:** constrain, repress, restrain; **DIRECT:**

lead, dominate, supervise, head, manage, govern
controversial *adj.* disputable, debatable, uncertain
controversy *n.* contention, debate, quarrel, difference
convene *v.* assemble, congregate, collect, gather
convenient *adj.* accessible, available, handy, close
convention *n.* **GATHERING:** assembly, convocation, meeting; **CUSTOM:** practice, habit, fashion
conventional *adj.* accepted, customary, typical, commonplace, traditional, formal
conversant *adj.* familiar, knowledgeable, experienced
conversation *n.* talk, discussion, discourse, speech
converse *v.* speak, talk, visit
converse *n.* antithesis, reverse, opposite
conversion *n.* change, turn, regeneration
convert *v.* alter, transform, change, reform
convey *v.* transport, transfer, communicate, send
convict *n.* captive, felon, criminal, prisoner
convict *v.* condemn, sentence, doom
conviction *n.* persuasion, confidence, belief, faith
convince *v.* persuade, establish, satisfy, teach
convincing *adj.* reasonable, plausible, likely
convivial *adj.* congenial, gregarious
cooperate *v.* conspire, participate, agree
copious *adj.* abundant, abounding
copy *v.* **IMITATE:** mimic, ape; **REPRODUCE:** duplicate, counterfeit, forge, depict, portray
cordial *adj.* friendly, genial, hearty, warm–hearted
core *n.* essence, gist, kernel, heart, center, hub
corporation *n.* enterprise, company, business
corporeal *adj.* material, tangible
corpse *n.* body, carcass, remains, cadaver
corral *v.* surround, capture

correct *adj.* **ACCURATE:** true, right; **PROPER:** suitable
correct *v.* adjust, remedy, rectify, amend, repair
correctness *n.* **ACCURACY:** precision, exactness; **PROPRIETY:** decency, decorum, fitness
correlation *n.* interdependence, equivalence
correspond *v.* **BE SIMILAR:** compare, match, resemble, conform; **COMMUNICATE:** write, reply, answer
correspondence *n.* **LIKENESS:** conformity, equivalence, similarity; **COMMUNICATION:** message, letter
corroborate *v.* confirm, prove, support, strengthen
corrupt *adj.* immoral, underhanded, fraudulent, crooked, nefarious, unscrupulous, shady, dishonest
corrupt *v.* debase, pervert, adulterate, taint, spoil
cost *n.* price, value, expense, payment, charge
costly *adj.* expensive, splendid, high–priced, precious
costume *n.* dress, clothing, attire, apparel, garb
couch *n.* sofa, lounge, davenport, chair
council *n.* group, cabinet, directorate, committee
counsel *n.* **ADVICE:** guidance, instruction, suggestion; **ADVISER:** lawyer, attorney, barrister
countenance *n.* appearance, aspect
countenance *v.* approve, endorse
counter *v.* react, respond
counter *n.* board, shelf, ledge, bench, table
counteract *v.* mitigate, check, invalidate, hinder
counterfeit *adj.* forged, fraudulent, fictitious, false
countermand *v.* cancel, reverse
countersign *n.* authentication, confirmation, sign
countless *adj.* innumerable, incalculable, infinite
coup *n.* feat, achievement
couple *n.* pair, two, set, brace,
couple *v.* join, unite, link, copulate

courage *n.* valor, boldness, spirit, audacity, mettle, stoutheartedness, gallantry, daring, spunk, strength

course *n.* route, passage, pathway, road

court *n.* SQUARE: patio, yard; ARENA: rink, ring, field

courteous *adj.* well–mannered, courtly, affable, polite

courtesy *n.* affability, politeness, refinement

covenant *n.* agreement, contract

cover *v.* WRAP: envelop, enshroud, encase; PROTECT: shield, screen, house, shelter; HIDE: screen, mask, disguise; INCLUDE: embrace, comprise, incorporate; TRAVEL: traverse, cross; FLOOD: drench, engulf; REPORT: recount, narrate, relate, broadcast, record

covert *adj.* hidden, disguised

cower *v.* cringe, shrink, quake, tremble, shake, snivel, flinch, quail, grovel

coy *adj.* shy, demur, evasive, bashful, humble

cozy *adj.* comfortable, secure, sheltered, snug, safe

crabby *adj.* grouchy, ill–humored

crack *n.* OPENING: crevice, cleft, fissure, rift; BLOW: hit, thwack, stroke; COMMENT: retort, jest, joke, remark

crack *v.* BREAK: cleave, burst, split, sever; DAMAGE: injure, hurt, impair; SOLVE: answer, decode

craft *n.* TRADE: occupation, career, work, job; SKILL: proficiency, competence, aptitude, ability

craftsman *n.* artisan, journeyman, machinist, artist

craggy *adj.* rough, steep, irregular

cramp *n.* spasm, crick, pang, pain

cramped *adj.* confined, restraining, restricted

crank *n.* DEVICE: bracket, bend, arm, handle; PERSON: eccentric, character, complainer, grouch

cranky *adj.* irritable, ill–tempered, disagreeable

crash *v.* FALL: plunge, tumble, drop; COLLIDE: jostle,

bump, jolt, hit; **MAKE NOISE:** clatter, bang, smash;
BREAK: shatter, splinter, smash; **GO UNINVITED:** invade, intrude, interrupt, meddle
crate *n.* box, carton, cage, container, package
crater *n.* depression, hollow, opening, abyss, hole
craving *n.* need, longing, yearning, desire
crawl *v.* creep, wriggle, squirm, slither, writhe, grovel
crazy *adj.* crazed, demented, mad, insane, foolish
cream *n.* lotion, cosmetic, jelly, salve, emulsion
creamy *adj.* smooth, buttery, rich, soft
create *v.* originate, build, fashion, shape, fabricate
creative *adj.* imaginative, inventive, artistic, original
creature *n.* being, creation, beast, animal
credibility *n.* likelihood, probability, chance
credible *adj.* plausible, believable, reliable
creditor *n.* lender, mortgagor, banker
creed *n.* belief, doctrine, dogma, faith
creep *v.* slither, writhe, crawl
creepy *adj.* apprehensive, uneasy
crestfallen *adj.* saddened, shamed, disheartened
crevice *n.* crack, chasm, cleft, slit, gap
crew *n.* company, troupe, squad, organization, team
crime *n.* transgression, wrongdoing, offense, violation
criminal *adj.* illegal, felonious, bad
criminal *n.* lawbreaker, felon, crook, gangster, thief
cringe *v.* cower, shrink, flinch, quail, wince, crawl
crisis *n.* straits, plight, predicament, trauma, pickle
crisp *adj.* **INVIGORATING:** brisk, fresh, bracing, stimulating; **FRESH:** green, plump, ripe
criterion *n.* basis, foundation, standard, principle
critic *n.* **REVIEWER:** commentator, analyst, examiner;
FAULTFINDER: detractor, complainer, mud–slinger

critical *adj.* **DISAPPROVING:** condemning, censuring, disparaging, sarcastic; **ANALYTICAL:** perceptive, discerning, observant; **CRUCIAL:** decisive, significant

criticize *v.* **EVALUATE:** study, analyze, examine; **FIND FAULT:** chastise, reprove, reprimand, blame

crook *n.* **CRIMINAL:** swindler, thief, rogue; **BEND:** notch, fork, angle, bend

crooked *adj.* **CURVED:** bowed, twisted, bent; **DISHONEST:** iniquitous, devious, corrupt, nefarious

crop *v.* trim, cut, clip

cross *adj.* angry, cranky, pettish, critical, irritable

cross *v.* **INTERSECT:** divide, traverse, span; **INTERBREED:** mingle, cross–pollinate, mix

crucial *adj.* **CRITICAL:** decisive, climatic, deciding; **SEVERE:** trying, taxing, hard, difficult

crude *adj.* unrefined, rough, unpolished, coarse

cruel *adj.* heartless, malevolent, vicious, savage

cruise *v.* travel, voyage, navigate, coast, sail

crumb *n.* piece, fragment, particle, scrap, pinch, bit

crumble *v.* decay, disintegrate, collapse

crumple *v.* collapse, rumple, crush, crease, wrinkle

crush *v.* **SUBDUE:** defeat, overwhelm, annihilate; **BREAK:** smash, pulverize, powder, grind

crust *n.* hull, rind, piecrust, shell, edge, border

cry *v.* weep, sob, wail, sorrow, grieve

cuddle *v.* embrace, snuggle, huddle, nestle

cuddly *adj.* affectionate, lovable

cue *n.* signal, hint, prompt

cuff *n.* slap, blow, punch, hit

culminate *v.* finish, close, end

cultivate *v.* nurture, educate, refine, improve, teach

cultivation *n.* horticulture, agriculture, gardening

cultural *adj.* educational, enlightening, enriching

culture *n.* FOLKWAYS: convention, custom, mores; RE-FINEMENT: breeding, gentility, manners, polish

cunning *adj.* sly, crafty, clever, skillful, ingenious

cure *v.* restore, heal, remedy

curious *adj.* INQUISITIVE: interested, inquiring, questioning; UNUSUAL: strange, odd, rare, queer, unique

current *adj.* prevailing, contemporary, fashionable

current *n.* drift, flow, tide

curt *adj.* brusque, brief, concise, terse, short

curtain *n.* hanging, screen, drape, drapery, shutter

curve *n.* arc, bow, arch

curve *v.* deviate, vow, crook, twist, bend

custodian *n.* caretaker, attendant, gatekeeper

custody *n.* care, protection, guardianship

custom *n.* tradition, practice, convention, ritual

customary *adj.* usual, habitual, conventional

cut *v.* REDUCE: shorten, curtail, lessen, decrease; SEVER: separate, cleave; CROSS: intersect, pass

cutback *v.* reduce, curtail, shorten, decrease

cycle *n.* sequence, series, succession, period

cynic *n.* skeptic, mocker, scoffer, detractor, critic

cynical *adj.* sardonic, unbelieving, sneering, sarcastic

dabble *v.* dally, trifle, putter

daffy *adj.* silly, ridiculous

dainty *adj.* delicate, fragile, petite, airy, lacy, cute

dally *v.* dawdle, trifle with, putter, dabble

dam *v.* obstruct, check, restrict, restrain

damage *v.* injure, scratch, mar, deface, break

damages *n.* compensation, reparations, costs, reimbursement, expense

damp *adj.* moist, humid, sodden, soggy, wet

danger *n.* risk, peril, jeopardy, threat, menace

dangerous *adj.* perilous, serious, vital, hazardous, risky, deadly, precarious, treacherous, unsafe

dangle *v.* hang, droop, sway, suspend

dank *adj.* damp, clammy

dare *n.* dare, challenge, defy

dare *v.* **VENTURE:** undertake, endeavor, hazard, risk, try; **DEFY:** confront, oppose, brave, challenge, face

daring *adj.* bold, courageous, fearless, brave

dark *adj.* **SINISTER:** evil, bad, gloomy, dismal, immoral, corrupt; **UNLIT:** dim, shadowy, somber, indistinct, dusky, murky, gloomy, obscure, shady, hazy

darken *v.* cloud, shade, shadow, blacken, shade

darkness *n.* **GLOOM:** murkiness, dimness, nightfall, night; **EVIL:** wickedness, sin, corruption; **SECRECY:** concealment, isolation, obscurity, seclusion, privacy

dart *n.* missile, barb, arrow, weapon

dart *v.* shoot, speed, plunge, thrust, hurtle, fling, heave, pitch, dash, spurt, skim, fly, scoot

dash *n.* little, sprinkle, scattering, grain, trace

dash *v.* **RUSH:** race, sprint, speed, hurry, run; **DISCOURAGE:** smash, dampen, dismay, dispirit

dashing *adj.* adventurous, dapper

data *n.* information, details, facts, statistics, figures

date *n.* **APPOINTMENT:** rendezvous, engagement, call, visit; **COMPANION:** partner, friend, lover

date *v.* **ACCOMPANY:** court, escort, accompany

dawn *n.* start, sunrise, daybreak, morning, beginning

daze *n.* stupor, bewilderment, distraction, confusion

daze *v.* stun, bewilder

dazzle *v.* blind, amaze,

dead *adj.* **LIFELESS:** deceased, perished, inanimate, defunct, still; **NUMB:** insensible, anesthetized; **EXHAUSTED:** wearied, worn, spent, tired

deaden *v.* anesthetize, dull, chloroform, numb

deafening *adj.* thunderous, overpowering, loud

deal *n.* agreement, pledge, pact, contract

deal *v.* trade, barter, bargain, buy, sell, distribute

dealer *n.* vendor, businessman, merchant

debar *v.* exclude, prohibit, restrict

debatable *adj.* disputable, unsettled, controversial, questionable

debate *v.* discuss, contend, contest, dispute, argue

debris *n.* remains, rubble, rubbish, wreckage, trash

debt *n.* obligation, liability, mortgage, note

debtor *n.* purchaser, borrower, mortgagor, buyer

decadent *adj.* immoral, wicked, degenerate, bad

deceit *n.* misrepresentation, trickery, fraud, duplicity, deception, dishonesty

deceitful *adj.* tricky, cunning, insincere, dishonest

deceive *v.* mislead, swindle, delude, defraud, victimize, betray, hoodwink, dupe, fleece, bilk

deceiver *n.* conniver, swindler, impostor, cheat

decent *adj.* seemly, respectable, nice, proper, ethical, virtuous, trustworthy, upright, good

deception *n.* trickery, craftiness, treachery, betrayal, pretense, deceit, duplicity, dishonesty

deceptive *adj.* misleading, misrepresenting

decide *v.* settle, determine, judge, select, pick

decipher *v.* interpret, decode, translate, explain, solve

decision *n.* judgment, resolution, result, opinion

decisive *adj.* conclusive, resolved, final, definitive, absolute, definite, determined

declaration *n.* statement, assertion, affirmation,

proclamation, affidavit, testimony, announcement

declare *v.* state, assert, tell, affirm, maintain, testify, certify, contend, allege, profess, swear

decline *v.* DETERIORATE: decrease, degenerate, backslide; REFUSE: desist

decorate *v.* adorn, beautify, renovate, brighten, enhance, embellish, elaborate

decoration *n.* EMBELLISHMENT: adornment, ornamentation, design; CITATION: medal, ribbon, emblem

decorative *adj.* ornamental, aesthetic, embellishing, beautifying, florid, ornate

decrease *v.* lessen, diminish, decline, subside, shrink, reduce, check, curb, restrain, blunt, curtail

decree *n.* proclamation, edict, pronouncement, declaration, judgment

decrepit *adj.* worn, aged

dedicate *v.* devote, apportion, assign

dedication *n.* sanctification, devotion, celebration

deduce *v.* conclude, infer

deduction *n.* SUBTRACTION: reduction, abatement, decrease, discount; REASONING: inference, thought; CONCLUSION: answer, judgment, opinion

deed *n.* ACTION: act, commission, accomplishment; DOCUMENT: release, agreement, charter, title

deep *adj.* IMMERSED: subterranean, underground; COMPREHENSIVE: penetrating, acute, profound

default *n.* failure, neglect, shortcoming, insufficiency

defeat *v.* conquer, overcome, vanquish, subdue, best, overthrow, crush, overwhelm, repulse, decimate

defect *n.* imperfection, fault, deficiency, flaw

defect *v.* abandon, forsake, desert, leave

defective *adj.* imperfect, inadequate, faulty, poor

defend *v.* **PROTECT:** shield, shelter, screen; **JUSTIFY:** plead, alibi, endorse, recommend, support

defender *n.* champion, patron, guardian, protector

defense *n.* **RESISTANCE:** protection, security, backing; **PLEA:** denial, alibi, explanation, justification, proof

defer *v.* postpone, shelve, delay, suspend

deference *n.* regard, veneration, homage, reverence

deferent, deferential *adj.* respectful, obedient

defiance *n.* insubordination, rebellion, insurgence, disobedience

defiant *adj.* resistant, obstinate, rebellious

deficient *adj.* lacking, defective, insufficient, skimpy, meager, inadequate,

deficit *n.* shortage, paucity, deficiency, lack

defile *v.* corrupt, debase, ravish, violate, molest

define *v.* **LIMIT:** bound, confine, circumscribe, edge; **DESCRIBE:** designate, characterize, represent, exemplify, explain, name

definite *adj.* **EXACT:** fixed, precise, positive, decisive, specific, categorical; **CLEAR:** sharp, distinct, unmistakable, obvious, plain; **POSITIVE:** sure, certain

definition *n.* meaning, terminology, signification, translation, explanation, description

definitive *adj.* conclusive, precise, final, absolute

deform *v.* damage, disfigure, deface, injure

deformity *n.* malformation, ugliness, unsightliness

defraud *v.* hoax, dupe, cheat, deceive

deft *adj.* skillful, dexterous

defy *v.* resist, oppose, insult, face, dare

degenerate *adj.* corrupted, depraved, immoral, bad

degradation *n.* depravity, corruption, degeneration, evil

degrade *v.* disgrace, debase, demote, discredit, diminish, humble
degraded *adj.* disgraced, debased, depraved, bad
degree *n.* MEASURE: gradation, size, dimension, gauge; RANGE: extent, quality, potency, proportion, intensity, scope; DIPLOMA: baccalaureate, doctorate, sheepskin,
dehydrate *v.* dry, desiccate, parch, drain
deify *v.* exalt, idealize, worship
deity *n.* god, divinity
dejected *adj.* dispirited, depressed, sad
delay *v.* postpone, defer, deter, impede, detain, check, curb, procrastinate, suspend, interrupt
delectable *adj.* delicious, pleasing, tasty
delegate *n.* legate, emissary, proxy, deputy, consul, minister, ambassador, agent, representative
delegate *v.* authorize, appoint, commission, name, nominate, select, choose, assign, deputize
deliberate *adj.* intentional, conscious, studied, planned, willful, considered, calculated, intended, purposeful, premeditated, designed, unhurried
deliberate *v.* confer, consider, ponder
delicacy *n.* FINENESS: daintiness, flimsiness, softness, lightness; FOOD: tidbit, morsel, delight, import
delicate *adj.* FINE: dainty, fragile, frail, subtle, tactful; SICKLY: susceptible, feeble, weak
delicious *adj.* tasty, savory, appetizing, delectable
delight *n.* enjoyment, joy, pleasure, happiness
delight *v.* fascinate, amuse, please, entertain
delightful *adj.* charming, amusing, clever, pleasant
delineate *v.* depict, describe
delinquent *adj.* LAX: tardy, negligent, derelict, remiss,

careless; **OVERDUE:** owed, due, unpaid

delirious *adj.* demented, crazy, irrational, insane

delirium *n.* hallucinations, confusion

deliver *v.* **BRING FORTH:** produce, provide; **FREE:** liberate, save; **TRANSFER:** pass, remit, give; **SPEAK:** present, address; **DISTRIBUTE:** allot, dispense

delude *v.* mislead, deceive

deluge *v.* flood, overwhelm

delusion *n.* phantasm, hallucination, fancy, illusion

demand *v.* request, charge, direct, command, ask

demanding *adj.* challenging, difficult, fussy, imperious, exacting, critical

demean *v.* debase, humble

demented *adj.* crazy, bemused, unbalanced, insane

demolish *v.* destroy, wreck, devastate, obliterate

demolition *n.* extermination, annihilation, wrecking, destruction, explosion

demonstrate *v.* **PROVE:** show, confirm; **ILLUSTRATE:** exhibit, manifest, parade, display

demonstration *n.* **EXHIBITION:** showing, presentation, display; **RALLY:** march, sit-in, protest

demoralize *v.* dishearten, confuse, weaken, unman, enfeeble, discourage

demure *adj.* modest, reserved

denial *n.* refusal, repudiation, rejection, refutation

denounce *v.* condemn, accuse, charge, blame, revile, reproach, rebuke, scold, reprimand

dense *adj.* **COMPACT:** thick, opaque, solid, impenetrable; **SLOW-WITTED:** stupid, dull, ignorant

deny *v.* contradict, disagree, disavow, disclaim, repudiate, controvert, renounce

depart *v.* leave, go, quit, withdraw

departure *n.* embarkation, evacuation, exodus, exit
dependable *adj.* trustworthy, steady, sure, reliable
dependent *adj.* **HELPLESS:** poor, immature, clinging, weak; **CONTINGENT:** conditional
depict *v.* represent, picture,
depletion *n.* exhaustion, consumption, deficiency
deplorable *adj.* tragic, distressing
deport *v.* exile, expel, banish
deposit *v.* **PLACE:** drop, put, install, leave; **PRESENT FOR SAFEKEEPING:** invest, store, bank, entrust
depreciate *v.* deteriorate, lessen, worsen, decrease
depreciation *n.* harm, reduction, shrinkage, loss
depress *v.* **PRESS DOWN:** squash, flatten; **DISMAY:** dampen, sadden, deject, oppress, discourage
depressed *adj.* discouraged, disheartened, sad
deprive *v.* strip, despoil, divest, seize
deputy *n.* assistant, lieutenant, aide, delegate
deranged *adj.*; disturbed, demented, crazy, insane
derelict *adj.* abandoned, negligent, delinquent
deride *v.* mock, ridicule, scorn, jeer
derivation *n.* root, source, beginning, origin
derive *v.* obtain, determine, conclude, assume
derivative *adj.* borrowed, learned
derogatory *adj.* disparaging, belittling, faultfinding, detracting, critical, sarcastic
descend *v.* plunge, sink, dip, plummet, tumble
descendants *n.* offspring, kin, children, family
descent *n.* **MOTION:** drop, sinking, reduction, tumble, decline, fall; **INCLINE:** declivity, slide, hill, inclination; **RELATIONSHIP:** extraction, origin, lineage, family
describe *v.* recount, portray, depict, picture, specify, illustrate, name, define, explain

description *n.* story, portrayal, account, characterization, brief, summary, depiction

descriptive *adj.* lifelike, vivid, picturesque, eloquent

desert *n.* waste, wastelands, wilderness

desert *v.* abandon, defect, leave

deserter *n.* runaway, fugitive, defector, traitor

deserve *v.* merit, earn, rate

deserved *adj.* justified, merited, rightful, fitting, just

deserving *adj.* needy; rightful, fitting, worthy

design *n.* plan, schematic, rendering, pattern, layout, diagram, drawing, sketch, blueprint, plan

design *v.* invent, devise, outline, sketch, plan

designate *v.* specify, appoint, indicate, name, choose

designation *n.* classification, appellation, class, name

designer *n.* planner, draftsman, modeler, architect, artist, sculptor

desire *n.* aspiration, longing, craving, lust, wish, mania, hunger, yearning, hankering, itch, yen, passion

desire *v.* want, wish, covet, crave, need

desist *v.* cease, abstain

desolate *adj.* forsaken, dreary, deserted, uninhabited, abandoned, isolated, disconsolate, forlorn,

desolation *n.* barrenness, devastation

despair *n.* hopelessness, depression, discouragement, desperation, gloom

despairing *adj.* despondent, miserable, sad

desperate *adj.* **HOPELESS:** despairing, downcast; **RECKLESS:** foolhardy, incautious, wild, careless, rash

despicable *adj.* detestable, contemptible, abject, base

despise *v.* disdain, scorn, condemn, hate

despondent *adj.* dejected, discouraged, depressed

destiny *n.* fate, future, fortune, doom

destitute *adj.* lacking, impoverished, poverty-stricken, penniless, poor

destroy *v.* ruin, demolish, raze, eradicate, annihilate, obliterate, extinguish, finish

destruction *n.* **DEMOLITION:** ruin, annihilation, eradication, liquidation, extermination, elimination; **REMAINS:** ashes, wreck, remnant, ruins

destructive *adj.* **HARMFUL:** hurtful, injurious, troublesome; **DEADLY:** fatal, ruinous, devastating, vicious

detach *v.* disconnect, remove, separate, divide

detached *adj.* **ALOOF:** impartial, disinterested, apathetic, uninvolved, unconcerned, indifferent; **CUT OFF:** separated, loosened, divided, disjoined

detail *n.* particular, trait, feature, aspect, minutia

detail *v.* itemize, catalogue, analyze, describe

detain *v.* delay, hold, keep, inhibit, restrain

detect *v.* distinguish, recognize, identify, discover

detection *n.* exposure, disclosure, discovery

detention *n.* custody, quarantine, arrest, confinement, restraint

deter *v.* discourage, caution, dissuade, prevent, warn

deteriorate *v.* worsen, depreciate, lessen, degenerate

determination *n.* resolution, persistence, obstinacy, resolve, conviction, firmness, purpose

determine *v.* **DEFINE:** circumscribe, delimit, restrict; **ASCERTAIN:** learn, discover; **RESOLVE:** settle, conclude, decide

detest *v.* dislike, loathe, abhor, despise, hate

detestable *adj.* disgusting, abhorrent, despicable

detract *v.* diminish, lessen, depreciate, discredit

detriment *n.* damage, loss

devastate *v.* ravage, sack, pillage, destroy

devastation *n.* destruction, defoliation, waste

develop *v.* **IMPROVE:** enlarge, expand, extend, promote, cultivate, intensify; **GROW:** mature, evolve; **REVEAL:** unfold, disclose, unravel, uncover, explain

deviate *v.* deflect, digress, wander, stray, differ

deviation *n.* change, alteration, difference, variation

device *n.* **APPARATUS:** instrument, contrivance, mechanism, appliance, contraption, implement, utensil, gadget; **METHOD:** artifice, scheme, design, dodge, trick, ruse, plan, technique

devious *adj.* deceptive, crafty, indirect, foxy, insidious, shrewd, dishonest

devoid *adj.* lacking, empty

devote *v.* assign, apply, consecrate, bless, dedicate

devotion *n.* affection, allegiance, consecration, faithfulness, fidelity, loyalty, worship

devour *v.* eat, gulp, swallow, gorge, absorb

devout *adj.* religious, sincere, devoted, pious, reverent, faithful, holy

diabolical *adj.* fiendish, wicked

diagnosis *n.* analysis, determination, investigation, summary

diagram *n.* sketch, drawing, layout, picture, description, design, plan

dialect *n.* idiom, jargon, cant, vernacular, patois

dialogue *n.* conversation, talk, exchange, remarks

diaphanous *adj.* fine, transparent, thin, airy

diary *n.* journal, chronicle, log, record

diatribe *n.* tirade, denunciation

dicker *v.* barter, bargain, trade, argue

dictator *n.* ruler, autocrat, despot, tyrant, oppressor

diction *n.* enunciation, articulation, vocabulary

die *v.* **EXPIRE:** perish, succumb, croak; **DECLINE:** fade, ebb, wither, decay, weaken, vanish

die–hard *n.* zealot, reactionary, extremist

diet *v.* reduce, fast, starve, abstain

differ *v.* vary, diverge, contrast, conflict, contrast

difference *n.* **VARIANCE:** deviation, departure, exception; **DISAGREEMENT:** divergence, opposition, dissimilarity, diversity, departure, differentiation, contrast

different *adj.* **UNLIKE:** diverse, separate, miscellaneous, assorted, various; **UNUSUAL:** unconventional, strange, startling

difficult *adj.* **LABORIOUS:** strenuous, exacting, arduous, labored, demanding, onerous, challenging, exacting, formidable; **INTRICATE:** involved, perplexing, puzzling, mystifying, bewildering, profound, complicated, deep, ambiguous, obscure

difficulty *n.* **OBSTACLE:** obstruction, impediment, misfortune, distress, barricade, hindrance, barrier; **DISTURBANCE:** trouble, distress, anxiety, frustration

diffident *adj.* shy, insecure

diffuse *v.* spread, disperse

digest *v.* **CONDENSE:** summarize, recap; **EAT:** absorb, consume; **UNDERSTAND:** learn, study

digit *n.* finger, toe, unit, symbol, numeral, number

dignify *v.* honor, exalt, elevate, praise

dignity *n.* poise, bearing, air, stateliness, splendor, majesty, class, pride

digress *v.* stray, deviate

dilemma *n.* predicament, quandary, difficulty

dilettante *n.* dabbler, trifler

diligence *n.* earnestness, perseverance, industry, vigor, carefulness, intensity, attention, care

diligent *adj.* industrious, painstaking

dilute *v.* thin, weaken, add, mix, reduce

diminish *v.* reduce, lessen, depreciate, decrease

dingy *adj.* drab, dirty, grimy, muddy, soiled

diplomacy *n.* finesse, tact, artfulness, skill, discretion

diplomat *n.* ambassador, consul, minister, legate, emissary, envoy, agent, representative, statesman

diplomatic *adj.* tactful, gracious, calculating, conciliatory, conniving, subtle, discreet, politic, polite

dire *adj.* serious, desperate, dreadful, terrible, horrible, frightful

direct *adj.* IMMEDIATE: prompt, succeeding, resultant; SINCERE: frank, straightforward, outspoken, candid; STRAIGHT: undeviating, unswerving

direct *v.* POINT OUT: guide, conduct, show, lead; COMMAND: instruct, order, govern, manage, charge; AIM: sight, train, level

direction *n.* TENDENCY: bias, bent, proclivity, inclination; SUPERVISION: management, superintendence, control, administration; POSITION: objective, bearing

directly *adv.* instantly, at once, quickly, immediately

directory *n.* reference, list, register, record, roster

disability *n.* feebleness, incapacity, injury, weakness

disable *v.* incapacitate, cripple, impair, damage

disadvantage *n.* obstacle, restraint, handicap, inconvenience, drawback, weakness

disagree *v.* DIFFER: dissent, object, oppose, quarrel; EFFECT: nauseate, bother

disagreeable *adj.* obnoxious, offensive, irritable, rude, bothersome, upsetting, disturbing, offensive

disagreement *n.* DISCORD: contention, strife, conflict, controversy, opposition, hostility, clash, quarrel;

disappear

INCONSISTENCY: discrepancy, dissimilarity, disparity

disappear *v.* fade, die, escape, evaporate, vanish

disappearance *n.* departure, desertion, escape, exodus, disintegration, evaporation

disappoint *v.* dissatisfy, disillusion, frustrate, miscarry, thwart, foil, baffle

disapprove *v.* condemn, chastise, reprove, denounce

disarray *n.* confusion, disorder

disaster *n.* calamity, mishap, debacle, misadventure, defeat, failure, tragedy, cataclysm, catastrophe

disastrous *adj.* calamitous, ruinous, harmful

disburse *v.* pay, expend, use, contribute, spend

discard *v.* reject, expel, dispossess, relinquish

discerning *adj.* discriminating, perceptive, penetrating, discreet

discharge *v.* **UNLOAD:** remove, unpack, empty; **RELEASE:** liberate, free, fire

discipline *v.* **TRAIN:** control; **PUNISH:** chastise, correct

disclose *v.* reveal, confess, publish

disclosure *n.* exposé. confession, admission

discomfort *n.* annoyance, uneasiness, trouble, displeasure, embarrassment

disconcert *v.* confuse, embarrass

disconnect *v.* detach, separate, disengage, cut, divide

disconsolate *adj.* dejected, gloomy, inconsolable,

discontinue *v.* stop, end, finish, close, cease

discord *n.* conflict, strife, contention, disagreement

discount *v.* **REBATE:** allow, deduct, lower, reduce; **MINIMIZE:** reject, diminish, discredit, decrease

discourage *v.* dissuade, repress, scare, dampen, daunt, demoralize, depress, frighten

discourse *v.* converse, write, speak

discourteous *adj.* impolite, rude, boorish, crude

discourtesy *n.* impudence, vulgarity, rudeness

discover *v.* invent, ascertain, detect, recognize, determine, observe, uncover, find, learn

discovery *n.* detection, disclosure, determination

discredit *v.* question, disbelieve, distrust, doubt

discreet *adj.* prudent, cautious, discerning, reserved, wary, watchful, circumspect, politic, diplomatic

discrepancy *n.* variance, inconsistency

discrete *adj.* unconnected, distinctive

discretion *n.* caution, wariness, prudence, tact

discriminate *v.* differentiate, separate, distinguish

discrimination *n.* PERCEPTION: acuteness, judgment; PARTIALITY: unfairness, bias, bigotry, prejudice

discuss *v.* talk, argue, debate, dispute, confer, reason

discussion *n.* conversation, exchange, contention, dialogue, dispute

disease *n.* sickness, malady, ailment, illness, infirmity

disfavor *n.* disapproval, displeasure, disappointment

disfigure *v.* deface, mar, mutilate, damage, hurt

disgrace *v.* dishonor, debase, shame, degrade, discredit, humble, stigmatize

disgraceful *adj.* dishonorable, disreputable, shocking, offensive, shameful

disguise *n.* mask, costume, masquerade, façade

disguise *v.* alter, conceal, cloak, cover, obscure

disgust *v.* offend, repel, revolt, nauseate, sicken, shock, upset, disturb

disgusting *adj.* repugnant, revolting, sickening, offensive

disheveled *adj.* untidy, rumpled

dishonest *adj.* deceitful, backbiting, treacherous,

sneaky, deceptive, underhanded, unscrupulous, disreputable, mean, low, contemptible, false

dishonor *n.* shame, ignominy, abasement, disgrace

disillusion *v.* disenchant, disappoint

disinclined *adj.* hesitant, reluctant

disinfect *v.* sanitize, sterilize, purify, fumigate, clean

disintegrate *v.* separate, disperse, crumble, dissolve

disinterested *adj.* impartial, indifferent, unconcerned

disjointed *adj.* disconnected, unattached, separated; incoherent, rambling

dislike *v.* detest, deplore, abhor, hate, abominate, loathe, despise, scorn

dislodge *v.* eject, evict, uproot, oust, remove

disloyalty *n.* treason, betrayal, dishonesty

dismal *adj.* dreary, bleak, gloomy, melancholy, desolate, morbid, ghastly, gruesome, cheerless, dusky, dingy, murky, bleak, somber, creepy, spooky

dismantle *v.* disassemble, undo, demolish, level, ruin, raze, fell, destroy

dismay *n.* terror, dread, anxiety, fear

dismiss *v.* reject, repudiate, disperse, expel, abolish, dispossess, exile, expatriate, banish, deport

dismissal *n.* expulsion, removal

disobedience *n.* insubordination, defiance, insurgence, mutiny, revolt, noncompliance, rebellion

disobedient *adj.* insubordinate, refractory, defiant, rebellious, unruly

disobey *v.* balk, decline, refuse, disregard, defy

disorder *n.* confusion, disarray, turmoil, chaos, anarchy, rebellion, trouble

disorder *v.* disarrange, clutter, scatter, disorganize

disorderly *adj.* CONFUSED: jumbled, scattered, messy,

untidy, cluttered, unkempt, disorganized; **UNRULY:**
intemperate, drunk, rowdy
disorganize *v.* disperse, scatter, litter, disrupt
disorient, disorientate *v.* confuse, bewilder
disown *v.* disinherit, repudiate, deny
disparage *v.* discredit, belittle
disparate *adj.* dissimilar, diversified
dispatch *v.* **SEND:** transmit, express, forward; **END:**
finish, conclude, kill
dispel *v.* disperse, dissipate, distribute, scatter
dispensable *adj.* unnecessary, trivial, useless
dispense *v.* distribute, apportion, assign, allocate
disperse *v.* scatter, separate, disband
displace *v.* **REMOVE:** transpose, dislodge; **MISLAY:**
misplace, disarrange, lose
display *n.* exhibition, exhibit, presentation, demonstration, performance, parade, pageant
display *v.* show, exhibit, uncover, present, unveil
displease *v.* dissatisfy, annoy, vex, provoke, anger
displeasure *n.* disapproval, annoyance, resentment,
anger
disposed *adj.* prone, inclined, apt, likely
disposition *n.* **ARRANGEMENT:** distribution, organization, plan; **TEMPERAMENT:** character, temper, mood
disproportionate *adj.* uneven, irregular
disprove *v.* refute, invalidate, deny
disputable *adj.* doubtful, dubious, questionable
dispute *n.* conflict, squabble, disturbance, feud
dispute *v.* argue, debate, contradict, quarrel, discuss
disqualify *v.* preclude, disentitle, disbar
disregard *v.* ignore, neglect
disreputable *adj.* offensive, shameful

disrespect n. discourtesy, insolence, irreverence
disrespectful adj. discourteous, impolite, rude
disrupt v. intrude, obstruct, break, interrupt
disruption n. disturbance, agitation, confusion
dissatisfaction n. displeasure, disapproval, objection
disseminate v. scatter, spread, sow, propagate, broadcast, distribute
dissension n. disagreement, difference, dispute
dissent v. disagree, refuse, contradict, differ, oppose
disservice n. wrong, injury, injustice, insult
dissident adj. hostile, opposed
dissipated adj. scattered, dispersed, strewn, disseminated, wasted, squandered, spent, depleted
dissolution n. dissolving, termination
dissolve v. liquefy, evaporate, disintegrate: disappear
distant adj. RESERVED: aloof; AFAR: abroad, removed
distasteful adj. unpleasant, disagreeable, repugnant
distend v. inflate, stretch, enlarge, widen, distort
distinct adj. PERCEPTIBLE: clear, sharp, enunciated, audible lucid, plain, obvious, clear, definite; DISCRETE: separate, disunited
distinction n. DEFINITION: separation, difference; ACHIEVEMENT: repute, renown, prominence, fame
distinctive adj. unique, peculiar, distinguishing, characteristic
distinguish v. DISCERN: detect, notice, discover; HONOR: celebrate, acknowledge, admire, praise
distinguished n. MARKED: characterized, labeled, identified, unique, conspicuous, separated; NOTABLE: celebrated, eminent, illustrious, venerable, renowned, prominent, reputable, famous
distort v. alter, pervert, misinterpret, misconstrue

distortion *n.* **DEFORMITY:** twist, malformation, mutilation, contortion, **MISREPRESENTATION:** perversion, lie
distract *v.* detract, amuse, entertain, mislead
distracted *adj.* distraught, frenzied, troubled
distraction *n.* **CONFUSION:** perplexity, abstraction, complication, confusion; **DIVERSION:** amusement, pastime, preoccupation, entertainment, game
distraught *adj.* troubled, distressed
distress *n.* pain, anxiety, worry, sorrow, wretchedness, suffering, ordeal, anguish, grief, trouble
distress *v.* irritate, disturb, upset, bother
distribute *v.* disburse, dispense, issue, allocate
distributor *n.* wholesaler, jobber, merchant
district *n.* area, neighborhood, community, vicinity
distrust *v.* mistrust, suspect, disbelieve, doubt
distrustful *adj.* doubting, fearful, suspicious
disturb *v.* trouble, worry, perplex, startle, alarm, arouse, depress, distress, provoke, irritate, harass
diverge *v.* radiate, veer, swerve, deviate
divers *adj.* several, varied
diverse *adj.* dissimilar, assorted, different, distinct
diversify *v.* vary, expand, alter, change, increase
diversion *n.* entertainment, amusement, recreation, play, sport
divert *v.* deflect, redirect, avert, turn; distract, disturb
dividend *n.* bonus, profit, share
divine *adj.* godlike, sacred, hallowed, consecrated, anointed, sanctified, ordained, revered, venerated
division *n.* **PARTITION:** section, compartment, parcel, branch; **RIFT:** disagreement, difficulty, dispute
divulge *v.* reveal, disclose, impart, confess, expose
do *v.* **EXECUTE:** complete, fulfill, obey, perform, act,

work, labor, produce, create, accomplish, succeed, perform; **SUFFICE:** serve, satisfy

docile *adj.* submissive, meek, mild, tractable, pliant, willing, obliging, manageable, tame, obedient

doctor *n.* physician, surgeon, intern, veterinarian, chiropractor, homeopath, osteopath, healer, shaman, quack, anesthetist, dentist, pediatrician, gynecologist, oculist, obstetrician, psychiatrist, psychoanalyst, orthopedist, neurologist, cardiologist, pathologist, dermatologist, endocrinologist, opthamologist, urologist, hematologist

doctor *v.* treat, attend, administer

doctrine *n.* policy, conviction, tradition, canon

document *n.* record, paper, diary, report

documentary *n.* book, movie, report

dogmatic *adj.* authoritarian, dictatorial, stubborn, intolerant, opinionated, domineering, tyrannical

dolt *n.* simpleton, nitwit, blockhead, fool

domain *n.* territory, dominion, field, specialty, area

domestic *adj.* indigenous, native, homemade

domesticate *v.* control, adapt, tame, breed, housebreak, teach, train

domicile *n.* residence, home

dominant *adj.* commanding, authoritative, assertive, aggressive, powerful

dominate *v.* control, rule, manage, subjugate, govern

domineering *adj.* assertive, overbearing, despotic, imperious, oppressive

dominion *n.* sovereignty, region, district, state, nation

donate *v.* contribute, grant, bestow, bequeath, distribute, give, provide

donation *n.* contribution, offering, present, gift

donor *n.* benefactor, contributor, patron, philanthropist, giver

dote *v.* adore, pet, admire, love

doubt *n.* uncertainty, skepticism, mistrust, suspicion, misgiving, apprehension

doubt *v.* wonder, question

doubtful *adj.* UNCERTAIN: dubious, questioning, unsure, wavering, hesitating, unresolved, suspicious; IMPROBABLE: questionable, unconvincing

doubtless *adj.* positively, certainly, unquestionably, surely

douse *v.* immerse, wet, submerge, drench, soak

dowdy *adj.* shabby, untidy, slovenly, plain

doze *v.* sleep, nap, drowse, slumber

drab *adj.* dismal, dingy, colorless, dreary, dull

draft *n.* SKETCH: layout, plans, blueprint, design; CURRENT: breeze, gust, puff, wind; SELECTION: conscription, induction

drag *n.* IMPEDANCE: restraint, hindrance, burden, impediment, barrier; TIRESOME: bother, annoyance, hang-up, nuisance

drag *v.* PULL: haul, move, transport, draw; LAG: straggle, dawdle, loiter, pause; SLOW: crawl, delay

drain *n.* duct, channel, sewer, conduit, pipe

drain *v.* EXHAUST: weary, tire, spend, weaken; EMPTY: exude, trickle, ooze, dry, flow

drama *n.* play, production, dramatization, show, melodrama, tragicomedy, opera, operetta, mystery

dramatic *adj.* tense, climactic, moving, exciting

dramatist *n.* playwright, author, writer

dramatize *v.* enact, perform, exaggerate

drastic *adj.* extreme, extravagant, exorbitant, radical

draw *v.* **PULL:** drag, attract, lug, tow, haul; **PORTRAY:** sketch, outline, trace, depict

drawback *n.* disadvantage, shortcoming, hindrance

dread *n.* awe, horror, terror, fear

dreadful *adj.* unpleasant, hideous, fearful, shameful, frightful

dreary *adj.* bleak, dismal, dull. damp, raw, cold

dribble *v.* trickle, spout, squirt, drop

drift *n.* tendency, bent, trend, inclination, impulse, bias, leaning, disposition

drift *v.* wander, stray, gravitate, flow

drink *v.* swallow, gulp, sip, guzzle, imbibe

drive *n.* **RIDE:** trip, outing, airing, tour, excursion, jaunt, spin, journey; **PATH:** driveway, approach, avenue, boulevard, road; **FORCE:** energy, effort, enthusiasm, vigor, impulse

drive *v.* urge, impel, propel, compel, coerce, induce, force, press, stimulate, provoke, push

drop *n.* **SMALL AMOUNT:** speck, dash, dab, bit; **DECLINE:** fall, tumble, reduction, decrease, slump, lowering

drowsy *adj.* sleepy, sluggish, languid, indolent, lazy

drug *n.* pills, medicine, sedative, potion, essence, salts, powder, tonic, opiate, downers,

drug *v.* anesthetize, desensitize, dope, deaden

drunk *adj.* intoxicated, inebriated, befuddled, tipsy, smashed, tanked, soused, pickled, stewed, tight

dry *adj.* **ARID:** parched, desiccated, barren, dehydrated, drained; **BORING:** uninteresting, tedious, dull; **HUMOROUS:** sarcastic, cynical, biting, funny

dry *v.* evaporate, dehydrate, blot, sponge, scorch

dubious *adj.* **DOUBTFUL:** indecisive, perplexed, hesitant, uncertain, questionable; **VAGUE:** ambiguous, indefinite, unclear, obscure

due *adj.* SCHEDULED: expected; FITTING: deserved; COLLECTABLE: unsatisfied, outstanding, unpaid

dull *adj.* COLORLESS: gloomy, somber, drab, dismal, dark, dingy, dusky, plain, gray, flat; UNINTELLIGENT: slow, retarded, witless, stupid; UNINTERESTING: prosaic, hackneyed, monotonous, humdrum, tedious, dreary, dismal, insipid, boring, ordinary, uninspiring, tame, routine, repetitious

duly *adv.* properly, rightfully, decorously, justly

dumb *adj.* simple–minded, dull, stupid

dumfound *v.* astonish, shock

dungeon *n.* cell, vault

duplicity *n.* deception

durability *n.* stamina, persistence, endurance

durable *adj.* strong, form, enduring, permanent

duration *n.* interval, span, term

duress *n.* threat, coercion, compulsion, control, pressure, restraint

dusk *n.* gloom, twilight, dawn, night

dutiful *adj.* obedient, devoted, respectful, conscientious, faithful

duty *n.* obligation, liability, burden, responsibility

dwell *v.* reside, live, inhabit, stay, lodge, settle, remain, continue, occupy

dweller *n.* inhabitant, tenant, occupant, resident

dwelling *n.* house, establishment, lodging, home

dynamic *adj.* forceful, intense, energetic, compelling, vigorous, magnetic, electric, effective, influential, charismatic, active, powerful

dynasty *n.* succession, sovereignty

eager *adj.* impatient, anxious, keen, fervent, zealous

early *adj.*, *adv.* primitive; premature, preceding, unexpected, punctual

earn *v.* **DESERVE:** win, merit, gain; **PAYMENT:** obtain, attain, get, procure, realize, acquire, secure

earnest *adj.* serious, intense, important, ardent, zealous, warm, enthusiastic

earthly *adj.* human, mortal, global, mundane

earthy *adj.* coarse, dull, crude, unrefined, natural

ease *n.* **COMFORT:** rest, peace, prosperity, leisure, calm, tranquillity; **WITHOUT DIFFICULTY:** snap, breeze, cinch, pushover

ease *v.* relieve, alleviate, allay, comfort, soothe, unburden, release, soften, calm, pacify

easily *adv.* readily, effortlessly, smoothly

easy *adj.* **UNTROUBLED:** secure, prosperous, leisurely, calm, peaceful, tranquil, contented, carefree, unhurried, relaxing; **MANAGEABLE:** simple, smooth, simple, pushover; **LAX:** lenient, indulgent, kind

eat *v.* **DEVOUR:** chew, swallow, feast, dine, gorge, feed; **REDUCE:** erode, corrode, waste, rust, spill

ebb *v.* decline, recede, subside, decrease

ebullient *adj.* exuberant enthusiastic

eccentric *adj.* unconventional, odd, queer, strange, unusual

eccentricity *n.* peculiarity, abnormality, idiosyncrasy

eclipse *v.* darken, diminish, obscure

economic *adj.* business, financial, commercial

economical *adj.* **CAREFUL:** thrifty, prudent, frugal, miserly, watchful, tight; **INEXPENSIVE:** cheap, reasonable, fair, moderate; **EFFICIENT:** practical, methodical

economist *n.* statistician, analyst, expert

economize *v.* husband, manage, stint, conserve,

scrimp, skimp
ecstasy *n.* joy, rapture, delight, happiness
ecumenical *adj.* general, universal,
edible *adj.* palatable, good, delicious, satisfying, savory, tasty, nutritious, digestible
edict *n.* decree, order
educate *v.* teach, train, inform, refine, tutor, instruct
education *n.* **LEARNING:** schooling, study, instruction, guidance, apprenticeship, tutelage, reading, indoctrination; **KNOWLEDGE:** learning, wisdom, scholarship
educational *adj.* enlightening, instructive, enriching, cultural
educator *n.* pedagogue, instructor, tutor, teacher
effect *n.* conclusion, consequence, outcome, result
effect *v.* produce, cause, make, begin
effective *adj.* efficient, serviceable, useful, adequate, productive, competent, practical
effectual *adj.* adequate, efficient, qualified, effective
effervescent *adj.* bubbly, lively, vivacious
efficiency *n.* productivity, capability, ability
efficient *adj.* competent, fitted, able, capable, qualified, skilled, adept, experienced, practical, productive, economical, effective, expedient, streamlined
effort *n.* attempt, undertaking, struggle, try, venture
effortless *adj.* simple, offhand, smooth, easy
effrontery *n.* boldness, insolence
egotism *n.* conceit, vanity, pride, self–love, arrogance, overconfidence, haughtiness
egotistical *adj.* conceited, vain, boastful, pompous, arrogant, insolent, affected, self–centered, blustering, proud, pretentious, overbearing
egregious *adj.* bad, outrageous

eject *v.* discard, reject, oust, evict

elaborate *adj.* ORNAMENTED: gaudy, decorated, showy, fussy, dressy, flowery, flashy, ornate; DETAILED: intricate, complicated, involved, complex

elect *v.* choose, name, select

elective *adj.* optional, voluntary, selective

elegance *n.* taste, cultivation, polish, splendor, beauty, gracefulness, magnificence, courtliness, charm, sophistication, style

elegant *adj.* ornate, polished, perfected, elaborate, adorned, embellished, artistic, rich

element *n.* substance, component, portion, particle, detail, part

elementary *adj.* primary, introductory, rudimentary, easy, fundamental, essential, basic

elevate *v.* RAISE: lift, hoist, heave, tilt; PROMOTE: advance, appoint, further

elevated *adj.* towering, tall, high, raised

eligibility *n.* fitness, acceptability, capability, ability

eligible *adj.* qualified, suitable, fit, usable

eliminate *v.* remove, reject, exclude, disqualify, oust, discard, dismiss, drop

elongate *v.* prolong, lengthen, extend, stretch

eloquence *n.* fluency, wit, wittiness, expressiveness, diction, articulation, delivery, poise

eloquent *adj.* vocal, articulate, outspoken, fluent

else *adj.* different, other, more

elude *v.* evade, escape, dodge, shun, avoid

elusive *adj.* fleeting, fugitive, temporary

embargo *n.* restriction, prohibition, impediment, restraint

embarrass *v.* distress, disconcert, chagrin, confound,

trouble, disturb, fluster, shame

embarrassment *n.* chagrin, mortification, discomfiture, humiliation, awkwardness

embezzle *v.* thieve, forge, pilfer, steal

embezzlement *n.* fraud, misappropriation, theft

embezzler *n.* thief, robber, defaulter, criminal

embrace *v.* hug, enfold, squeeze, grip

emerge *v.* rise, arrive, appear, form, evolve

emergency *n.* crisis, predicament, difficulty

emigrant *n.* exile, expatriate, colonist, migrant, pilgrim, refugee

emigrate *v.* migrate, immigrate, quit, leave

emigration *n.* departure, leaving, displacement, exodus, movement, migration, settling

eminence *n.* standing, prominence, distinction, fame

eminent *adj.* renowned, exalted, celebrated, prominent, dignified, distinguished

emissary *n.* intermediary, ambassador, consul, agent

emotion *n.* excitement, sentiment, passion

emotional *adj.* hysterical, demonstrative, ardent, enthusiastic, passionate, excitable, impulsive, impetuous, temperamental, irrational, sentimental, affectionate, neurotic, high-strung

emphatic *adj.* definite, assured, strong, determined, forceful, earnest, positive, dynamic

employ *v.* USE: operate, manipulate, apply; ENGAGE: contract, procure, hire

employer *n.* owner, manager, proprietor, director, executive, superintendent, supervisor, businessman

employment *n.* job, profession, vocation, business, trade, work

emulate *v.* imitate, equal, compete, follow

encompass *v.* include, encircle, gird, surround

encounter *n.* **MEETING:** interview, rendezvous, appointment; **VIOLENCE:** conflict, clash, collision, fight

encourage *v.* support, inspire, cheer, praise, fortify, help, aid, reassure, reinforce, back, strengthen

encouraging *adj.* bright, good, promising, hopeful

endeavor *n.* effort, undertaking

endeavor *v.* attempt, aim, try

endorse *v.* **SIGN:** countersign, underwrite, subscribe, notarize; **SUPPORT:** approve, sanction, acknowledge

endorsement *n.* support, sanction, permission

endurable *adj.* tolerable, supportable, bearable

endurance *n.* sufferance, fortitude, tolerance, perseverance, stamina

endure *v.* **CONTINUE:** sustain, prevail, stay, persist; **BEAR UP:** suffer, tolerate, allow, permit, withstand

engross *v.* absorb, busy, fill, occupy

enhance *v.* embellish, magnify, amplify, increase

enigma *n.* problem, riddle, parable, puzzle

enjoy *v.* relish, luxuriate, delight, like

enjoyable *adj.* agreeable, welcome, genial, pleasant

enjoyment *n.* satisfaction, gratification, diversion, entertainment, indulgence

enlighten *v.* inform, divulge, acquaint, teach, tell

enormous *adj.* monstrous, immense, huge, large

enterprise *n.* undertaking, endeavor, affair, business

entertain *v.* **AMUSE:** cheer, delight, beguile, charm, captivate, stimulate, satisfy, distract, indulge; **HOST:** receive, invite, welcome

entertainer *n.* performer, player, artist, actor

entertaining *adj.* diverting, amusing, engaging, enchanting, witty, clever, interesting, captivating, stimulating, absorbing

entertainment *n.* amusement, enjoyment, diversion

enthusiasm *n.* excitement, interest, fervor, ardor, eagerness, zeal

enthusiast *n.* ZEALOT: fanatic, fan, believer; FOLLOWER: partisan, supporter, participant

enthusiastic *adj.* interested, excited, exhilarated, eager, ardent, spirited, zestful, fervent

entrance *n.* access, entry, passage, approach, admittance, introduction, debut, enrollment

entrance *v.* delight, enchant

envelop *v.* encompass, contain, hide, surround, wrap

envelope *n.* pouch, pocket, container, wrapper

enviable *adj.* good, superior, excellent

envious *adj.* covetous, resentful, desiring, wishful, greedy, jealous

envy *v.* begrudge, covet, crave

episode *n.* event, happening, occurrence, event

equilibrium *n.* balance, stability

equip *v.* outfit, train, furnish, implement, provide

equipment *n.* tools, implements, utensils, apparatus, devices, tackle, machinery, fittings

equitable *adj.* fair, impartial, just, moral

equity *n.* FAIRNESS: impartiality; ASSETS: investment, money, property

equivalent *adj.* equal, corresponding, commensurate, comparable, similar

eradicate *v.* destroy, eliminate, exterminate

erase *v.* remove, delete, obliterate, cut, eradicate

erect *adj.* vertical, upright, perpendicular, straight

erect *v.* construct, fabricate, build

erection *n.* building, construction

erratic *adj.* **WANDERING:** rambling, roving; **STRANGE:** eccentric, queer, unusual; **VARIABLE:** deviating, inconsistent, unpredictable, irregular

erroneous *adj.* inaccurate, incorrect, untrue, false

erudite *adj.* scholarly, learned

erupt *v.* eruct, eject, emit, explode

eruption *n.* burst, outburst, flow, explosion

escape *n.* flight, retreat, evasion, avoidance

escape *v.* elude, avoid, flee, evade, disappear, vanish

escort *n.* guide, attendant, guard, companion

escort *v.* accompany, attend, date

espouse *v.* marry, advocate, adopt, uphold, support

essay *n.* dissertation, treatise, tract, writing

essence *n.* pith, core, kernel, gist, nature, basis, substance, nucleus, germ

essential *adj.* **BASIC:** fundamental, primary; **NECESSARY:** imperative, required, indispensable

establish *v.* **FOUND:** institute, organize, erect, build; **PROVE:** verify, authenticate, confirm; **SECURE:** fix, stabilize, fasten

establishment *n.* business, organization, company, corporation, enterprise

ethical *adj.* moral, humane, respectable, decent, honest, noble

ethics *n.* morality, mores, decency, integrity, honor

etiquette *n.* conduct, manners, behavior

euphoria *n.* relaxation, health, well–being, happiness

evade *v.* avoid, dodge, shun, elude, baffle, shift, conceal, deceive, veil, hide

evasion *n.* subterfuge, equivocation, lie, trick

evasive *adj.* vague, fugitive, shifty, sly

event *n.* occasion, incident, occurrence, happening,

affair, function, experience, situation

eventful *adj.* momentous, memorable, important

eventual *adj.* inevitable, ultimate, consequent

eventually *adv.* ultimately, finally

evolve *v.* unfold, emerge, develop, grow

exact *adj.* ACCURATE: precise, correct, perfect, definite; CLEAR: sharp, distinct

exacting *adj.* precise, careful, critical, difficult

exactness *n.* precision, scrupulousness, accuracy

exaggerate *v.* overstate, misrepresent, falsify, magnify, amplify, heighten, intensify, distort, stretch, overdo, elaborate, color, fabricate

exaggerated *adj.* overwrought, extravagant, melodramatic, distorted, pronounced

exaggeration *n.* misrepresentation, elaboration

examination *n.* SCRUTINY: inspection, analysis, study; TEST: review, questionnaire, quiz, exam, midterm

examine *v.* INSPECT: analyze, scrutinize, explore, probe; TEST: question, interrogate

exasperate *v.* annoy, irritate

exceed *v.* excel, outdo

exceedingly *adv.* greatly, remarkable, very

excel *v.* surpass, transcend, exceed

excellence *n.* superiority, distinction, perfection

excellent *adj.* outstanding, exceptional, first–class, choice, select, exquisite, high–grade

excess *n.* ABUNDANCE: profusion, surplus; OVER-INDULGENCE: prodigality, dissipation, intemperance, greed, waste

excessive *adj.* immoderate, extravagant, exorbitant, extreme

excitable *adj.* sensitive, high–strung, nervous

excite *v.* provoke, stimulate, inflame, arouse, stir, provoke, incite

excitement *n.* disturbance, tumult, turmoil, stir, agitation, stimulation, commotion, fuss

exclaim *v.* shout, call, yell

exclamation *n.* yell, clamor, cry

exclude *v.* except, reject, ban, bar

exclusion *n.* prohibition, repudiation, separation, eviction, expulsion

execute *v.* perform, act, do, effect

exemplify *v.* illustrate, represent

exempt *adj.* privileged, excused, unrestricted

exemption *n.* exception, immunity, privilege

exhaust *v.* debilitate, tire, weaken, weary; deplete, use

exhaustion *n.* weariness, fatigue, depletion

exhilaration *n.* elation, excitement

exhort *v.* entreat, beg

exist *v.* live, survive, be, endure

existence *n.* being, actuality, reality, presence

exorbitant *adj.* excessive, extravagant, wasteful

exotic *adj.* FOREIGN: imported, extrinsic; PECULIAR: strange, different, fascinating, unusual

expand *v.* extend, augment, dilate, grow

expanse *n.* extent, reach, area, space, span, spread, scope, range

expansion *n.* enlargement, augmentation, extension, increase

expect *v.* ANTICIPATE: await, hope; REQUIRE: demand, exact; ASSUME: presume, suppose, suspect

expectancy *n.* hope, prospect, likelihood, anticipation

expectant *adj.* hopeful, awaiting, anticipating, eager

expedient *adj.* convenient, profitable, useful, practical

expedite *v.* speed, quicken

expel *v.* EJECT: dislodge, evict; DISMISS: suspend, discharge, oust

expenditure *n.* outgo, payment, expense

experience *n.* background, skill, knowledge, practice, maturity, judgment, know–how

experience *v.* undergo, feel, endure

expert *adj.* skillful, practiced, proficient, able

expert *n.* graduate, master, specialist

explain *v.* interpret, elucidate, illustrate, clarify, illuminate, expound, teach, demonstrate, define

explainable *adj.* explicable, accountable, intelligible, understandable

explanation *n.* account, justification, analysis, commentary, brief, breakdown, proof

expletive *n.* exclamation

explicit *adj.* clear, express, sure, plain, definite, understandable

exploit *n.* deed, venture, escapade, achievement

exploit *v.* utilize, employ, use

exploration *n.* investigation, research, search

explore *v.* examine, search, hunt, seek

explorer *n.* adventurer, traveler, pioneer, voyager, seafarer, mountaineer, scientist, navigator

explosion *n.* detonation, blast, burst, discharge

explosive *adj.* stormy, fiery, forceful, raging, violent, uncontrollable, frenzied, savage

expose *v.* UNCOVER: disclose, reveal, unmask, unfold; ENDANGER: imperil

exposition *n.* MAKING CLEAR: elucidation, delineation, explication, explanation; EXHIBITION: exhibit, showing, performance, display

exposure *n.* disclosure, betrayal, display, publication, unveiling

express *v.* declare, tell, signify, utter

expression *n.* appearance, cast, character, looks, grimace, smile, smirk, mug, sneer, pout, grin

expressive *adj.* eloquent, demonstrative, dramatic, stirring, articulate, spirited, lively, stimulating

expulsion *n.* ejection, suspension, purge, removal

exquisite *adj.* fine, scrupulous, precise, dainty

extemporaneous *adj.* spontaneous, impromptu

extend *v.* enlarge, lengthen, increase, reach, continue, spread

extension *n.* section, branch, addition

extensive *adj.* wide, broad, great

extent *n.* SIZE: span, space, area, expanse, bulk; DEGREE: scope, reach, range, magnitude, intensity

exterior *adj.* outer, outlying, outermost, outside

exterminate *v.* annihilate, eradicate, abolish, destroy

extinction *n.* extermination, destruction

extinguish *v.* smother, choke, quench, douse, stifle

extort *v.* extract, wrench, force, steal

extortion *n.* fraud, blackmail, theft

extra *adj.* additional, other, spare, reserve, supplemental, auxiliary, added, more

extract *v.* evoke, derive, secure, obtain

extract *n.* distillation, infusion, concentration, essence

extraneous *adj.* foreign; incidental

extraordinary *adj.* unusual, remarkable, curious, amazing

extravagance *n.* excess, lavishness, improvidence, waste

extravagant *adj.* lavish, prodigal, immoderate, wasteful

extreme *adj.* outermost, utmost, immoderate, excessive, outrageous, preposterous, exaggerated

extremist *n.* zealot, fanatic, die–hard, radical

exuberance *n.* fervor, eagerness, exhilaration, zeal

exuberant *adj.* ardent, vivacious, passionate, zealous

eye *n.* APPRECIATION: perception, taste, discrimination; CENTER: focus, core, heart, kernel, nub

eyesore *n.* distortion, deformity, ugliness

eyewitness *n.* onlooker, passer–by, observer

fable *n.* story, allegory, tale, parable

fabric *n.* cloth, textile, stuff, material, goods

fabricate *v.* PRODUCE: construct, erect, make, form, build, manufacture, devise; LIE: misrepresent, contrive, prevaricate

fabulous *adj.* fictitious, remarkable, amazing, immense, unusual

façade *n.* face, appearance, look, front

face *n.* VISAGE:, countenance, appearance, features, silhouette, profile; SURFACE: front, finish; PRESTIGE: status, standing, reputation

face *v.* CONFRONT: defy, meet, challenge, encounter, endure, suffer, bear; REFINISH: front, redecorate, cover, paint

facet *n.* surface, aspect, face, side, plane

facetious *adj.* humorous, whimsical, ridiculous, funny

facile *adj.* easy, simple, obvious, apparent, fluent

facilitate *v.* promote, aid, simplify, help

facility *n.* EQUIPMENT: material, tools, plant, buildings; AGENCY: department, bureau, company, office

facsimile *n.* copy, duplicate, reproduction, mirror

fact *n.* **CERTAINTY:** truth, actuality, reality, evidence, **EVENT:** action, deed, happening, occurrence, manifestation, experience, act, episode, incident

faction *n.* party, clique, gang, crew, wing, block, lobby, sect, cell

factious *adj.* turbulent, contentious

factor *n.* agent, cause, part, portion, constituent, determinant

factory *n.* manufactory, plant, shop, industry, mill, foundry, forge

factual *adj.* exact, specific, descriptive, accurate

faculty *n.* **ABILITY:** aptitude, peculiarity, strength, forte; **TEACHERS:** instructors, mentors, professors, tutors, lecturers, advisers, scholars, fellows

fad *n.* fancy, style, craze, fashion, eccentricity, innovation, vogue, fashion

fade *v.* **PALE:** bleach, blanch, dim, vanish; **DIMINISH:** hush, quiet, sink, decrease

fail *v.* miss, falter, flounder, fizzle, flop, lessen, worsen, sink, decrease

failure *n.* **DEFAULT:** fiasco, bankruptcy, miscarriage, breakdown, stoppage, collapse, downfall, flop, washout; **UNSUCCESSFUL PERSON:** incompetent, underachiever, dropout, dud

faint *adj.* **FALTERING:** shaky, dizzy, weak, **VAGUE:** thin, hazy, indistinct, dull; **SUBDUED:** low, soft, quiet, muffled, hushed

faint *v.* swoon, drop, collapse, succumb

fair *adj.* **JUST:** forthright, impartial, scrupulous, honest, decent, honorable, righteous, reasonable, evenhanded, principled, trustworthy; **AVERAGE:** ordinary, mediocre, commonplace; **PLEASANT:** clear, sunny, bright, calm, placid, tranquil, favorable, balmy, mild

fair *n.* exposition, carnival, bazaar, festival, market

fairly *adv.* **HONESTLY:** reasonably, honorably, justly; **SOMEWHAT:** moderately, reasonably, adequately

fairy *n.* spirit, sprite, elf, nymph, pixy

faith *n.* **TRUST:** confidence, credence, assurance, acceptance, conviction, sureness, reliance; **FORMAL BELIEF:** creed, doctrine, dogma, tenet, revelation, credo, gospel, canon, theology

faithful *adj.* reliable, dependable, incorruptible, honest, honorable, scrupulous, firm, sure, unswerving, conscientious, steadfast

fake *adj.* pretended, fraudulent, bogus, false

fake *n.* counterfeit, copy, imitation, fraud, fabrication, forgery; cheat, charlatan

fake *v.* feign, simulate, disguise, pretend

fall *v.* **DROP:** decline, sink, topple, settle, droop, stumble, trip, plunge, descend, totter, recede, ebb, diminish, flop; **SUBMIT:** yield, surrender, succumb, resign, capitulate

fallacy *n.* inconsistency, mistake, ambiguity, paradox, miscalculation, quirk, flaw, heresy, error

fallibility *n.* imperfection, misjudgment, frailty, uncertainty

fallible *adj.* frail, imperfect, erring, unreliable, questionable, wrong

fallow *adj.* unplowed, unplanted, unproductive

false *adj.* **UNFAITHFUL:** treacherous, disloyal, underhanded, deceitful, unscrupulous, untrustworthy; **SPURIOUS:** fanciful, untruthful, deceptive, fallacious, misleading, erroneous, inaccurate, fraudulent;

COUNTERFEIT: fabricated, bogus, forged, faked, contrived, phony

falsehood *n.* deception, prevarication, story, lie

falsify *v.* misrepresent, adulterate, counterfeit, deceive, lie, forge

falter *v.* waver, fluctuate, be undecided, hesitate

fame *n.* renown, glory, distinction, eminence, esteem, name, note, greatness, rank, position, standing, preeminence, regard, popularity

familiar *adj.* everyday, customary, accustomed, common, ordinary, informal, commonplace

familiarity *n.* friendliness, acquaintanceship, fellowship, friendship; comprehension, awareness, experience

familiarize *v.* acquaint, accustom

family *n.* household, relatives, clan, relations, tribe, dynasty, descendants, forbears, heirs, genealogy, descent, parentage, extraction, kinship, lineage

famine *n.* starvation, want, misery, hunger

famished *a.* starving, hungering, starved, hungry

famous *adj.* known, renowned, eminent, foremost, famed, celebrated, noted, prominent, reputable, renowned, notable, notorious

fan *n.* supporter, follower, amateur, devotee

fanatical *adj.* enthusiastic, obsessed, passionate, devoted, zealous

fanciful *adj.* unreal, incredible, whimsical, fantastic

fancy *adj.* elaborate, ornamental, intricate, elegant, embellished, rich, adorned, ostentatious, gaudy, showy, baroque, lavish, ornate

fancy *n.* **WHIMSY:** imagination, caprice, levity, humor; **WHIM:** notion, impulse, idea; **INCLINATION:** wishes, will, preference, desire

fantastic *adj.* fanciful, whimsical, capricious, strange, odd, queer, quaint, peculiar, outlandish, wonderful, exotic, ludicrous, ridiculous, preposterous, grotesque, absurd

fantasy *n.* illusion, flight, figment, fiction

far *adj.* distant, faraway, remote

farce *n.* satire, travesty, burlesque

fare *n.* FOOD: menu, rations, meals; FEE: charge, passage, passage, tariff, expense

fare *v.* experience, prosper, happen

farewell *n.* good–bye, valediction, parting, departure

farfetched *adj.* strained, unbelievable, fantastic

farm *v.* cultivate, till, garden, ranch, homestead

farmer *n.* planter, grower, stockman, agriculturist, rancher, homesteader, peasant, peon, herdsman, plowman, sharecropper, gardener, horticulturist

farsighted *adj.* aware, perceptive, sagacious

farthest *adj.* remotest, ultimate, last, furthest

fascinate *v.* charm, captivate, entrance, enchant, bewitch, enrapture, delight, please, attract, lure, seduce, entice, intoxicate, tantalize

fascination *n.* charm, enchantment, attraction

fashion *n.* manner, custom, convention, vogue, mode, usage, observance, style, craze

fashion *v.* make, model, shape, form, create, mold, adapt

fashionable *adj.* smart, stylish, chic

fast *adj.* RAPID: swift, fleet, quick, speedy, brisk, accelerated, hasty, nimble; FIXED: attached, immovable, firm

fasten *v.* lock, fix, tie, lace, close, bind, tighten,

attach, secure, anchor, grip, clasp, clamp, pin, nail, tack, bolt, rivet, set, weld, cement, glue

fat *adj.* portly, stout, obese, corpulent, fleshy, plump, bulky, heavy

fatal *adj.* mortal, lethal, deadly

fatality *n.* casualty, death

fate *n.* destiny, fortune, luck, doom

fated *adj.* lost, destined, elected, doomed

fateful *adj.* MOMENTOUS: portentous, critical, decisive, crucial; FATAL: destructive, ruinous, lethal, deadly

father *n.* PARENT: sire, progenitor, procreator, forebear, ancestor; ORIGINATOR: founder, inventor, promoter, author; PRIEST: pastor, ecclesiastic, parson

fatigue *n.* weariness, exhaustion, lassitude

fatten *v.* feed, stuff, plump, cram, fill

fault *n.* DELINQUENCY: wrongdoing, transgression, crime, impropriety, misconduct, malpractice, failing; ERROR: defect, blunder, mistake, misdeed; RESPONSIBILITY: liability, accountability, blame

favor *v.* indulge, prefer, pick, choose, value, prize, esteem

favorable *adj.* well–disposed, kind, well–intentioned, propitious, beneficial

favorite *adj.* beloved, favored, preferred, adored

favorite *n.* darling, pet

favoritism *n.* bias, partiality, inequity, inclination

faze *v.* discourage, bother, intimidate, worry, disturb

fear *n.* dread, fright, dismay, awe, anxiety, foreboding, concern, alarm

fearful *adj.* timid, shy, apprehensive, cowardly

fearless *adj.* bold, daring, courageous, dashing, brave

feasible *adj.* expedient, worthwhile, convenient,

practicable, possible, attainable

feast *n.* banquet, entertainment, festival, fiesta, barbecue, picnic, dinner

feast *v.* eat, entertain

feat *n.* deed, act, effort, achievement

feature *n.* ATTRACTION: highlight, specialty; ARTICLE: editorial, story; CHARACTERISTIC: quality, peculiarity

federation *n.* confederacy, alliance

fee *n.* price, remuneration, salary, charge, pay

feeble *adj.* weak, faint, fragile, puny, strengthless

feeble-minded *adj.* foolish, retarded, senile, dull

feed *n.* fodder, provisions, supplies, pasture, forage

feed *v.* feast, nourish, dine, fatten, cater, serve

feel *v.* TOUCH: caress, fondle, paw, grasp; EXPERIENCE: sense, perceive; BELIEVE: consider, hold, think

feeling *n.* SENSATION: sensibility, sensitiveness, perception, receptivity, responsiveness, awareness, enjoyment, sensuality, pain, pleasure, reflex; REACTION: opinion, thought, outlook, attitude; SENSITIVITY: taste, tenderness, discrimination, discernment, refinement, culture, faculty, judgment

feign *v.* pretend, dissemble, imagine, fabricate

fellow *n.* YOUTH: chap, lad, boy, stripling, apprentice, adolescent, juvenile, youngster, kid; ASSOCIATE: member, peer, colleague, friend

fellowship *n.* COMRADESHIP: conviviality, sociability, intimacy, friendliness, affability, camaraderie; PAYMENT: stipend, scholarship, honorarium, subsidy

felon *n.* criminal, outlaw, delinquent, convict

felony *n.* crime, misconduct, offense, transgression

feminine *adj.* soft, delicate, gentle, ladylike, matronly, maidenly, tender, womanly

fence n. hedge, divider, barrier, backstop, railing, barricade, barrier

ferment v. effervesce, foam, froth, bubble, seethe, fizz, work, ripen, rise

ferocious adj. savage, fierce, wild

ferocity n. fierceness brutality barbarity cruelty

ferry n. ferryboat passage boat barge packet boat

ferry v. carry, convey

fertile adj. productive, inventive, fruitful, rich, productive, fat, teeming, yielding, arable, flowering

fertility n. fruitfulness, virility, productiveness

fertilization n. **IMPREGNATION:** pollination, breeding, propagation, procreation

fervent adj. zealous, eager, ardent, enthusiastic

fervor n. ardor, enthusiasm, zeal

festival n. celebration, festivity, feast

festive adj. gay, merry, joyful, happy

festivity n. revelry, amusement, entertainment

fetch v. get, retrieve, carry

fetish n. fixation, craze, mania, obsession

fetter n. shackle, restraint

fetus n. embryo, organism, child

feud n. quarrel, strife, bickering, fight

feverish adj. burning, hot

few adj. sparse, scanty, scattering, inconsiderable

fib n. prevarication, fabrication, misrepresentation, lie

fiber n. thread, filament, cord, string, strand

fibrous adj. veined, hairy, coarse, stringy

fickle adj. inconstant, capricious, whimsical, mercurial, changing

fiction n. novel, tale, romance, story

fictitious adj. imaginary, made–up, untrue, false

fidelity *n.* faithfulness, fealty, loyalty, devotion

fidget *v.* stir, twitch, worry, wiggle

field *n.* pasture, meadow, acreage, plot, patch, garden, grasslend, tract

fiend *n.* **MONSTER:** barbarian, brute, beast, devil; **ADDICT:** fan, aficionado, monomaniac

fierce *n.* ferocious, savage, wild, untamed, brutal, monstrous, vicious, dangerous, violent, threatening

fiery *adj.* impetuous, hotheaded

fight *n.* **CONFLICT:** struggle, battle, strife, contention, feud, quarrel, dispute, confrontation, brawl, fracas, altercation, bickering, wrangling, argument, debate, conflict, clash, scuffle, engagement; **METTLE:** hardihood, boldness, courage

fight *v.* conflict, battle, oppose, grapple

figurative *adj.* metaphorical, allegorical, illustrative

figure *n.* **FORM:** design, statue, shape, structure; **TORSO:** body, frame, development, build, posture, attitude, pose, carriage; **SUM:** total, number; **PRICE:** value, worth

figure *v.* **COMPUTE:** calculate, reckon, number, count; **CONCLUDE:** suppose, think, opine, decide

file *v.* **SMOOTH:** abrade, rasp, scrape, finish; **ARRANGE:** classify, index, categorize, catalogue, register, list

fill *v.* pack, stuff, charge, inflate

filter *v.* strain, purify, sieve, refine, clarify, separate

filth *n.* dirt, contamination, pollution, muck, slop, squalor, grime, garbage, sludge

filthy *adj.* dirty, foul, squalid, nasty, corrupt

final *adj.* last, terminal, concluding, ultimate, decisive

finance *n.* business, commerce, economics

finances *n.* resources, money, capital, funds, wealth

financial *adj.* economic, business, monetary, commercial

financier *n.* capitalist, banker, merchant, executive

find *v.* discover, detect, notice, perceive, discern, uncover, expose

finding *n.* verdict, decision, sentence, judgment

fine *adj.* EXACT: precise, accurate, definite; SMALL: thin, subtle; LIGHT: powdery, granular

fine *n.* punishment, penalty, damage, forfeit

fine *v.* penalize, exact, tax, levy, punish

finish *v.* END: perfect, achieve; POLISH: wax, stain, cover, paint; COMPLETE: cease, close, end, stop

fire *n.* burning, flame, blaze, embers, sparks, glow, warmth, combustion, conflagration

fire *v.* INFLAME: kindle, enkindle, ignite, light, burn, rekindle, relight, animate; DISCHARGE: shoot, set, off, hurl; DISMISS: discharge, eject

firm *adj.* FIXED: stable, solid, rooted, immovable, fastened, motionless, secured; HARD: solid, dense, compact, impenetrable, impervious, rigid, hardened, inflexible, unyielding; SETTLED: determined, steadfast, resolute, constant

firmament *n.* sky, heavens

first *adj.* beginning, original, primary, prime, initial, earliest, introductory

first-rate *adj.* prime, very, good, choice, excellent

fishy *adj.* improbable, dubious, implausible, unlikely

fit *adj.* APPROPRIATE: suitable, proper, practicable, advantageous, beneficial, desirable; HEALTHY: trim, competent, robust

fit *n.* ADJUSTMENT: adaptation; CONVULSION: attack, rage, spasm, seizure, stroke, paroxysm; TANTRUM:

burst, rush, outburst, huff, rage, spell

fit *v*. **ADAPT:** arrange, alter, adjust; **QUALIFY:** belong, conform, relate, match, correspond

fitting *n*. connection, component, constituent

fixture *n*. equipment, convenience, appliance, machine, device, equipment

fizzle *n*. disappointment, fiasco, defeat, failure

flabby *adj*. soft, yielding, limp, tender, fat

flag *n*. banner, standard, colors, emblem

flagrant *adj*. obvious, notorious, disgraceful, infamous, outrageous

flair *n*. talent, aptitude, gift, ability

flamboyant *adj*. bombastic, ostentatious, ornate

flame *n*. blaze, flare, flash, fire

flame *v*. burn, blaze, oxidize

flange *n*. edge, rim

flap *n*. fold, tab, cover, appendage, tag

flap *v*. flutter, flash, swing, wave

flare *v*. blaze, glow, burn, flash

flash *v*. gleam, glimmer, sparkle, glitter, glisten, glare, shine, glow, twinkle, reflect, radiate, flicker

flashy *adj*. gaudy, showy, ostentatious, ornate

flask *n*. bottle, decanter, jug, canteen

flat *adj*. **LEVEL:** even, smooth, extended, prostrate, horizontal, prone; **TASTELESS:** unseasoned, insipid, flavorless

flatter *v*. adulate, glorify, praise

flattery *adj*. adulation, compliments, praise, tribute, fawning, blarney

flaunt *v*. display, vaunt, brandish, boast

flavor *n*. taste, tang, relish

flavor *v*. season, salt, pepper, spice,

flavoring *n.* essence, extract, seasoning, additive
flaw *n.* defect, imperfection, stain, blemish
flaw *v.* mar, crack
fleck *n.* spot, mite, dot, bit
flee *v.* run, desert, escape, retreat
fleet *adj.* swift, transient
flexibility *n.* pliancy, suppleness, elasticity, litheness
flexible *adj.* limber, lithe, supple, elastic, malleable, pliable, tractable
flicker *v.* sparkle, twinkle, glitter, flash, shine
flight *n.* ESCAPE: fleeing, retreat; STEPS: stairs, staircase, ascent; SOARING: flying, aviation, aeronautics, gliding
flighty *adj.* capricious, fickle, whimsical, changing
flimsy *adj.* thin; weak; slight, infirm, frail, insubstantial, fragile, decrepit
flinch *v.* wince, start, blench
fling *n.* escapade, indulgence, party, celebration
fling *v.* hurl, toss, sling, dump, throw
flippant *adj.* pert, frivolous, impudent, saucy, rude
flirt *n.* coquette, tease, siren
flirt *v.* trifle, tease, seduce
float *v.* waft, drift
flock *n.* congregation, group, pack, litter, herd
flock *v.* gather, throng, congregate, crowd
flog *v.* beat, lash
flood *v.* inundate, swamp, overflow, deluge, submerge, immerse
floor *n.* DECK: tiles, planking, carpet, rug, linoleum; LEVEL: story, landing, basement, mezzanine, downstairs, upstairs, loft, attic, garret, penthouse
flop *v.* FALL: tumble, slump, drop; FAIL: miscarry,

founder, bomb

flounder *v.* struggle, wallow, blunder

flourish *v.* THRIVE: increase, wax, succeed, adorn;
BRANDISH: wave

flout *v.* sneer, disregard

flow *n.* current, tide, movement, progress

flow *v.* stream, course, move, run, rush, whirl, surge,
spurt, squirt, gush, trickle, spew

flower *n.* spray, cluster, shoot, posy, herb, vine, annual, perennial, plant

flower *v.* bloom, open, blossom, blow

flowery *adj.* elaborate, ornamented, rococo, ornate

fluctuate *v.* waver, vacillate, falter, hesitate

fluctuation, *n.* variation, inconstancy, change

fluent *adj.* eloquent, glib, smooth, verbose, chatty,
articulate, persuasive, silver–tongued

fluid *adj.* flowing, liquid, watery, molten, liquefied

fluid *n.* liquid, liquor, solution

flunk *v.* fail, miss, drop

fluster *v.* disconcert, confuse

flutter *v.* flap, ripple, wiggle, wave

flutter *n.* agitation, motion

fly *v.* FLEE: escape, retreat, withdraw; SOAR: float,
glide, hover, swoop, drift, circle; RUSH: dart, speed

foam *n.* froth, fluff, bubbles, lather

focus *v.* ATTRACT: converge, convene, center; CLEAR:
adjust, detail, sharpen

foe *n.* enemy, opponent, antagonist, adversary

fog *n.* mist, haze, cloud, film, steam, wisp, smoke,
soup, smog

foggy *adj.* dull, misty, gray, hazy

foible *n.* failing, weakness

fold

fold *v.* DOUBLE: crease, crimp, ruffle, pucker, gather, lap, overlap, overlay; FAIL: bankrupt, close

folder *n.* circular, pamphlet, paper, bulletin, advertisement, brochure, throwaway

foliage *n.* leaves, greenery

folk *n.* people, race, nation, community, tribe, society, population, settlement, clan, confederation

folklore *n.* customs, superstitions, traditions, tales, lore, legends, folkways, myth

folks *n.* family, kin, relatives, relations

follow *v.* COME AFTER: ensue, postdate, succeed; IMITATE: conform, copy, mirror, reflect, mimic; OBSERVE: heed, regard, watch, comply; UNDERSTAND: comprehend, catch, realize; RESULT: happen, ensue

follower *n.* attendant, companion, lackey, helper, partisan, disciple, pupil, protégé, supporter, backer, devotee, believer, member, admirer

following *adj.* subsequent, succeeding, next, ensuing

following *n.* clientele, audience, adherents, supporters, patrons

foment *v.* encourage, incite

fond *adj.* loving, enamored, attached, affectionate

food *n.* victuals, foodstuffs, nutriment, refreshment, edibles, comestibles, provisions, stores, sustenance, rations, board, cuisine, nourishment, fare

fool *n.* nitwit, simpleton, dunce, oaf, ninny, nincompoop, dolt, buffoon, blockhead, clown

fool *v.* deceive, trick, dupe, mislead

foolish *adj.* silly, simple, half–witted, stupid

foothold *n.* ledge, footing, niche, step

forbear *v.* abstain, stop

forbearance *n.* patience, clemency

forbid *v.* prohibit, debar, restrain, inhibit, preclude, oppose, obstruct, bar, prevent, outlaw, disallow, ban

forbidding *adj.* unpleasant, offensive, repulsive, grim

force *n.* STRENGTH: energy, power, might; DOMINANCE: forcefulness, competency, energy, persistence, willpower, drive, determination, authority; ORGANIZATION: group, band, unit

force *v.* compel, coerce, press, drive, make, impel, oblige, require, demand, command, impose, exact

forceful *adj.* commanding, dominant, powerful

forebode *v.* apprehend, foretell

foreboding *n.* premonition, dread, presentiment, anticipation, apprehension

forecast *n.* prognosis, divination, foresight, prophecy

forecast *v.* predict, predetermine, foretell

forefather *n.* ancestor, progenitor, forebear, father, parent, sire, forerunner, predecessor, originator, precursor, procreator, patriarch, founder, kinsman

foregoing *n.* prior, former, previous, preceding

foreign *adj.* alien, remote, exotic, strange, distant, different, alien, imported, borrowed, abroad

foreigner *n.* stranger, immigrant, newcomer, alien

foreman *n.* overseer, manager, supervisor, superintendent, head, boss

foremost *adj.* original, primary, first

forerunner *n.* herald, harbinger, precursor, sign

foresee *v.* prophesy, understand, predict, foretell

foresight *n.* carefulness, husbandry, prudence

forestall *v.* thwart, prevent, preclude, hinder

foretell *v.* prophesy, predict, divine, foresee, forebode, augur, portend, foreshadow

forethought *n.* provision, planning, foresight

forever *adv.* always, everlastingly, perpetually, eternally, endlessly, forevermore

forewarn *v.* admonish, alarm, warm

forfeit *v.* lose, sacrifice, relinquish, abandon

forge *v.* counterfeit, falsify, fabricate, feign, imitate, copy, duplicate, reproduce

forgery *n.* imitation, copy, counterfeit, fake

forget *v.* neglect, overlook, ignore, slight, disregard, skip, exclude

forgetful *adj.* inattentive, neglectful, heedless, careless, distracted

forgive *v.* pardon, overlook, excuse, exonerate

forgiveness *n.* absolution, pardon, acquittal, exoneration, dispensation, reprieve, amnesty, respite

forgo *v.* quit, relinquish, waive, abandon

fork *v.* branch, divide

form *n.* **SHAPE:** figure, appearance, arrangement, configuration, formation, structure, contour, profile, silhouette; **CEREMONY:** manner, mode, custom, method; **PATTERN:** model, die, mold; **DOCUMENT:** chart, questionnaire, application

form *v.* **SHAPE:** mold, model, make, fashion, construct, devise, design, produce, build, create; **INSTRUCT:** rear, breed, teach; **DEVELOP:** accumulate, harden, set, rise, appear, grow, mature, materialize

formal *adj.* **REGULAR:** orderly, precise, set; **POLITE:** reserved, distant, stiff, conventional

formality *n.* decorum, etiquette, correctness, behavior

format *n.* arrangement, construction, form

formation *n.* form, structure, arrangement, composition, development, fabrication, generation, creation, genesis, constitution

former *adj.* earlier, previous, foregoing, preceding
formerly *adj.* before, once, previously, earlier
formula *n.* equation, recipe, directions, method
formulate *v.* systematize, express, form
forsake *v.* desert, abandon, leave, quit
fort *n.* fortress, stronghold, citadel, acropolis
fortification *n.* stronghold, fort, fortress, defense, barricade, battlement, stockade, bastion, bulwark
fortify *v.* strengthen, barricade, entrench, buttress
fortitude *n.* strength, firmness, valor, fearlessness, determination
fortress *n.* stronghold, fort
fortune *n.* CHANCE: luck, fate, uncertainty; WEALTH: riches, possessions, inheritance, estate
fortunate *adj.* lucky, favorable
forward *adj.* bold, presumptuous, impertinent, fresh
fossil *n.* remains, specimen, skeleton, relic
foster *v.* nurse, raise, cherish, nourish, encourage
foul *adj.* FILTHY: impure, disgusting, nasty, vulgar, coarse, offensive; UNFAIR: inequitable, unjust
found *v.* institute, establish, endow
foundation *n.* BASIS: reason, justification, authority; BASE: footing, pier, groundwork, bed, substructure, underpinning; INSTITUTION: organization, endowment, institute, society, charity
founder *n.* originator, patron
foxy *adj.* sly, crafty
fraction *n.* fragment, section, portion, part, division
fractious *adj.* cross, irritable
fracture *n.* rupture, shattering, breach, dislocation, shearing, separating
fracture *v.* break, crack

fragile *adj.* frail, brittle, delicate, dainty, weak
fragment *n.* piece, scrap, remnant, bit
fragrance *n.* perfume, aroma, smell
fragrant *adj.* aromatic, sweet, perfumed
frail *adj.* fragile, feeble, breakable, tender, dainty
frame *n.* SKELETON: framework, scaffolding, support; BORDER: margin, fringe, hem, trim, outline
frame *v.* MAKE: construct, erect, raise, build; SURROUND: encircle, confine, enclose
franchise *n.* right, privilege
frank *adj.* candid, open, sincere, direct, ingenuous, forthright, outspoken, straightforward, blunt
frantic *adj.* excited, distracted, frenetic, frenzied
fraternity *n.* society, brotherhood, fellowship
fraud *n.* DECEIT: trickery, duplicity, guile, deception; TRICKSTER: impostor, pretender, charlatan, cheat
fraudulent *adj.* deceitful, tricky, dishonest
freak *n.* monstrosity, rarity, malformation, oddity, aberration, curiosity
free *adj.* SOVEREIGN: independent, autonomous, liberated, democratic; UNIMPEDED: unobstructed, unconstrained, unhampered, loose; GRATIS: gratuitous, complimentary
free *v.* release, discharge, rescue, extricate, undo, acquit, dismiss, pardon, redeem, disentangle
freedom *n.* LIBERTY: independence, sovereignty, autonomy; EXEMPTION: privilege, immunity, license, indulgence, latitude
freeway *n.* turnpike, superhighway, road
freeze *v.* SOLIDIFY: congeal, harden; CONTROL: seal, terminate, immobilize
freight *n.* CARGO: load, encumbrance, consignment,

goods, tonnage

frenzy *n.* excitement, rage, craze, furor, insanity

frequency *n.* repetition, recurrence, reiteration, regularity

frequent *adj.* **OFTEN:** habitual, customary, intermittent, periodic, commonplace; **REGULAR:** repeated, recurrent, incessant, continual

frequent *v.* visit, attend

fresh *adj.* **NEW:** green, recent, current, late, untried; **NOT PRESERVED:** unsalted, uncured, unsmoked; **UNSPOILED:** uncontaminated, preserved; **COLORFUL:** vivid, bright; **POTABLE:** drinkable, cool, clear, pure, clean, sweet, safe; **REFRESHED:** rested, restored, relaxed, reinvigorated, revived; **INEXPERIENCED:** untrained, untried, unskilled

fret *v.* worry, irritate, agitate, vex, bother

friction *n.* **RUBBING:** attrition, abrasion, erosion, grinding; **ANTAGONISM:** trouble, animosity, quarrel, discontent, hatred

friend *n.* schoolmate, playmate, roommate, companion, intimate, confidant, comrade, fellow, pal, chum, crony, buddy, side-kick

friendly *adj.* kindly, amiable, neighborly, sociable, civil, affectionate, attentive, agreeable, accommodating, pleasant, cordial, congenial

fright *n.* fear, panic, terror, dread, horror, shock

frighten *v.* terrify, scare, intimidate, threaten, badger, petrify, terrorize

frightful *adj.* **FEARFUL:** awful, dreadful, terrible; **UNPLEASANT:** calamitous, shocking, offensive

frill *n.* ruffle, frivolity, ornamentation

frisky *adj.* spirited, dashing, playful, active

frivolous *adj.* unimportant, slight, trifling, superficial, petty, trivial
frock *n.* dress, garment
frontier *n.* boundary, wilderness, hinterland
frosting *n.* covering, coating, icing
frosty *adj.* frigid, freezing, chilly, cold
froth *n.* foam, bubbles, fizz, effervescence, lather
frown *v.* scowl, grimace, pout, glare, sulk, glower
frugal *adj.* thrifty, economical, sparing, saving, parsimonious, careful
fruitful *adj.* prolific, productive, fecund, fertile
fruitless *adj.* vain, unprofitable, empty, futile
frustrate *v.* defeat, thwart, foil, balk, prevent
frustration *n.* disappointment, impediment, failure
fry *v.* sauté, sear, singe, brown, pan–fry
fudge *n.* candy, penuche, chocolate, divinity
fuel *n.* coal, gas, oil, charcoal, propane, peat, firewood, kindling, gasoline, kerosene
fugitive *adj.* fleeting, passing
fugitive *n.* outlaw, runaway, exile, outcast
fulfill *v.* complete, accomplish, effect, achieve
full *adj.* **SATURATED:** crammed, packed, stuffed, jammed, glutted, gorged, loaded; **ABUNDANT:** copious, ample, plentiful, sufficient, adequate, lavish, extravagant, profuse
fumble *v.* mishandle, bungle, mismanage, botch
fun *n.* amusement, relaxation, diversion, entertainment, pleasure, celebration, holiday, enjoyment
function *n.* duty, employment, capacity, use; action, event, party
function *v.* perform, run, work, operate
functional *adj.* utilitarian, practical

fund *n.* money, capital, endowment, gift
fundamental *adj.* basic, underlying, primary, rudimentary, elemental, structural, original
funds *n.* capital, wealth, cash, collateral, money, assets, currency, savings, revenue, wherewithal, stocks, bonds, property, means, affluence, belongings, resources, securities, profits
funeral *n.* interment, burial, entombment, requiem
funny *adj.* **COMIC:** laughable, comical, whimsical, amusing, entertaining, diverting, humorous, witty, jocular, droll; **SUSPICIOUS:** curious, unusual, odd
fur *n.* pelt, hide, hair, coat, brush
furbish *v.* polish, spruce, renovate
furious *adj.* raging, enraged, fierce, angry
furnace *n.* heater, boiler, kiln, stove, forge
furnish *v.* supply, equip, stock, provide
furor *n.* tumult, excitement, stir, disturbance
further *adj.* additional, more, distant
further *v.* promote, advance
fury *n.* rage, anger, wrath
fuse *v.* meld, blend
fuss *n.* quarrel, complaint, bother, disturbance, stir
fuss *v.* wrangle, whine, whimper, object, complain
fussy *adj.* fastidious, particular, meticulous, careful
futile *adj.* useless, vain, fruitless, hopeless, impractical, unsuccessful, purposeless, ineffective, ineffectual, unproductive, empty, hollow
future *adj.* impending, imminent, destined, fated, prospective, expected, approaching, ultimate
fuzz *n.* nap, fluff, fur, hair
gab *vi.* talk, chatter, gossip, jabber, babble
gabble *v.* jabber, cackle

gadget *n.* device, contrivance, object, contraption

gag *v.* **RETCH:** sicken, choke, vomit; **MUZZLE:** muffle, silence, stifle, throttle

gaiety *n.* merriment, jollity, mirth, exhilaration

gain *n.* profit, increase, accrual, accumulation

gain *v.* **INCREASE:** augment, expand, enlarge, grow; **ADVANCE:** progress, overtake; **ACHIEVE:** attain, realize, reach, succeed

gait *n.* walk, step, stride, pace, carriage, movement

gale *n.* wind, hurricane, blow, typhoon, storm

gallant *adj.* noble, brave, courteous, bold, courageous, intrepid

gallantry *n.* heroism, valor, bravery, courage

gallery *n.* **ONLOOKERS:** spectators, audience, public; **MUSEUM:** salon, studio, hall, showroom

gallop *v.* leap, run, spring, bound, hurdle, swing, stride, lope, amble, trot

gamble *v.* bet, wager, plunge, speculate, risk, chance

gambol *v.* leap, play

game *adj.* spirited, hardy, resolute, brave

game *n.* **ENTERTAINMENT:** sport, play, recreation; **MEAT:** fish, fowl, quarry, prey, wildlife

gang *n.* band, group, horde, troop, organization

gangster *n.* criminal, gunman, racketeer

gap *n.* **BREACH:** cleft, rift, hole; **BREAK:** hiatus, recess, lull, pause; **PASS:** chasm, hollow, ravine, gorge, canyon, gully, gulch

garbage *n.* refuse, trash, waste

garden *n.* patch, field, plot, bed, terrace, oasis

garish *adj.* showy, gaudy, ostentatious, ornate

garment *n.* dress, attire, apparel, clothes

garnish *v.* adorn, decorate, embellish, beautify, deck

gaseous *adj.* vaporous, effervescent, aeriform, light

gash *n.* wound, slash, slice, cut

gasp *v.* gulp, pant, puff, wheeze, blow, snort

gate *n.* entrance, ingress, passage, barrier, doorway

gather *v.* COLLECT: aggregate, amass, accumulate, assemble, garner; INFER: conclude, deduce, assume; ASSEMBLE: meet, congregate, flock, convene, collect, reunite, converge, concentrate

gathering *n.* assembly, meeting, conclave, caucus, parley, council, conference, congregation, rally, throng, collection, huddle, turnout, convention, reunion, meet

gaudy *a.* showy, flashy, tawdry, ornate

gauge *v.* measure, check, weigh, calibrate, calculate

gaunt *adj.* thin, lean, haggard, emaciated, scraggy

gauze *n.* fabric, veil, bandage, dressing

gawk *v.* stare, ogle, gaze, look

gay *adj.* lively, showy, merry, cheerful, vivacious

gaze *v.* stare, watch, gape, look

gazette *n.* journal, newspaper

gear *n.* COG: pinion, sprocket; BELONGINGS: equipment, material, tackle

gem *n.* stone, jewel, bauble, ornament

genealogy *n.* derivation, lineage, extraction, family

general *adj.* COMPREHENSIVE: broad, universal, extensive, ecumenical, ubiquitous; COMMON: usual, customary, prevailing; NOT SPECIFIC: indefinite, uncertain, imprecise, vague

generality *n.* abstraction, principle

generalize *v.* theorize, speculate, postulate

generally *adj.* commonly, ordinarily, regularly

generate *v.* produce, form, make, beget, create

generosity *n.* hospitality, benevolence, charity, philanthropy, altruism, unselfishness, kindness

generous *adj.* bountiful, lavish, profuse, prodigal, unstinting, magnanimous

genesis *n.* generation, creation

genial *adj.* cordial, kind, warmhearted, friendly

genius *n.* talent, intellect, intelligence, gift, aptitude, astuteness, acumen, capability

gentility *n.* decorum, propriety, refinement, behavior

gentle *adj.* **SOFT:** tender, smooth; **KIND:** tender, considerate, benign; **TAMED:** domesticated, trained;

genuine *adj.* **AUTHENTIC:** actual, original, authenticated; **SINCERE:** unaffected, reliable, staunch, trustworthy, certain, valid, positive, frank

germ *n.* microbe, bacterium, micro–organism, virus, parasite, bug

germinate *v.* sprout, begin, generate

gesture *n.* movement, indication, intimation, sign

get *v.* **OBTAIN:** procure, capture, take, grab, attain, gain, secure, collect, purchase, receive, possess, acquire; **BECOME:** grow, develop; **RECEIVE:** take, accept; **BEAT;** vanquish, overpower, defeat; **PREPARE:** make, arrange; **CONTRACT:** succumb, catch; **UNDERSTAND:** comprehend, perceive, know; **IRRITATE:** annoy, provoke, vex, bother

ghastly *adj.* terrifying, hideous, horrible, frightening, frightful, repulsive, disgusting, abhorrent, offensive

ghost *n.* spirit, apparition, vision, specter, phantom, spook, devil

giant *adj.* monstrous, colossal, enormous, large

giant *n.* colossus, behemoth, monster, leviathan

gibberish *n.* jargon, chatter, claptrap, nonsense

gibe *v.* sneer, mock, taunt

giddy, *adj.* high, towering, lofty, steep

gift *n.* PRESENT: donation, grant, endowment, bequest, legacy, reward, remembrance, bonus, subsidy, contribution; TALENT: aptitude, faculty, capacity, capability, ability

gigantic *adj.* massive, huge, immense, large

giggle *v.* laugh, titter, chuckle, snicker

gimmick *n.* device, stratagem, catch, method, trick

girdle *n.* belt, cinch, sash, underwear

girdle *v.* bind, enclose, encircle, clasp, surround

girl *n.* schoolgirl, lass, woman, coed, lassie, damsel, maid, maiden

girth *n.* circumference, size

gist *n.* substance, essence, significance, basis

give *v.* BESTOW: donate, grant, confer, impart, present, endow, bequeath, award, contribute, convey; YIELD: retreat, collapse, fall, contract, shrink, recede

glacial *adj.* icy, frozen, polar, cold

glad *adj.* exhilarated, animated, jovial, happy

glamour *n.* allurement, charm, attraction, beauty

glance *v.* LOOK: see, peep, glimpse; RICOCHET: skip, rebound, bounce

glare *v.* SHINE: light, beam, glow, radiate; STARE: pierce, glower, scowl, frown

glaring *adj.* SHINING: blinding, dazzling, blazing, bright; OBVIOUS: evident, conspicuous, obtrusive

glass *n.* tumbler, goblet, beaker, chalice, cup

gleam *v.* glow, flash

glee *n.* joy, gaiety, joviality, merriment, mirth

glib *adj.* fluent, pat

glide *v.* float, drift, waft, skim, fly, flit, soar

glimmer *n.* gleam, flash, flicker, light
glimpse *n.* view, flash, impression, sight
glisten *v.* sparkle, glitter, shimmer, flicker, shine
glitter *n.* luster, brilliancy, sparkle, shimmer, gleam
glitter *v.* glare, shimmer, sparkle, shine
globule *n.* drop, particle
gloom *n.* **DARKNESS:** cloudiness; **SADNESS:** depression, dejection, melancholia, despondency, morbidity, pessimism, foreboding, misgiving, mourning
gloomy *adj.* dreary, depressing, discouraging, dismal
glorify *v.* laud, commend, acclaim, praise
glorious *adj.* splendid, excellent, exalted, grand, illustrious, celebrated, remarkable
glory *n.* **SPLENDOR:** grandeur, majesty, brilliance, richness, beauty, fineness; **HONOR:** renown, distinction, reputation, fame
glory *v.* triumph, exult, boast
gloss *n.* brightness, sheen
glossy, *adj.* shining, reflecting, lustrous, bright
glow *v.* shine, gleam, redden, radiate, burn
glower *v.* stare, scowl
glue *n.* adhesive, paste, gum, cement, repair
glue *v.* paste, join
glum *adj.* sullen, moody, morose, sad
glut *v.* **OVEREAT:** stuff, cram, gorge, feast, devour; **OVERSUPPLY:** overwhelm, overstock, fill, flood
gluttony *n.* voracity, edacity, intemperance, greed
gnarled *adj.* knotted, twisted, contorted, bent
gnaw *v.* tear, crunch, champ, masticate, bite, chew
go *v.* **LEAVE:** withdraw, depart, vacate, flee, fly, run, escape; **PROCEED:** advance, progress, move; **FUNCTION:** run, perform, operate; **SUIT:** conform,

accord, harmonize, agree, fit; **EXTEND:** stretch, cover, reach; **ELAPSE:** transpire, pass; **DIE:** depart, succumb

goad *v.* prod, urge, prompt, spur, drive, press, push, impel, force, stimulate, provoke, encourage

goal *n.* aim, ambition, object, intent, end, purpose

go–between *n.* middleman, referee, mediator, agent

god *n.* deity, divinity, spirit

godly *adj.* righteous, devout, pious, holy

gone *adj.* moved, withdrawn, retired, departed, dissolved, decayed, extinct

good *adj.* **MORAL:** upright, honest, respectable, noble, ethical, fair, pure, decent, honorable; **KIND:** considerate, tolerant, generous; **RELIABLE:** trustworthy, dependable, loyal; **SOUND:** safe, solid, stable, reliable; **PLEASANT:** agreeable, satisfying, enjoyable; **HEALTHY:** sound, normal, vigorous; **OBEDIENT:** dutiful, tractable, well–behaved; **GENUINE:** valid, real, sound; **DELICIOUS:** tasty, flavorful, tasteful

good–for–nothing *n.* loafer, vagabond, bum, vagrant

good–looking *adj.* clean–cut, attractive, impressive, beautiful, handsome

good–natured *adj.* cordial, kindly, amiable, friendly

goodness *n.* decency, morality, honesty, virtue

goof *v.* err, flub, fail

gorge *n.* chasm, abyss, crevasse, ravine

gorge *v.* glut, surfeit, stuff, eat, fill

gorgeous *adj.* beautiful, dazzling, superb, sumptuous, impressive, grand

gory *adj.* blood–soaked, bloodstained, offensive

gossip *n.* **RUMOR:** scandal, meddling, hearsay, slander, defamation; **TALEBEARER:** snoop, meddler, tattler, scandalmonger, muckraker, backbiter

gossip

gossip *v.* tattle, chat, report, blab, babble, repeat

govern *v.* rule, administer, oversee, supervise, dictate, tyrannize

governmental *adj.* political, administrative, executive, regulatory, bureaucratic, supervisory

gown *n.* dress, garment, garb, clothes, dress

grab *v.* seize, clutch, grasp, take

grace *n.* **CHARM:** nimbleness, agility, poise, dexterity, symmetry, balance, style, harmony; **MERCY:** forgiveness, love, charity

graceful *adj.* **SUPPLE:** agile, lithe, nimble, dexterous, sprightly, elegant; **WELL–PROPORTIONED:** elegant, neat, trim, dainty, comely, slender, exquisite, statuesque; **CULTURED:** seemly, becoming, polite

gracious *adj.* **GENIAL:** amiable, courteous, condescending, polite; **MERCIFUL:** tender, loving, charitable, kind

grade *n.* **RANK;** class, category, classification; **SLOPE:** incline, gradient, slant, inclination, pitch, ascent, descent, ramp, climb, elevation, height, hill; **EMBANKMENT:** fill, causeway, dike, dam

grade *v.* arrange, rate, assort, rank

gradual *adj.* creeping, regular, continuous, regulated

grand *adj.* splendid, stately, dignified, regal, noble, illustrious, august, majestic, overwhelming

grandeur *n.* splendor, magnificence, pomp, glory, luxury, stateliness, beauty, ceremony, majesty

grandstand, *n.* seats, spectators

grant *n.* gift, boon, reward, present, allowance, stipend, donation, endowment, bequest

grant *v.* **BESTOW:** impart, allow; **ADMIT:** concede, accede, acquiesce, acknowledge

graph *n.* diagram, chart, design, plan

graphic *adj.* **PICTORIAL:** illustrated, visual, sketched, pictured; **VIVID:** clear, picturesque, comprehensible, striking, expressive, eloquent, poetic

grasp *n.* grip, hold, clutch, cinch

grasp *v.* **SEIZE:** clutch, enclose, clasp, grip, hold; **UNDERSTAND:** comprehend, perceive, apprehend, follow

grassland *n.* plains, meadow, prairie, field

grate *v.* rub, rasp, grind, abrade

grateful *adj.* thankful, appreciative, pleased, obliged

gratify *v.* please, satisfy

gratitude *n.* appreciation, acknowledgment, thanks

gratuitous *adj.* free, voluntary

gratuity *n.* present, tip

grave *adj.* **WEIGHTY:** important, momentous, consequential, critical; **SOMBER:** solemn, serious, sober

grave *n.* vault, sepulcher, tomb, crypt, mausoleum, catacomb

gravity *n.* importance, seriousness, significance

gravy *n.* juices, sauce, dressing

graze *v.* **FEED:** browse, nibble, forage, eat, munch, ruminate; **PASS LIGHTLY:** brush, scrape, rub, touch

greasy *adj.* creamy, fatty, oily

great *adj.* **LARGE:** numerous, big, commanding, vast; **EXCELLENT:** exceptional, surpassing, transcendent; **EMINENT:** grand, majestic, exalted, famous, renowned, celebrated, distinguished, noted

greedy *adj.* avid, grasping, rapacious, selfish, miserly, intemperate, mercenary, covetous

green *adj.* **VERDANT:** growing, leafy, sprouting, grassy, flourishing, lush; **IMMATURE:** young, unripe, maturing, developing; **INEXPERIENCED:** youthful, callow

greet *v.* hail, welcome, address, recognize, embrace,

nod, acknowledge, bow

greeting *n.* salutation, welcome, regards

gregarious *adj.* companionable, friendly

grief *n.* sorrow, sadness, melancholy, mourning, misery, anguish, despondency, heartache, gloom

grievance *n.* hardship, injury, complaint, objection

grieve *v.* lament, bewail, regret, sorrow, mourn

grill *v.* broil, roast, sauté, barbecue, cook

grim *adj.* SULLEN: gloomy, sulky, morose, glum; STERN: austere, strict, harsh, severe; RELENTLESS: implacable, inexorable

grimace *n.* smirk, smile, sneer

grime *n.* dirt, soil, smudge, filth

grin *n.* smile, simper, smirk, wry

grin *v.* smirk, simper, beam, smile

grind *v.* crush, powder, mill, granulate, crumble

grip *n.* GRASP: hold, clutch, clasp, catch, clench, embrace, handshake; SUITCASE: valise, satchel, bag

grip *v.* grasp, clutch, clasp, seize

gripe *n.* complaint, grievance, beef, objection

gripe *v.* grumble, mutter, fuss, complain

grit *n.* pluck, courage; sand, dust

gritty *adj.* rough, abrasive, sandy, granular, scratchy

groan *n.* moan, sob, grunt, cry

groan *v.* moan, murmur, keen, cry

groceries *n.* food, edibles, comestibles, foodstuffs

groggy *adj.* sleepy, dizzy, reeling, tired

groom *v.* tend, rub, down, comb, brush

groove *n.* furrow, rut, channel, trench, depression, furrow, gutter, ditch

grope *v.* feel, search, fumble, touch, feel

gross *adj.* WHOLE: total, entire; FAT: corpulent, obese, huge; **OBSCENE:** indecent, lewd, coarse, shameful

grotesque *adj.* ludicrous, odd, bizarre, malformed, ugly, distorted, deformed

grotto *n.* cave, cavern, hollow

grouch *n.* complainer, grumbler, growler, bear, sourpuss, sorehead, crab, crank, bellyacher

grouch *v.* mutter, grumble, gripe, complain

grouchy *adv.* surly, ill–tempered, crusty, irritable

group *n.* **GATHERING:** assemblage, cluster, crowd; **COLLECTION:** accumulation, assortment, combination; **ORGANIZATION:** association, club, society

group *v.* assemble, file, assort, arrange, classify

grovel *v.* crawl, wallow, beg, kneel, crouch, kowtow, cower, snivel

grow *v.* **INCREASE:** expand, swell, wax, thrive, enlarge, multiply, flourish; **CHANGE:** become, develop, evolve, progress, age, ripen, blossom, mature; **CULTIVATE:** raise, tend, foster, produce, plant, breed

growl *v.* snarl, grumble, bark, grunt, cry

grown *adj.* aged, adult, mature

grub *v.* dig, root

grudge *n.* enmity, spite, rancor, animosity, hatred

grudge *v.* envy, begrudge, covet

gruel *n.* porridge, cereal

gruesome *adj.* horrible, ghastly, grim, grisly, frightful

gruff *adj.* bluff, churlish, harsh, grating, hoarse

grumble *v.* complain, growl, whine, protest, fuss

grumpy *adj.* sullen, grouchy, cantankerous, irritable

grunt *v.* snort, groan, mutter, grumble

guarantee *n.* surety, promise, bond

guarantee *v.* pledge, endorse, warrant, insure

guaranty *n.* warranty, contract, certificate

guard *n.* sentry, sentinel, watchman

guard *v.* protect, watch, patrol, picket, tend

guarded *adj.* **PROTECTED:** secured, defended, safe; **CAUTIOUS:** circumspect, attentive, careful

guardian *n.* protector, overseer, trustee, custodian, keeper, defender, supervisor, baby–sitter

guess *v.* estimate, presume, infer, speculate, imagine, surmise, theorize, venture, suppose, presume

guest *n.* visitor, caller

guidance *n.* direction, leadership, supervision

guide *n.* leader, pilot, pathfinder, scout, escort, director, conductor, pioneer

guide *v.* lead, direct, conduct, escort

guilt *n.* responsibility, culpability, blame, error, fault, liability, weakness, failing

guilty *adj.* condemned, censured, incriminated, indicted, judged, damned, reproachable, chargeable

guise *n.* appearance, disguise

gulch *n.* ravine, gully, ditch, gorge

gulf *n.* **CHASM:** abyss, abysm, depth, ravine, **BAY:** inlet, sound, cove

gull, *v.* deceive, trick, cheat

gullible *adj.* innocent, trustful, simple, naïve

gully *n.* channel, ditch, chasm, crevasse, ravine

gulp *v.* swallow, gasp, swig

gurgle *v.* babble, ripple, murmur

guru *n.* teacher, instructor, mentor

gush *v.* **FLOW:** pour, well, spew

gust *n.* blast, burst, blow, breeze, wind

gusto, *n.* enjoyment, zest, zeal, fervor, ardor

gutter *n.* channel, gully, sewer, drain, trough

guttural *adj.* throaty, gruff, deep, hoarse

guy *n.* **MAN:** chap, lad, fellow; **GUIDE:** rope, chain, cable

guzzle *v.* swill, quaff, swig, drink

gymnasium *n.* arena, coliseum, ring, rink, pit, gym

gymnast *n.* acrobat, tumbler, jumper, athlete

gypsy *n.* wanderer, tramp, vagrant, traveler

habiliments *n.* dress, garments

habit *n.* **CUSTOM:** mode, practice, fashion, manner; **DRESS:** costume; **OBSESSION:** addiction, fixation

habitat *n.* environment, territory, surroundings

habitual *adj.* customary, frequent, periodic, continual, routine, rooted, systematic, recurrent, repeated, accustomed, established, repetitious, stereotyped

hack *adj.* routine, trite

hack *v.* chop, whack, mangle, cut

hackneyed *adj.* commonplace, trite

hag *n.* crone, shrew, ogress, hellcat, fishwife, harridan, witch

haggard *adj.* gaunt, worn, tired

haggle *v.* bargain, wrangle, deal, argue, buy, sell

hail *v.* call, greet, salute, cheer, welcome, honor

halfhearted *adj.* indecisive, irresolute, indifferent

half-truth *n.* lie, deception

halfway *adj.* partial, midway, incomplete, partially, imperfectly, insufficiently, moderately, middling

halfway *adv.* half, partly

hall *n.* **PUBLIC ROOM:** chamber, assembly, arena, ballroom, church, clubhouse, salon, lounge, gymnasium, amphitheater, gallery; **ENTRANCE:** foyer, corridor, hallway

hallmark *n.* label, endorsement, seal, emblem

hallow *v.* bless, sanctify

hallucination *n.* delusion, vision

hallway *n.* foyer, entrance, way, corridor, entrance
halt *n.* stop, cessation
halt *v.* check, terminate, suspend, interrupt, block, stem, deter, stall, curb, restrict, arrest, suppress, intercept, obstruct, hinder, impede, squelch
halve *v.* divide, split, bisect
ham *n.* overacter, amateur, nonprofessional
hamlet *n.* town, village
hamper *v.* hinder, slow, thwart, embarrass
hand *n.* WORKMAN: helper, worker, laborer; PENMANSHIP: calligraphy, script; APPLAUSE: ovation, reception, handclapping; CARDS: deal, round, game
handbag *n.* pocketbook, bag, purse
handbook *n.* textbook, directory, guidebook
handcuff *v.* restrain, shackle
handicap *n.* disadvantage, obstacle, impediment, affliction, hindrance, disorder, injury
handicap *v.* encumber, hinder
handily *adv.* easily, skillfully, smoothly, cleverly
handkerchief *n.* napkin, hanky
handle *v.* HOLD: touch, finger, check, examine, feel; MANAGE: manipulate, operate, use, work; DEAL: retail, market, sell
handsome *adj.* attractive, impressive, stately, robust, well–dressed, slick, beautiful
hand–to–mouth *adj.* marginal, minimal, borderline
handwriting *n.* penmanship, hand, writing, script, scrawl, scribble, calligraphy, scratching
handy *adj.* CONVENIENT: near, nearby; DEXTEROUS: able; USEFUL: beneficial, advantageous, gainful, helpful, profitable, usable
hang *v.* SUSPEND: dangle, droop, drape; WAVE: flap,

swing; **KILL:** execute, lynch

hanging *adj.* **DANGLING:** swaying, swinging, overhanging, pendulous, drooping; **TENTATIVE:** uncertain

hang–out *n.* bar, joint, hole, headquarters, room

hang–up *n.* problem, predicament, difficulty

haphazard *adj.* accidental, random, offhand, casual, slipshod, reckless, irregular, unplanned, aimless

happen *v.* befall, occur, ensue, arise, transpire

happening *n.* incident, affair, accident, event

happily *adv.* joyously, gladly, cheerily, gaily, merrily, brightly, blissfully, cheerfully, gleefully

happiness *n.* mirth, merrymaking, cheer, merriment, delight, gladness, hilarity, gaiety, cheerfulness, rejoicing, exhilaration

happy *adj.* joyous, merry, mirthful, gay, laughing, contented, genial, satisfied, cheery, jolly, sparkling, blissful, exhilarated, pleased, gratified, ecstatic, overjoyed, radiant, smiling, elated

happy–go–lucky *adj.* easygoing, unconcerned, thoughtless, irresponsible

harangue *n.* speech, tirade

harass *v.* annoy, attack, tease, vex, irritate, bother

harbor *n.* refuge, port, pier, inlet, wharf, dock

harbor *v.* **PROTECT:** shelter, secure, defend, lodge; **CONSIDER:** entertain, cherish, regard

hard *adj.* **COMPACT:** unyielding, solid, impermeable, tough, dense, firm; **DIFFICULT:** arduous, tricky, trying, tedious, complex, abstract, puzzling, troublesome, laborious; **CRUEL:** perverse, unrelenting, vengeful; **SEVERE:** harsh, exacting, grim

hard–core *adj.* inflexible, dedicated, steadfast, unwavering, faithful

harden v. steel, temper, solidify, crystallize, clot, petrify, compact, concentrate, fossilize, toughen

hardheaded adj. willful, stubborn, headstrong

hardhearted adj. cold, unfeeling, heartless, cruel

hardly adv. scarcely, barely, imperceptibly, infrequently, somewhat, rarely, slightly, sparsely

hardship n. trial, sorrow, worry, difficulty, grief

hardware n. appliance, fixture, casting, metalware, implement, tool, fitting, utensil, equipment

hardy adj. tough, resistant, solid, staunch, seasoned, fit, acclimatized, rugged, robust, hearty, hale, vigorous, powerful, sturdy, solid, substantial, strong

hark, harden v. listen, heed

harm n. INJURY: infliction, impairment, damage; EVIL: wickedness, outrage, abuse

harm v. injure, wreck, cripple, hurt

harmful adj. injurious, detrimental, hurtful, noxious, evil, adverse, sinister, virulent, corroding, toxic, painful, crippling, malicious, malignant, unwholesome, corrupting, menacing, damaging, catastrophic, disastrous, destructive, unhealthy, mortal

harmless adj. pure, innocent, powerless, controllable, manageable, safe, trustworthy, sanitary

harmonious adj. HARMONIC: tuneful, musical, melodic; CONGRUOUS: agreeable, corresponding, suitable, adapted, similar, like, cooperative, friendly, conforming, balanced, symmetrical

harp v. carp, nag, repeat, pester, complain

harridan n. witch, hag, nag

harrow v. torment, distress

harry v. plunder, harass

harsh adj. rough, severe, discordant, jangling,

cacophonous, grating, dissonant, creaking, clashing, jarring, clamorous, hoarse, rasping, screeching, ear-splitting, tuneless, shrill

harvest *n.* crops, yield, fruit, grain, produce, vegetable

harvest *v.* glean, gather, accumulate, collect, garner, cut, pluck, pick, cull, hoard, mow

hasp *n.* fastener, latch

hassle *n.* dispute, squabble

haste *n.* speed, dispatch, precipitation, rashness, impetuousness, foolhardiness, recklessness, hastiness, carelessness, heedlessness

hasten *v.* HURRY: rush, fly, sprint; EXPEDITE: accelerate, quicken, push, urge, goad, press

hasty *adj.* HURRIED: quick, speedy, swift, fast; CARELESS: precipitate, foolhardy, careless, rash

hat *n.* headgear, headpiece, helmet, chapeau, bonnet, cap, derby, sombrero, topper, bowler, Panama, fedora, beret, turban, hood, cowl, beret

hatch *v.* produce, originate, bear

hatchway *n.* hatch, door, entrance

hate *n.* dislike, animosity, enmity, hatred

hate *v.* DETEST: abhor, abominate, loathe, despise, dislike, resent

hateful *adj.* odious, detestable, repugnant, offensive

hatred *n.* dislike, abhorrence, loathing, rancor, repugnance, repulsion, disgust, contempt, displeasure, bitterness, antagonism, animosity, pique, grudge, malice, malevolence, spleen, hostility, alienation

haughty *adj.* disdainful, arrogant, proud, egotistic

haul *n.* PULL: tug, lift, wrench; DISTANCE: voyage, trip; SPOILS: take, find, booty

haul *v.* drag, pull, bring, draw

haunt v. **FREQUENT:** habituate, visit; **OBSESS:** torment, possess, trouble, hound, terrify, plague, vex, harass, worry, frighten, annoy, bother, disturb

haunting *adj.* eerie, unforgettable, seductive, frightful

have v. **OWN:** keep, retain, use, maintain, control, treasure, hold, possess; **BEAR:** beget, produce

haven n. harbor, port, refuge, shelter

havoc n. destruction, confusion, devastation, plunder

hazard n. chance, risk, peril, jeopardy, danger

hazard v. chance, try, guess, gamble, risk

haze n. fog, mist, smog, cloudiness

hazy *adj.* vague, cloudy, foggy, murky, misty, unclear, overcast, filmy, gauzy, vaporous, smoky, dim, indistinct, dusky, obscure, veiled, blurred, faint

head n. **SKULL:** brainpan, scalp, crown, bean, noggin, noodle; **LEADER:** chief, commander, officer, ruler; **TOP:** summit, peak, crest; **BEGINNING:** front, start, source, origin; **INTELLIGENCE:** brains, foresight, ingenuity, judgment

head v. lead, direct, oversee, supervise, manage

headache n. **PAIN:** migraine, neuralgia; **PROBLEM:** vexation, mess, difficulty, trouble

headway n. progress, advance, increase, promotion

heal v. cure, restore, renew, regenerate, remedy, rejuvenate, medicate, revive, rehabilitate, resuscitate, salve, help, ameliorate, doctor

health n. vigor, wholeness, healthfulness, fitness, bloom, hardiness, stamina, energy, strength

healthy *adj.* sound, trim, robust, vigorous, well, hearty, athletic, able–bodied, virile, blooming, sturdy, firm, lively, flourishing, good, fit, rugged

heap n. pile, mass, stack, quantity

heap *v.* pile, add, lump, load, pack
hear *v.* **LISTEN:** attend, catch, apprehend, eavesdrop, perceive, overhear; **TRY:** judge, examine, referee
hearsay *n.* rumor, scandal, report, gossip
heart *n.* **FEELING:** response, sympathy, sensitivity, emotion; **CENTER:** core, middle, pith; **SPIRIT:** courage, fortitude, gallantry
heartache *n.* sorrow, pain, despair, anguish, grief
heartless *adj.* cruel, unkind, insensitive, ruthless
hearty *adj.* warm, zealous, sincere, cheery, cheerful, jovial, animated, ardent, genial, enthusiastic, genuine, passionate, intense, exuberant, devout, unfeigned, fervent, responsive, friendly
heat *n.* **WARMTH:** fever, sultriness; **FERVOR:** ardor, passion, excitement, desire
heat *v.* warm, inflame, kindle, thaw, boil, sear, singe, scorch, ignite
heated *adj.* **WARMED:** cooked, fried, baked **FERVENT:** fiery, ardent, avid, excited, passionate
heathen *adj.* infidel, atheist, barbarian
heave *v.* **THROW:** toss; **MOVE:** rock, bob, pitch, lurch, roll, reel, sway, throb, slosh
heavenly *adj.* **DIVINE:** celestial, supernal, angelic, holy; **BLISSFUL:** sweet, enjoyable, excellent, pleasant
heavy *adj.* **WEIGHTY:** ponderous, huge, stout, dense, substantial, hefty, large; **BURDENSOME:** troublesome, oppressive, vexatious, difficult, disturbing, onerous; **DULL:** listless, slow, apathetic, indifferent; **GLOOMY:** dejected, cloudy, overcast, dark, dismal, sad
heavy-handed *adj.* oppressive, harsh, cruel, severe
heckle *v.* torment, disturb, pester, bother, ridicule
hectic *adj.* frantic, unsettled, boisterous, restless,

confused, disordered

hector *v.* bully, annoy, tease, vex

heed *n.* notice, care

height *n.* altitude, elevation, prominence, loftiness, highness, tallness, stature, expanse, extent, length

heighten *v.* **INCREASE:** sharpen, redouble, emphasize, strengthen; **RAISE:** uplift, elevate, lift

heinous *adj.* hateful, atrocious, wicked

heir *n.* inheritor, successor, descendent, heiress, beneficiary, inheritor, prince

heirloom *n.* legacy, inheritance, bequest, gift, antique

heist *n.* robbery, burglary

heist *v.* rob, steal

helm *n.* leadership, control

help *n.* **ASSISTANCE:** advice, comfort, aid, support, gift, charity, encouragement, subsidy, service, relief, endowment, cooperation, guidance; **EMPLOYEE:** aid, representative, assistant, faculty, staff; **RELIEF:** maintenance, sustenance, nourishment, remedy

help *v.* assist, advise, encourage, cooperate, intercede, befriend, accommodate, sustain, benefit, bolster, promote, back, advocate, abet, stimulate, uphold, further, boost, support

helpful *adj.* **USEFUL:** valuable, significant, serviceable, profitable, advantageous, favorable, convenient, suitable, practical, operative, usable, applicable, desirable, convenient; **CURATIVE:** healthy, salutary, restorative, healthful; **OBLIGING:** accommodating, considerate, neighborly, kind

helping *n.* portion, serving, plateful, share

helpless *adj.* **INCOMPETENT:** incapable, unfit, inexpert; **DEPENDENT:** feeble, unable, weak, vulnerable

hem *n.* border, skirting, edging, edge, fringe, rim
henpeck *v.* nag, bully, suppress, intimidate, bother
herald *n.* proclaimer, forerunner
herd *n.* flock, group, drove, pack, brood, swarm, lot, bevy, covey, gaggle, nest, brood, flight, school, clan
herdsman *n.* shepherd, herder, rancher
hereditary *adj.* inherited, genetic, paternal
heredity *n.* ancestry, inheritance, genetic
heresy *n.* dissent, nonconformity, dissidence, sectarianism, schism, unorthodoxy, secularism
heretic *n.* schismatic, apostate, sectarian, cynic
heritage *n.* **INHERITANCE:** legacy, birthright, ancestry, dowry, share, endowment, status, heredity; **TRADITION:** culture, custom, fashion, system
hermit *n.* ascetic, recluse
hero *n.* champion, model, conqueror, god, martyr, warrior, saint, star, knight–errant
heroic *adj.* valiant, valorous, fearless, brave, noble
heroism *n.* fortitude, valor, bravery, courage, strength
hesitancy *n.* indecision, wavering, procrastination, delay, pause
hesitant *adj.* **DOUBTFUL:** skeptical, irresolute, uncertain; **SLOW:** delaying, wavering, dawdling, lazy
hesitate *v.* pause, stop, falter, vacillate, flounder, ponder, delay, weigh, consider, deliberate, linger
hesitation *n.* **DOUBT:** equivocation, skepticism, irresolution, uncertainty; **DELAY:** wavering, dawdling
hex *n.* spell, curse
hex *v.* curse, enchant
hiatus *n.* break, pause
hidden *adj.* secluded, private, covert, concealed, occult, masked, screened, veiled, clouded, obscured,

hide

disguised, unseen, camouflaged, shrouded, shadowy, clandestine, cloistered, surreptitious

hide *n.* skin, pelt, rawhide, fur, leather

hide *v.* conceal, shroud, curtain, veil, camouflage, cover, mask, cloak, screen, suppress, withhold, shield, secrete, hoard, closet, obscure, disguise

hideous *adj.* frightful, shocking, revolting, hateful, ghastly, grisly, ugly

hideout *n.* lair, den, refuge, retreat, shelter

hierarchy *n.* government, authority, ministry, regime

high *adj.* **TOWERING:** tall, gigantic, big, colossal, tremendous, great, giant, huge, formidable, immense, steep, elevated, lofty, soaring, raised; **EXALTED:** eminent, leading, powerful, distinguished, noble; **EXPENSIVE:** costly, precious, **EXTRAORDINARY:** great, special, unusual; **SHRILL:** piercing, sharp, penetrating; **DRUNK:** intoxicated, tipsy, inebriated

high–flown *adj.* lofty, exalted, pretentious

high–pressure *adj.* forceful, compelling, powerful

high–spirited *adj.* daring, dauntless, reckless, brave

high–strung *adj.* nervous, tense, impatient, restless

highway *n.* roadway, parkway, freeway, turnpike

hijack *v.* rob, steal, privateer, capture, seize

hike *n.* walk, tour, trek, trip, backpack, journey

hike *v.* **TRAMP:** tour, explore, travel, walk; **RAISE:** lift, advance, increase

hilarious *adj.* gay, merry, funny, amusing, lively, witty, entertaining

hill *n.* mound, knoll, butte, bluff, promontory, precipice, rising, headland, upland, inclination, slope, ascent, grade, incline, rise, foothill, dune, climb, elevation, hillside, hilltop

hinder *v.* stop, impede, obstruct, check, retard, fetter, block, thwart, bar, clog, encumber, burden, inhibit, shackle, interrupt, arrest, curb, oppose, deter, hamper, frustrate, intercept, prohibit, stall, slow, down, smother, disappoint, spoil, gag, annul

hindrance *n.* obstacle, barrier, interference

hinge *n.* joint, pivot, juncture, articulation, link

hinge *v.* hang, turn, depend, connect, couple, join

hint *n.* allusion, mention, inkling, implication, reference, observation, notice, tip, clue, omen, scent, notion, taste, suspicion, innuendo, sign, impression, indication, suggestion

hint *v.* intimate, inform, imply, infer, acquaint, remind, recall, cue, prompt, insinuate, indicate, wink, advise, suggest

hip *n.* **AWARE:** informed, enlightened, knowledgeable, cognizant; **FASHIONABLE:** modern, stylish

hire *v.* engage, secure, enlist, appoint, delegate, authorize, retain, commission, empower, select, pick, contract, procure

historic *adj.* factual, traditional, chronicled, old

history *n.* account, annals, records, archives, chronicle, writings, evidence, record

hit *adj.* struck, slugged, cuffed, smacked, clouted, banged, smashed, tapped, rapped, swatted, hurt

hit *n.* **STROKE:** blow, slap, rap, punch; **SUCCESS:** favorite, sellout, knockout

hit *v.* **STRIKE:** knock, sock, slap, bump, thump, collide, punch, hammer, whack, jab, tap, pelt, cuff, clout, club; **REACH:** find, win

hitch *n.* **KNOT:** loop, noose, tie; **DIFFICULTY:** obstacle, hindrance, block

hitch

hitch *v.* hook, unite, yoke, hook, fasten, join
hoard *n.* cache, treasure
hoard *v.* amass, acquire, keep, accumulate, save
hoary *adj.* white, old
hoax *n.* trick, fabrication, deceit, deception, lie
hobby *n.* pursuit, avocation, pastime, diversion, interest, activity, pursuit, sport, amusement, craft
hobo *n.* vagrant, vagabond, wanderer, beggar
hock *v.* sell, pledge, deposit, pawn
hod *n.* trough, scuttle
hodgepodge *n.* mixture, jumble, combination, mess
hoist *n.* lift, crane, derrick, elevator
hoist *v.* raise, lift
hokum *n.* nonsense, trickery, chicanery
hold *v.* **POSSESS:** keep, retain, have, accept; **SUPPORT:** sustain, brace, buttress, prop; **GRASP:** grip, clutch, embrace, squeeze, hug, seize; **CONFINE:** imprison, enclose, restrain; **RESIST:** persevere, continue, endure; **ADHERE:** cling, fasten, stick
holdout *n.* die–hard, objector, resister, resistance
holdover *n.* remnant, relic, surplus, remainder
holdup *n.* robbery, burglary, stick–up, crime, theft
hole *n.* **CAVITY:** perforation, puncture, slot, eyelet, split, tear, cleft, opening, fissure, gap, gash, rift, rupture, aperture, breach, eye, crater, gorge, hollow, chasm, crevasse, **BURROW:** den, lair; **DIFFICULTY:** impasse, tangle, mess, crisis, emergency
holiday *n.* festival, fiesta, carnival, jubilee, anniversary, celebration
holiness *n.* devoutness, humility, saintliness, devotion, worship
hollow *adj.* **CONCAVE:** sunken, depressed, excavated,

142

indented; **CAVERNOUS:** deep, resonant, booming, rumbling, reverberating, muffled, dull, resounding; **UNSOUND:** empty, pretentious

hollow *n.* cavity, dale, bowl, basin, valley

hollow *v.* scoop, excavate, indent, dig, shovel

holocaust *n.* loss, fire, destruction

holy *adj.* devout, pious, righteous, moral, just, good, angelic, godly, reverent, venerable, humble, saintly, innocent, godlike, saintlike, perfect, faultless, chaste, upright, virtuous, dedicated, devoted, spiritual, religious

homage *n.* loyalty, worship, respect, adoration, deference, devotion, reverence

home *n.* **DWELLING:** residence, habitation, abode, lodging, quarters, domicile, shelter; **ASYLUM:** orphanage, sanitarium, hospital

homecoming *n.* welcome, celebration, entry, arrival

homely *adj.* **UNPRETENTIOUS:** plain, snug, simple, cozy, modest; **PLAIN:** unattractive, uncomely

homespun *adj.* hand–crafted, domestic, homemade

homestead *n.* property, house, ranch, estate, home

homogenize *v.* blend, combine

homologous *adj.* equivalent, associated

honest *adj.* **TRUTHFUL:** trustworthy, unimpeachable, legitimate, straight; **FRANK:** candid, straightforward, aboveboard; **FAIR:** just, equitable, impartial

honesty *n.* fidelity, scrupulousness, candor, openness, morality, goodness, virtue

honk *v.* blare, trumpet, bellow, sound

honor *n.* distinction, recognition, attention, reputation, tribute, integrity

honor *v.* **RESPECT:** worship, sanctify, venerate, praise;

VALUE: admire, esteem, compliment; **ACCEPT:** clear, pass, acknowledge

honorable *adj.* reputable, creditable, distinguished, famous, noble

honorary *adj.* titular, nominal, complimentary

hood *n.* **COVERING:** cowl, shawl, bonnet, veil, capuchin, mantle; **CANOPY:** awning, cover; **HOODLUM:** criminal, gangster, crook

hoodlum *n.* rowdy, thug, gangster, crook, criminal

hook *n.* lock, catch, clasp, fastener

hook *v.* **BEND:** curve, angle, crook, arch; **CATCH:** pin, secure, fasten

hoot *n.* howl, whoop, boo, cry

hop *v.* leap, jump, skip, bounce

hope *n.* **FAITH:** expectation, anticipation; **DREAM:** desire, purpose, wish, goal

hope *v.* expect, desire, await, suppose, believe, anticipate, trust

hopeful *adj.* **OPTIMISTIC:** expectant, trustful, anticipating, trusting, confident; **ENCOURAGING:** promising, reassuring, favorable, cheering, propitious, auspicious, uplifting, heartening, inspiring

hopeless *adj.* unfortunate, bad, incurable, vain, irreversible, irreparable, disastrous, tragic, desperate

horde *n.* crowd, swarm, pack, throng, gathering

horizon *n.* range, border, limit, boundary, extent

horizontal *adj.* **LEVEL:** aligned, parallel, flat, straight; **EVEN:** flush, uniform, regular, smooth

horrible *adj.* repulsive, dreadful, disgusting, terrible, frightful, shameful, shocking, awful

horrid *adj.* shocking, hideous, disturbing, shameful, offensive, pitiful

horrify *v.* shock, terrify
horror *n.* fear, terror, awe, fright
hors d'oeuvre *n.* appetizer, canapé
horseman *n.* cavalryman, knight, dragoon, equestrian, jockey, cowboy, rider
horticulture *n.* cultivation, agriculture, farming
hospitable *adj.* kind, receptive, cordial, courteous, open, friendly
hospital *n.* clinic, infirmary, sanitarium, dispensary
hospitality *n.* companionship, fellowship, entertainment, welcome
hostile *adj.* unfriendly, antagonistic, hateful, opposed
hostility *n.* abhorrence, aversion, bitterness, hatred
hot *adj.* BURNING: fiery, flaming, blazing, baking, roasting, scorching, blistering, searing, sizzling, broiling, scalding, parching; AROUSED: furious, ill-tempered, indignant, angry
hotel *n.* motel, lodging, inn, hostel, resort, tavern
hotrod *n.* car, racer, dragster
hound *n.* dog, cur
hound *v.* bully, pester, badger, provoke, annoy
house *n.* HOME: habitation, dwelling, residence; FAMILY: line, tradition, ancestry; LEGISLATURE: congress, council, parliament
housekeeper *n.* caretaker, servant
hover *v.* remain, wait, float, linger
howl *v.* cry, wail, bawl, lament, yell
hub *n.* center, core, middle, focus, heart
hubbub *n.* uproar, bustle
huddle *v.* crowd, cluster, group, conference
hue *n.* color, tint, value, dye
huff *n.* anger, annoyance, pique

huff *v.* puff, blow, bluster, bully

huffy *adj.* offended, piqued, angry, insulted, irritable

hug *v.* embrace, hold, squeeze, clasp, press, cling, clutch, envelop, enfold, nestle, cuddle

huge *adj.* large, tremendous, enormous, immense

hulking *adj.* bulky, massive

humane *adj.* merciful, kind, benevolent, sympathetic, understanding, compassionate, kindhearted, tenderhearted, forgiving, charitable, tender, generous, lenient, tolerant, altruistic, philanthropic, magnanimous, unselfish, warmhearted

humanitarian *adj.* humane, kindly

humble *adj.* **MEEK:** submissive, gentle, diffident, retiring, bashful, shy, timid, reserved, deferential, mild, withdrawn, hesitant, fearful, tentative, obedient, passive, tame, restrained, subdued; **UNPRETENTIOUS:** unassuming, modest, seemly, becoming, homespun, natural, servile, shabby, beggarly, insignificant, plain, common, homely, simple

humble *v.* humiliate, shame, mortify, chasten, demean, demote, lower, crush, degrade, discredit, deflate, squelch, squash

humbug *n.* hoax, fraud, lie, deception, nonsense

humdrum *adj.* monotonous, common, uninteresting, dull

humid *adj.* moist, damp, stuffy, sticky, muggy, close

humiliate *v.* humble, shame, debase, chasten, mortify, degrade, dishonor, demean, conquer, vanquish, disgrace, embarrass

humiliation *n.* chagrin, mortification, disgrace, embarrassment, shame

humility *n.* meekness, timidity, submissiveness,

servility, subservience, resignation, shyness

humor *n.* **COMEDY:** entertainment, amusement, jesting, raillery; **WITTICISM:** pleasantry, banter, joke, mirth; **DISPOSITION:** wittiness, jolliness, gaiety, joyfulness, playfulness

humor *v.* indulge, pamper, gratify, please, appease, placate, comfort

humorous *adj.* amusing, funny, comical, entertaining

hunch *n.* intuition, notion, feeling, premonition, instinct, anticipation, clue, foreboding, portent, apprehension, misgiving, qualm, suspicion, inkling

hunger *n.* longing, yearning, lust, want

hunger *v.* crave, desire

hungry *adj.* starved, famished, ravenous, desirous, unsatisfied, unfilled, starving, voracious

hunk *n.* lump, chunk, mass, clod, slice, morsel

hunt *v.* **PURSUE:** follow, stalk, hound, trail, seek, track, chase; **INVESTIGATE:** search, probe, seek

hurdle *n.* obstacle, barricade, blockade, barrier

hurl *v.* throw, cast, fling, heave

hurrah *v.* applaud, cheer, approve

hurry *v.* **HASTEN:** scurry, scuttle, dash, sprint, rush, scoot, dart, spring, speed, fly, bustle, race; **URGE:** drive, push, spur, goad

hurt *adj.* injured, harmed, wounded, disfigured, suffering, distressed, tortured, unhappy

hurt *v.* **INJURE:** cut, bruise, slap, abuse, flog, whip, torture, stab, harm, wound, lacerate, bite, burn, punch, pinch, scourge, lash, cane, switch; **HARM:** maltreat, injure, spoil, damage, destroy; **PAIN:** ache, throb, sting

hurtful *adj.* aching, injurious, deadly, harmful

husband *v.* economize, conserve

hush *v.* calm, soothe, quiet, silence, gag, stifle

husky *adj.* **HOARSE:** rough, throaty, growling, gruff; **STRONG:** muscular, sinewy, strapping

hustle *v.* rush, push, hurry, race, run, speed

hut *n.* shanty, lean–to, shack, dugout, hovel

hygiene *n.* health, sanitation, cleanliness

hygienic *adj.* healthful, sanitary, clean, pure, sterile

hyperbole *n.* metaphor, exaggeration

hypnotic *adj.* narcotic, soporific, soothing

hypnotize *v.* mesmerize, fascinate, captivate, stupefy, soothe, anesthetize

hypocrisy *n.* pretense, affectation, bigotry, sanctimony, dishonesty, lie

hypocrite *n.* pretender, fraud, faker, deceiver, charlatan, trickster, rascal

hypothesis *n.* theory, supposition, assumption, guess, opinion

hypothetical *adj.* **SUPPOSED:** imagined, uncertain, vague, assumed, likely, **POSTULATED:** academic, philosophical, logical

hysteria, hysterics *n.* neurosis, emotionalism, delirium, agitation, confusion, excitement, nervousness

hysterical, *adj.* frantic, convulsed, raving, delirious, emotional, neurotic, distracted, distraught, unrestrained, convulsive, uncontrollable, agitated, frenzied, tempestuous, impassioned, overwrought

icon *n.* image, picture

iconoclast *n.* dissenter, rebel

idea *n.* **CONCEPT:** belief, theory, hypothesis, assumption, conjecture, notion, thought; **FANCY:** whimsy, whim, fantasy, imagination

ideal *adj.* **TYPICAL:** model, archetypal; **PERFECT:** best, theoretical, supreme, fitting, exemplary, excellent

ideal *n.* concept, paragon, goal, prototype, model

idealism *n.* principle, conscience, philosophy, ethics

identical *adj.* same, alike, twin, indistinguishable

identification *n.* **CLASSIFYING:** naming, cataloguing, description, classification; **CREDENTIALS:** passport, testimony, papers, badge

identify *v.* classify, catalog, analyze, describe, name

identity *n.* characteristics, identification, individuality, uniqueness, name

ideology *n.* philosophy, belief, doctrine, ethics

idiom *n.* expression, usage, jargon, argot

idiot *n.* simpleton, nincompoop, booby, fool

idiotic *adj.* thick–witted, dull, moronic, stupid

idle *adj.* unemployed, unoccupied, uncultivated, fallow, motionless, inert, resting

idle *v.* loiter, slack, shirk, loaf

idol *n.* image, icon, god, figurine, fetish, totem

idolatry *n.* worship, love, infatuation, fervor, zeal

idolize *v.* worship, glorify, adore, canonize

ignite *v.* fire, light, enkindle, burn

ignoble *adj.* mean, dishonorable

ignominy *n.* shame, disgrace

ignorance *n.* incomprehension, incapacity, inexperience, illiteracy, simplicity, shallowness

ignorant *adj.* **UNAWARE:** unconscious, shallow, superficial, inexperienced, unwitting, unintelligent, obtuse, dense, shallow, stupid; **UNTRAINED:** illiterate, uneducated, misguided, apprenticed, naïve

ignore *v.* disregard, reject, overlook, neglect

ilk *n.* type, kind

ill *adj.* **BAD:** harmful, evil, noxious, unfavorable; **SICK:** unwell, unhealthy, ailing

ill *n.* evil, depravity, misfortune, mischief, wrong

illegal *adj.* unlawful illicit banned outlawed unauthorized unlicensed, illegitimate, prohibited, forbidden, criminal

illegible *adj.* unreadable, faint, unintelligible, confused, obscure

illicit *adj.* unlawful, prohibited, unauthorized, illegal

illiteracy *n.* ignorance, stupidity, idiocy

illiterate *adj.* ignorant, uneducated, unenlightened

illness *n.* sickness, infirmity, disorder, attack, convalescence, complaint, collapse, breakdown, confinement, weakness, disease, ailment, malady

illogical *adj.* irrational, unreasonable, absurd, fallacious, incorrect, inconsistent, unscientific, contradictory, unsound, implausible

ill–tempered *adj.* cross, touchy, querulous, irritable

illuminate *v.* **BRIGHTEN:** lighten, illumine, decorate, light; **CLARIFY:** illustrate, explain, interpret, elucidate

illumination *n.* **LIGHT:** flame, brilliance, lighting; **CLARIFICATION:** instruction, teaching, education, information, knowledge

illusion *n.* deception, fancy, hallucination, mirage, apparition, delusion, trick, dream

illusory *adj.* deceiving, unreal

illustrate *v.* explain; picture, portray, depict

illustration *n.* explanation, picture, engraving, vignette, inset, newsphoto, chart, diagram

illustrative *adj.* symbolic, representative, pictorial, descriptive, explanatory, graphic

illustrious *adj.* distinguished, famous

image *n.* LIKENESS: idol, representation, effigy, form, drawing, portrait, photograph, replica, picture; CONCEPT: conception, perception, thought, idea

imagery *n.* metaphor, representation, comparison

imaginable *adj.* conceivable, comprehensible, sensible, possible, plausible, believable, reasonable, likely

imaginary *adj.* fancied, illusory, visionary, dreamy, hypothetical, theoretical, imagined, hallucinatory, whimsical, fabulous, nonexistent, mythological, legendary, fictitious, unreal

imagination *n.* inventiveness, conception, sensitivity, visualization, awareness, insight

imaginative *adj.* creative, inventive, artistic, original

imagine *v.* conceive, invent, picture, conjure, envision, invent, fabricate, formulate, devise, conceptualize, dream, perceive, create

imbalance *n.* unevenness, inequality, irregularity

imbecilic *adj.* foolish, silly

imbibe *v.* ingest, gorge, guzzle, drink, swallow

imbroglio *n.* commotion, entanglement, fracas

imbue *v.* permeate, invade, absorb

imitate *v.* MIMIC: impersonate, mirror, mime, ape, simulate, parody; COPY: duplicate, counterfeit, falsify, reproduce; RESEMBLE: simulate, parallel

imitation *n.* SIMULATION: duplication, mimicry, impersonation, copy; COUNTERFEIT: likeness, replica, substitution, forgery

imitative *adj.* deceptive, false, forged, sham

immaculate *adj.* pure, unsoiled, unsullied, spotless, stainless, bright, clean

immanent *adj.* deep–seated, inherent

immaterial *adj.* unimportant, insignificant

immature *adj.* childish, youthful, sophomoric, naïve
immediate *adj.* now, next, prompt, following
immense *adj.* large, gigantic, tremendous, enormous
immerse *v.* plunge, involve, submerge, douse, steep, soak, drench, dunk, souse
immigrant *n.* outsider, newcomer, alien
immigrate *v.* move, enter
immigration *n.* colonization, settlement, migration
imminent *adj.* impending, approaching, coming
immobility *n.* firm, fixed, motionless
immodest *adj.* brazen, shameless, bold, egotistic
immoral *adj.* sinful, corrupt, shameless, bad
immorality *n.* vice, depravity, dissoluteness, evil
immortal *adj.* **DEATHLESS:** undying, imperishable, endless, timeless, everlasting, indestructible, enduring, eternal; **ILLUSTRIOUS:** celebrated, eminent, glorious, famous
immovable *adj.* solid, stable, fixed, firm
immune *adj.* exempt, free, unsusceptible, privileged, excused, safe
immunity *n.* **EXEMPTION:** privilege, license, freedom; **IMMUNIZATION:** resistance, protection
immure *v.* confine, imprison
impact *n.* shock, impression, contact, collision
impair *v.* diminish, spoil, injure, hurt, break, damage
impart *v.* **GIVE:** bestow, grant, present, allow; **INFORM:** tell, announce, divulge, admit, reveal
impartial *adj.* unbiased, disinterested, equal, fair
impartiality *n.* objectivity, candor, equality, fairness
impasse *n.* deadlock, standstill, cessation, pause
impassioned *adj.* ardent, fervent, passionate
impassive *adj.* emotionless, unemotional, unmoved

impatience *n.* agitation, restlessness, anxiety, excitement, nervousness

impatient *adj.* anxious, eager, feverish, restless

impeach *v.* charge, arraign, denounce, indict, discredit, reprimand, blame, incriminate, try

impeccable *adj.* flawless, perfect

impede *v.* hinder, obstruct, slow

impediment *n.* obstruction, hindrance, obstacle, difficulty, barrier

impel *v.* drive, force, urge

impend *v.* approach, threaten

impenetrable *adj.* **DENSE:** impervious, hard, compact, firm, thick; **INCOMPREHENSIBLE:** unintelligible, inscrutable, unfathomable, obscure

impenitent *adj.* unrepentant, remorseless

imperative *adj.* **NECESSARY:** obligatory, mandatory; **AUTHORITATIVE:** masterful, commanding, dominant, aggressive, powerful

imperfect *adj.* flawed, incomplete, deficient, faulty

imperfection *n.* fault, flaw, stain, blemish

imperious *adj.* haughty, arrogant

impersonal *adj.* detached, disinterested, indifferent

impersonate *v.* portray, mimic, represent, imitate

impersonation *n.* role, enactment, performance

impertinent *adj.* impudent, saucy, insolent, rude

impervious *adj.* impassable, impermeable, impenetrable, watertight

impetuous *adj.* hasty, impulsive

impetus *n.* force, momentum, stimulus, incentive, purpose, reason

impinge *v.* encroach, infringe, strike, touch

impious *adj.* sinful, profane, blasphemous, bad

implement *n.* tool, instrument, appliance, utensil
implicate *v.* involve, connect, associate, link, relate
implication *n.* indication, inference, guess
implicit *adj.* **UNDERSTOOD:** implied; **DEFINITE:** certain, absolute, accurate, inevitable
imply *v.* indicate, intimate, suggest, hint, implicate, signify, mean, indicate
impolite *adj.* discourteous, churlish, rude, sullen
impolitic *adj.* imprudent, unwise
import *n.* meaning, signification
importance *n.* import, consequence, bearing, influence, emphasis, weight, relevance
important *adj.* **WEIGHTY:** significant, momentous, essential, critical, primary, foremost, marked, valuable, crucial, vital, serious, consequential; **EMINENT:** illustrious, well–known, influential, famous
importune *v.* urge, entreat
impose *v.* force, presume, burden, compel
imposing *adj.* stirring, overwhelming, impressive
imposition *n.* burden, pressure, encumbrance, demand, restraint
impossibility *n.* hopelessness, difficulty, futility
impossible *adj.* inconceivable, vain, unattainable, insurmountable, unworkable, futile, hopeless
impostor *n.* fraud, deceiver, pretender, charlatan
imposture *n.* ruse, deceit, hoax, sham
impotent *adj.* **WEAK:** powerless, inept, infirm, unable; **STERILE:** barren, frigid, unproductive
impound *v.* appropriate, take, usurp, seize
impoverish *v.* bankrupt, exhaust, destroy
impoverished *adj.* bankrupt, broke, poor, ruined
impractical *adj.* unrealistic, unworkable, improbable,

illogical, absurd, wild, impossible, idealistic

impregnable *adj.* invulnerable, unassailable

impregnate *v.* **PERMEATE:** fill, pervade, soak, infuse; **BEGET:** conceive, reproduce, fertilize

impress *v.* **MARK:** indent, emboss, imprint, dent, stamp; **FASCINATE:** affect, dazzle, stir, fascinate

impression *n.* **MARK:** imprint, dent, indentation, depression; **EFFECT:** response, reaction; **NOTION:** theory, conjecture, supposition, guess, opinion

impressionable *adj.* perceptive, receptive, affected

impressive *adj.* stirring, moving, inspiring, thrilling, intense, dramatic, absorbing, profound, remarkable, extraordinary, notable, momentous

imprint *n.* **IDENTIFICATION:** banner, trademark, emblem, signature; **IMPRESSION:** dent, indentation

imprint *v.* print, stamp, designate, mark

imprison *v.* jail, confine, incarcerate, detain, hold, intern, cage, enclose

improbable *adj.* doubtful, unlikely

improper *adj.* indecent, incongruous, inadvisable, untimely, inappropriate, unbefitting, unsuitable

improve *v.* update, refine, enrich, enhance, augment

improvement *n.* betterment, advancement, development, growth, enrichment, renovation, reorganization, amendment, revision, refinement, modernization, enhancement, remodeling, supplement

impudent *adj.* bold, insolent, forward, rude

impulse *n.* **THROB:** surge, pulsation, beat; **FANCY:** urge, stimulus, whim, caprice, spontaneity, notion, inclination, disposition

impulsive *adj.* impetuous, spontaneous

impure *adj.* adulterated, diluted, debased, tainted,

contaminated, polluted, corrupted, doctored
impute *v.* ascribe, assign, charge
inability *n.* incompetence, incapacity, shortcoming, failure, weakness, lack, frailty
inaccessible *adj.* distant, rare, remote, separated
inaccuracy *n.* mistake, exaggeration, deception, error
inaccurate *adj.* incorrect, inexact, fallacious, incorrect, mistaken, wrong
inactive *adj.* idle, lazy, dormant, still, motionless
inadequacy *n.* inferiority, weakness, defect, flaw, drawback, shortcoming, blemish, lack
inadequate *adj.* insufficient, lacking, scanty, meager, deficient, imperfect, defective, unsatisfactory
inane *adj.* senseless, pointless, foolish, silly
inanimate *adj.* lifeless, dull, inert, idle, motionless
inappropriate *adj.* improper, unsuitable
inapt *adj.* unfit, unsuitable
inarticulate *adj.* MUTE: reticent, speechless, wordless; INCOMPREHENSIBLE: obscure, unintelligible, vague
inattentive *adj.* preoccupied, indifferent, negligent, careless, diverted
inaugurate *v.* induct, begin, introduce, initiate, begin
incalculable *adj.* unpredictable, uncertain
incantation *n.* chant, charm, recitation, supplication
incapable *adj.* inadequate, incompetent, inexperienced, naïve, poor, unqualified, unsuited
incapacitate *v.* disable, disqualify, invalidate
incarcerate *v.* confine, imprison
incarnate *adj.* bodily, manifest, personified
incense *n.* scent, fragrance, essence, perfume
incense *v.* inflame, anger
incentive *n.* motive, spur, inducement, stimulus,

impetus, enticement, temptation, inspiration, encouragement, reason

incessant *adj.* continual, ceaseless, constant

inchoate *adj.* shapeless, formless

incidence *n.* range, occurrence, scope

incident *n.* occurrence, happening, episode, event

incidental *adj.* subsidiary, related, subordinate

incinerate *v.* burn, cremate

incise *v.* cut, engrave, dissect, chop, split, divide

incision *n.* cut, gash, slash, surgery

incisive *adj.* cutting, keen, sarcastic, trenchant

incite *v.* rouse, stir, stimulate, provoke, spur, goad, persuade, induce, urge, inspire

inclement *adj.* stormy, severe; cruel, merciless

inclination *n.* TENDENCY: bias, bent, propensity, predilection, penchant, leaning, disposition, preference, drift, trend; SLANT: pitch, slope, incline, angle, ramp, bank, lean, list, grade

incline *v.* LEAN: tilt, bow, nod; TEND: prefer, favor

inclined *adj.* leaning, sloping

include *v.* contain, embrace, involve, incorporate, constitute, interject, insert

inclusive *adj.* including, incorporating

incoherent *adj.* UNCONNECTED: disorganized; INDISTINCT: unintelligible, muddled, muttered, muffled

income *n.* revenue, earnings, salary, wages, profit, dividends, proceeds, receipts, commission

incommensurate *adj.* disproportionate, inadequate

incomparable *adj.* excellent, exceptional, matchless, perfect, superior, unequaled, unique, unusual

incompatible *adj.* irreconcilable, incongruous, contrary, clashing, contradictory, inconstant, discordant

incompetent *adj.* incapable, unfit, unskilled, bungling, ineffectual, clumsy, awkward, inexperienced
incomplete *adj.* imperfect, rough, unfinished
inconceivable *adj.* unthinkable, unbelievable
incongruous *adj.* inconsistent, contradictory
inconsequential *adj.* irrelevant, trivial, unnecessary
inconsiderate *adj.* thoughtless, boorish, impolite, discourteous, rude
inconsistent *adj.* illogical, contradictory, incoherent
inconspicuous *adj.* concealed, hidden, obscure
inconstant *adj.* varying, fickle
inconvenience *n.* trouble, discomfort, bother
incorporation *n.* embodiment, addition
incorrect *adj.* false, mistaken, unreliable, wrong
incorrigible *adj.* bad, difficult
increase *n.* growth, addition, development, spread, enlargement, expansion, escalation
increase *v.* extend, enlarge, expand, dilate, broaden, widen, thicken, deepen, build, lengthen, augment, escalate, amplify, supplement
incredible *adj.* unbelievable, improbable, ridiculous
incredulous *adj.* disbelieving, skeptical
incriminate *v.* charge, involve, implicate, blame
incumbent *adj.* binding, obligatory
incurable *adj.* fatal, serious, hopeless, deadly
incursion *n.* inroad, invasion
indebted *adj.* obligated, grateful, appreciative
indecent *adj.* offensive, immoral, bad, lewd, shameful
indecency *n.* vulgarity, impropriety
indecision *n.* hesitation, doubt, uncertainty
indecisive *adj.* irresolute, unstable
indefinite *adj.* vague, uncertain, unsure, unsettled

indelible *adj.* ingrained, enduring, strong, permanent

indemnify *v.* compensate, protect

indentation *n.* imprint, recession, depression, dent

independence *n.* freedom, sovereignty, license

indestructible *adj.* durable, immortal, permanent

index *v.* list, catalog, alphabetize, arrange, tabulate

indicate *v.* SIGNIFY: symbolize, betoken, intimate, mean; DESIGNATE: show, name, point

indication *n.* symptom, evidence, sign, hint

indicator *n.* dial, pointer

indictment *n.* accusation, detention, incrimination

indifferent *adj.* unconcerned, cool, unemotional, unsympathetic, heartless, unresponsive, unfeeling, nonchalant, impassive, detached, callous, stony, remote, reserved, distant, arrogant, unmoved

indigent *adj.* destitute, impoverished, poor

indignant *adj.* angry, upset, displeased, piqued

indignity *n.* affront, humiliation, injury, insult

indirect *adj.* devious, roundabout, tortuous, twisting, devious, sinister, rambling, oblique

indiscreet *adj.* imprudent, misguided, rash, tactless

indiscriminate *adj.* random, chaotic, aimless

indispensable *adj.* necessary, required, essential

indisposed *adj.* DISINCLINED: reluctant, unwilling; ILL: ailing, sickly, weak

indisputable *adj.* incontrovertible, undeniable, undoubted, unquestionable, certain

indistinct *adj.* vague, confused, indefinite, obscure

individual *adj.* personal, particular, solitary, distinctive, personalized, sole, private

indoctrinate *v.* instruct, implant, influence, teach

indomitable *adj.* invincible, unconquerable

induce *v.* begin, cause, effect, persuade, produce
inducement *n.* incentive, influence, motive
induct *v.* admit, recruit, enroll, conscript, draft
induction *n.* **REASONING:** rationalization, conjecture, reason; **INITIATION:** ordination, consecration
indulge *v.* humor, coddle, entertain, gratify
indulgence *n.* **HUMORING:** coddling, pampering, spoiling, placating, gratifying; **REVELRY:** intemperance, greed, waste
industrious *adj.* diligent, intent, involved, active, busy
industry *n.* activity, persistence, application, perseverance, enterprise, zeal, inventiveness, attention
inebriate *v.* exhilarate, intoxicate, stupefy
ineffective *adj.* inadequate, incompetent, weak
inefficient *adj.* prodigal, improvident, wasteful
ineligible *adj.* unqualified, unsuitable, unfit
inept *adj.* bungling, clumsy, incompetent, awkward
inert *adj.* inactive, sluggish, still, dormant, idle
inevitable *adj.* unavoidable, irresistible, fated, sure, inescapable, destined, unalterable, ordained
inexorable *adj.* rigid, stubborn, inflexible
inexperienced *adj.* unskilled, untried, youthful, new, immature, tender, raw, green
infallible *adj.* perfect, accurate, certain
infamous *adj.* notorious, wicked, heinous, offensive
infant *n.* baby, minor, child, tot
infantile *adj.* childlike, juvenile, childish, naïve
infect *v.* taint, defile, spoil
infer *v.* deduce, conclude, gather, assume
inferior *adj.* subordinate, mediocre, common, poor
inferiority *n.* deficiency, inadequacy, weakness
infernal *adj.* fiendish , devilish

infest *v.* **CONTAMINATE:** pollute, infect, corrupt; **INVADE:** crowd, jam, teem, flood, flock, overwhelm

infidelity *n.* unfaithfulness, adultery

infiltrate *v.* permeate, pervade, penetrate, join

infinite *adj.* endless, limitless, countless, incalculable, boundless, immense, endless

infinitesimal *adj.* tiny, small

infirm *adj.* sickly, weak

infirmary *n.* clinic, sickroom, hospital

infirmity *n.* disease, weakness, frailty, debility

inflame *v.* **AROUSE:** incense, disturb, excite; **HURT:** redden, swell; **BURN:** kindle, scorch, ignite

inflate *v.* **DISTEND:** expand, swell, bloat, balloon, widen; **EXAGGERATE:** magnify, overestimate, raise

inflection *n.* tone, enunciation, intonation, accent

inflexibility *n.* toughness, rigidity, stiffness, firmness

inflexible *adj.* rigid, unyielding, taut, firm, stiff

inflict *v.* impose, administer, deliver, strike, cause

influence *n.* power, authority, control, command, esteem, prominence, prestige, reputation

influence *v.* affect, impress, compel, urge, shape, convince, persuade, motivate

influential *adj.* prominent, substantial, powerful

inform *v.* tell, betray, instruct, relate, teach

informal *adj.* casual, intimate, relaxed

information *n.* **KNOWLEDGE:** facts, evidence, details, statistics, data; **NEWS:** report, notice, message

infraction *n.* violation, breach

infrequent *adj.* seldom, occasional, scarce, rare

infringe *v.* encroach, trespass, transgress, meddle

infuriate *v.* aggravate, enrage, provoke, anger

infuse *v.* fill, inspire; steep

ingenious *adj.* able, clever, cunning, gifted, intelligent, original, resourceful, shrewd, skillful

ingenuity *n.* cleverness, imagination, inventiveness, originality, productiveness, resourcefulness

ingenuous *adj.* candid, innocent, straightforward

ingrain *v.* imbue, fix, instill, teach

ingratiate *v.* charm, seduce, disarm

ingredient *n.* component, constituent, element

inhabit *v.* dwell, occupy, reside, stay

inhabitant *n.* occupant, dweller, lodger, roomer, boarder, tenant, resident

inherent *adj.* inborn, inbred, inherited, innate, intrinsic, native, natural

inherit *v.* acquire, receive, succeed, get

inheritance *n.* bequest, legacy, heritage, gift

inhibit *v.* check, restrain, repress, frustrate, hinder

inhibition *n.* restraint, hindrance, interference

inhuman *adj.* mean, heartless, cruel, fierce, ruthless

iniquity *n.* crime, evil, injustice, sin, wickedness

initial *adj.* beginning, starting, basic, primary, elementary, first, fundamental

initiate *n.* beginner, learner, novice

initiation *n.* **BEGINNING:** introduction; **INDOCTRINATION:** induction, orientation

initiative *n.* enterprise, responsibility

injure *v.* harm, damage, wound, hurt

injurious *adj.* harmful, detrimental, damaging

injury *n.* hurt, abrasion, wound, laceration, affliction

injustice *n.* infringement, violation, transgression, breach, infraction, wrong

inkling *n.* hint, indication, notion, innuendo, suspicion, suggestion

inmate *n.* occupant, patient, convict, prisoner

inn *n.* tavern, hostel, hotel, motel, resort

innate *adj.* inborn, native

innermost *adj.* intimate, private, secret

innocence *n.* honesty, simplicity, purity, naïveté, chastity, ignorance, virtue

innocent *adj.* **GUILTLESS:** blameless, faultless, honest; **OPEN:** guileless, frank, childish, naïve, natural, simple; **PURE:** unblemished, wholesome, upright, virtuous, righteous, angelic; **HARMLESS:** innocuous, inoffensive, safe

innovation *n.* change, newness, addition

innuendo *n.* hint, insinuation, aside, intimation

innumerable *adj.* countless, incalculable

inopportune *adj.* disadvantageous, ill–timed, inappropriate, awkward, untimely

input *n.* data, information, knowledge, facts

input *v.* add, enter

inquest *n.* inquiry, investigation

inquire *v.* ask, investigate, probe, interrogate

inquiry *n.* probe, analysis, hearing, examination

inquisitive *adj.* curious, questioning, meddling, analytical, prying, snoopy, nosy, interested

inquisitor *n.* examiner, questioner

inroad *n.* encroachment, invasion

insane *adj.* **DEMENTED:** crazed, frenzied, lunatic, balmy, psychotic, raving, deluded, possessed, obsessed; **FOOLISH:** madcap, daft, idiotic, stupid

insanity *n.* abnormality, dementia, psychosis, neurosis, phobia, mania

insatiate *adj.* ravenous, voracious

inscribe *v.* address, carve, dedicate, engrave, write

inscription *n.* dedication, engraving, legend
insecure *adj.* anxious, vague, uncertain, troubled
insert *v.* introduce, place, inject, include
insidious *adj.* treacherous, deceitful, harmful
insight *n.* perspicacity, shrewdness, intelligence
insignia *n.* badge, rank, ensign, symbol, decoration, emblem
insignificant *adj.* trivial, unimportant, irrelevant, petty, trifling
insincere *adj.* deceitful, pretentious, shifty, dishonest, false, hypocritical, sly
insinuate *v.* hint, suggest, imply, purport, mention
insipid *adj.* dull, flat, tasteless, uninteresting
insist *v.* persist, demand
insolent *adj.* disrespectful, insulting, rude
insolvent *adj.* bankrupt, broke, failed, ruined
inspect *v.* examine, scrutinize, probe, examine
inspiration *n.* IDEA: notion, whim, fancy, impulse, thought; STIMULUS: spur, influence, incentive
inspire *v.* encourage, enthuse, fire, invigorate, motivate, stimulate
install *v.* establish, introduce, inaugurate
installation *n.* induction, ordination, inauguration, launching, establishment
installment *n.* payment, part
instance *n.* example, case, situation, occurrence
instant *adj.* momentary, quick, pressing, current
instantly *adv.* urgently, directly, immediately
instigate *v.* incite, initiate, spur, urge
instill *v.* infuse, indoctrinate, implant, teach
instinct *n.* impulse, sense, intuition, feeling
instinctive *adj.* intuitive, spontaneous, natural

institute *n.* establishment, organization
institute *v.* establish, found, launch, organize
institution *n.* establishment, organization, company, association, business, university
instruct *v.* inform, teach, order, direct, educate
instruction *n.* guidance, direction, education
instructor *n.* professor, tutor, lecturer, teacher
instrument *n.* **UTENSIL:** apparatus, implement, device, tool; **CONTRACT:** deed, document
insubordinate *adj.* disobedient, mutinous, treacherous, defiant, rebellious
insufferable *adj.* difficult, intolerable, unbearable
insufficient *adj.* skimpy, meager, inadequate
insular *adj.* detached, isolated, narrow, provincial
insult *n.* affront, indignity, abuse, impudence, insolence, mockery, derision, impertinence, invective
insult *v.* offend, mock, annoy, provoke, taunt, ridicule
insurance *n.* security, indemnity, assurance, warrant
insure *v.* secure, warrant, protect, guarantee
insurrection *n.* uprising, rebellion, insurgence, revolt
intact *adj.* entire, whole, together
intangible *adj.* indefinite, uncertain, vague
integral *adj.* **WHOLE:** entire; **NECESSARY:** essential
integrate *v.* blend, combine, mix
integrity *n.* morality, honesty, uprightness, honor
intellect *n.* understanding, intelligence, mentality
intellectual *adj.* smart, creative, intelligent, learned
intellectual *n.* highbrow, genius, philosopher, academician, egghead, brain
intelligence *n.* **UNDERSTANDING:** discernment, comprehension, judgment; **INTELLECT:** mind, brain, mentality; **INFORMATION:** statistics, facts, news

intelligent *adj.* clever, bright, smart, brilliant, perceptive, keen, imaginative, knowledgeable, understanding, quick, sharp, comprehending, discerning

intelligentsia *n.* intellectuals, elite

intelligible *adj.* understandable, comprehensible, plain, clear, obvious

intend *v.* PROPOSE: purpose, aspire, aim, plan; MEAN: indicate, signify, denote

intense *adj.* deep, profound, heightened, vivid, impassioned, exaggerated, violent, excessive, keen, piercing, cutting, severe

intensify *v.* enhance, heighten, sharpen, emphasize, increase, strengthen

intensity *n.* concentration, strength, power, force, passion, fervor, ardor, severity, depth, magnitude

intensive *adj.* accelerated, hard, fast, severe

intent *adj.* fixed, absorbed

intent *n.* design, plan

intention *n.* purpose, aim, end, plan

intentional *adj.* deliberate, planned

inter *v.* bury, entomb

intercept *v.* obstruct, ambush, block, hijack

intercession *n.* entreaty, petition, mediation, plea

interchange *n.* BARTER: trade, exchange, substitution; INTERSECTION: cloverleaf, off–ramp

interest *n.* CONCERN: attention, excitement, curiosity, enthusiasm; SHARE: claim, right, stake

interest *v.* arouse, involve, fascinate, intrigue, attract, amuse, please, entertain

interested *adj.* AROUSED: stimulated, curious, affected, responsive, roused, stirred, attracted; OCCUPIED: engrossed, obsessed, absorbed, involved

interesting *adj.* intriguing, fascinating, engaging, absorbing, captivating

interfere *v.* meddle, intervene, interpose, interlope

interference *n.* **MEDDLING:** interruption, trespassing, tampering; **OBSTRUCTION:** check, obstacle, restraint

interior *adj.* within, inside, inland, inner, internal, inward, central, inside

interlope *v.* interfere, intrude, meddle

intermediate *adj.* intervening, medium, intermediary, median, central, middle

intermediary *n.* mediator, agent

intermission *n.* pause, interval, interim, recess

intermix *v.* mix, mingle

intermittent *adj.* cyclic, recurring, periodic, recurrent, changing, irregular

intern *v.* **CONFINE:** detain, imprison; **TEACH:** train, apprentice, tutor

internal *adj.* interior, inner, domestic, inside, inward, intrinsic, innate, inherent

interpret *v.* translate, explain, render, delineate, define, describe

interpretation *n.* rendition, description, representation, presentation, explanation

interrogate *v.* question, ask, examine

interrogation *n.* inquiry, investigation, examination

interrupt *v.* intervene, interfere, infringe

intersperse *v.* scatter, strew

interval *n.* time, period, interlude, interim, pause

intervene *v.* intercede, mediate, negotiate, reconcile

intervention *n.* intercession, interruption, interference, intrusion

interview *n.* meeting, audience, conference

interview v. interrogate, question, examine
intimacy n. closeness, familiarity, affection
intimate adj. familiar, close, trusted, secret, special
intimate n. friend, associate, companion, lover
intimate v. hint, allude
intimidate v. frighten, threaten
intolerable adj. insufferable, unendurable, unbearable, impossible, offensive, painful, undesirable
intolerant adj. dogmatic, bigoted, prejudiced
intoxicate v. inebriate, muddle, befuddle
intransigence n. obstinacy, stubbornness
intransigent adj. intolerant, uncompromising
intricacy n. elaborateness, complexity, difficulty
intricate adj. involved, complex, tricky, abstruse, difficult, obscure
intrigue v. plot, scheme, delight, please, attract, charm, entertain, fascinate
intrinsic adj. essential, inborn, inherent
introduce v. PRESENT: submit, advance, offer, propose, acquaint; ACQUAINT: present; INSERT: add, enter, include
introduction n. ADMITTANCE: initiation, installation, entrance; PRESENTATION: debut, acquaintance, start, awakening, baptism; PREFACE: preamble, foreword, prologue, overture
introductory adj. opening, early, starting, beginning, preparatory, primary, original
introvert n. loner, recluse
intrude v. encroach, trespass, interfere, meddle
intuition n. instinct, hunch, foreknowledge, feeling
intuitive adj. instinctive, automatic, natural
inure v. acclimate, accustom

inured *adj.* hardened, cold, unfeeling
invade *v.* attack, intrude. infringe, trespass, interfere
invader *n.* trespasser, alien, attacker, enemy
invalidate *v.* void, revoke, annul, refute, nullify
invaluable *adj.* priceless, expensive, dear, valuable
invariable *adj.* unchanging, uniform, static, constant
invective *adj.* railing, abusive
inveigh *v.* protest, rant
inveigle *v.* coax, entice, flatter
invent *v.* create, discover, originate, devise, fashion, form, design, improvise, contrive, build
invention *n.* contrivance, contraption, design
inventory *n.* **LIST:** itemization, register, index, record; **INSPECTION:** examination, summary
inverse *adj.* reversed, contrary
invert *v.* **UPSET:** overturn, tip; **REVERSE:** change, transpose, exchange
investigate *v.* inquire, review, examine, study
investigation *n.* inquiry search research examination
inveterate *adj.* addicted, well–established, persisting
invidious *adj.* envious, malicious, spiteful
invigorate *v.* animate, energize, enervate, enliven, excite, exhilarate, freshen, stimulate
invincible *adj.* impregnable, invulnerable, powerful, strong, unconquerable
inviolate *adj.* hallowed, holy, intact, pure, sacred
inviting *adj.* appealing, attractive, encouraging
invocation *n.* prayer, appeal
invoice *n.* notice, statement, bill, receipt
invoke *v.* implore, solicit, summon
involuntary *adj.* unintentional, uncontrolled, instinctive, automatic, habitual

involve *v.* associate, commit, connect, comprise, connect, entangle, implicate, include, link

involved *adj.* **COMPLICATED:** elaborate, entangled, intricate, sophisticated; **IMPLICATED:** connected, emotional, engrossed, incriminated

invulnerable *adj.* strong, invincible, secure, safe

iota *n.* jot, particle, trace, scrap, grain, bit, speck

irascible *adj.* irritable, temperamental, testy, touchy

irate *adj.* enraged, furious, incensed, angry

irk *v.* vex, annoy, harass, disturb, bother

irony *n.* satire, ridicule, mockery, derision, sarcasm

irrational *adj.* illogical, unreasoning, specious, fallacious, wrong, senseless, silly, ridiculous

irreconcilable *adj.* implacable, incompatible

irrefutable *adj.* conclusive, evident, indisputable, obvious, undeniable

irregular *adj.* **UNEVEN:** rough, fitful, random, occasional, fluctuating, wavering, intermittent, sporadic, variable, shifting; **UNCUSTOMARY:** unique, extraordinary, abnormal, unusual; **QUESTIONABLE:** strange, debatable, suspicious

irrelevant *adj.* immaterial, unrelated, extraneous, pointless, trivial, unnecessary

irreparable *adj.* incurable, hopeless, irreversible, destroyed, ruined

irresistible *adj.* compelling, overpowering, overwhelming, powerful

irresponsible *adj.* capricious, flighty, fickle, thoughtless, rash, unstable, lax, shiftless, unreliable

irrevocable *adj.* permanent, indelible, inevitable

irritable *adj.* cranky, testy, touchy, huffy, peevish, petulant, surly, moody, churlish, grouchy, grumpy

irritant *n.* annoyance, bother, burden, nuisance

irritate *v.* **BOTHER:** exasperate, pester, disturb, annoy; **INFLAME:** redden, chafe, sting, burn, hurt, itch

irritated *adj.* annoyed, disturbed, upset, bothered

island *n.* isle, bar, archipelago

isolate *v.* detach, insulate, confine, seclude, divide

isolation *n.* solitude, seclusion, segregation, confinement, separation

issue *n.* **DISTRIBUTION:** publication; **TOPIC:** subject, concern, argument; **EDITION:** number, copy

issue *v.* **EMERGE:** proceed, appear, begin; **RELEASE:** circulate, announce, advertise, declare, publish

itemize *v.* list, catalog, enumerate, number, detail

itinerant *adj.* traveling, roving, nomadic, wandering

itinerant *n.* wanderer, nomad, vagrant, tramp

jab *v.* poke, punch, hit, blow

jacket *n.* coat, tunic, jerkin, parka, cape

jackpot *n.* bonanza, winnings, luck, profit, success

jaded *adj.* cold, impassive, indifferent, nonchalant, world–weary

jail *n.* penitentiary, cage, cell, dungeon, bastille, stockade, prison, lockup

jam *n.* **PRESERVES:** conserve, marmalade, jelly; **TROUBLE:** dilemma, problem, difficulty

jam *v.* compress, bind, squeeze, push, pack, press

jar *n.* **CONTAINER:** crock, vessel, beaker, cruet, bottle, flagon, flask; **JOLT:** jounce, thud, thump, bump

jargon *n.* argot, patois, idiom, vernacular, colloquialism, localism, dialect, slang

jaunt *n.* excursion, trip, tour, journey, walk

jaunty *adj.* buoyant, chipper, dashing, frisky, rakish

jealous *adj.* envious, possessive, resentful

jeer *n.* derision, ridicule, taunt
jeer *v.* deride, insult, mock, ridicule, taunt
jell *v.* set, harden, stiffen, thicken
jeopardize *v.* endanger, imperil, expose, venture, risk
jeopardy *n.* danger, peril, hazard, chance
jerk *n.* **TWITCH:** tic, shake, quiver; **DOLT:** scamp, scoundrel, fool, rascal
jerk *v.* **SPASM:** quiver, shiver, shake, twitch; **PULL:** yank, snatch, seize
jest *v.* joke, tease
jester *n.* comedian, buffoon, joker, actor, clown, fool
jetty *n.* pier, wharf
jewel *n.* prize, bauble, gem, trinket
jewelry *n.* bangles, gems, baubles, trinkets, adornments, ornaments
jiggle *v.* shake, twitch, wiggle, jerk
jingle *n.* rhyme, verse
jingle *v.* tinkle, clink, rattle
jinx *n.* hex, spell
job *n.* **EMPLOYMENT:** situation, position, calling, vocation, career, pursuit, business, profession, trade; **TASK:** assignment, undertaking, project, chore, errand, duty; **ASSIGNMENT:** output, duty
jobber *n.* broker, wholesaler
jocular *adj.* comic, frolicsome, funny, witty
jocund *adj.* cheerful, happy, joyful, lighthearted
jog *v.* **TROT:** canter, lope, nudge, run; **NUDGE:** bump, jar, jostle, shake
join *v.* unite, blend, combine, connect, couple, attach, link, fuse, entwine, associate
joint *adj.* joined, shared, united
joint *n.* juncture, union, coupling, hinge, link,

connection, seam; **DIVE:** hangout, bar, tavern
joke v. jest, quip, banter, laugh, play, frolic, wisecrack
jolly adj. gay, merry, joyful, happy
jolt n. **BUMP:** jar, bounce, blow, jerk; **SURPRISE:** jar, start, shock, surprise
jostle v. push, elbow, nudge
jot n. bit, iota
jot v. write, note, scribble, record
journal n. **DIARY:** almanac, chronicle, record; **PERIODICAL:** publication, newspaper, magazine, daily
journalist n. columnist, commentator, reporter
journey n. trip, tour, excursion, jaunt, travel
jovial adj. affable, amiable, merry, happy
joy n. mirth, delight, playfulness, gaiety, geniality, merriment, levity, jubilation, laughter
joyful adj. elated, glad, happy, joyous, jubilant
joyous adj. blithe, glad, gay, happy
jubilant adj. ecstatic, elated, exuberant, delighted, rapturous, joyous
jubilee n. anniversary, celebration
judge n. **MODERATOR:** arbiter, referee, umpire; **CONNOISSEUR:** analyst, critic, expert, specialist
judge v. hear, decide, adjudicate, rule
judgment n. **DISCERNMENT:** discrimination, taste; **DECISION:** determination, analysis, pronouncement, conclusion, verdict
judgmental adj. biased, prejudiced, unfair
judicial adj. legalistic, administrative, lawful
judicious adj. prudent, discreet, sensible, discreet
jug n. crock, flask, pitcher, container
juice n. sap, extract, fluid, liquid
juicy adj. succulent, moist, watery, syrupy

jumble *n.* clutter, mess, hodgepodge, confusion

jump *v.* **LEAP:** vault, spring, lunge, bound, skip, hurdle; **PLUMMET:** plunge, dive, fall; **ACCOST:** attack

junction *n.* **MEETING:** joining, coupling, joint, union; **CROSSROADS:** crossing, intersection

juncture *n.* joining, junction

jungle *n.* tangle, wilderness, undergrowth, forest

junior *adj.* younger, lower

junk *n.* scrap, waste, garbage, filth, trash

junk *v.* abandon, discard

junket *n.* picnic, excursion, trip

jurisdiction *n.* authority, range, province, scope, domain, extent, empire, sovereignty

jurist *n.* judge, attorney, adviser, lawyer

jury *n.* council, committee, tribunal, panel

just *adj.* **PRECISELY:** exactly, correctly, perfectly, accurate; **HARDLY:** barely, scarcely; **ONLY:** merely, simply, plainly; **FAIR:** impartial, equal, righteous

justice *n.* **FAIRNESS:** right, truth, equity; **LAWFULNESS:** legality, legitimacy, sanction, constitutionality, authority, custom; **ADMINISTRATION:** adjudication, arbitration, hearing, trial, litigation, judgment; **JUDGE:** magistrate, umpire, chancellor

justification *n.* excuse, defense, reason, explanation

justify *v.* **VINDICATE:** absolve, acquit, clear, excuse, exonerate; **EXPLAIN:** apologize, excuse, defend

jut *adj.* extend, bulge, project

juvenile *adj.* childish, youthful, adolescent, teenage

juxtapose *v.* compare, contrast

keen *adj.* **SHARP:** pointed, edged; **ASTUTE:** clever, shrewd, intelligent; **EAGER:** ardent, intent, zealous

keep *v.* **HOLD:** retain, possess, have, seize, save;

MAINTAIN: preserve, conserve; **CONTINUE:** sustain, endure; **REMAIN:** stay, continue, abide, settle; **STORE:** hoard, preserve, reserve, stash, cache

keepsake *n.* memento, token, remembrance, reminder

keg *n.* cask, drum, vat, barrel

kernel *n.* seed, grain, core, nut, germ

kettle *n.* vessel, cauldron, saucepan, stewpot, pot

key *n.* **OPENER:** latchkey, passkey; **SOLUTION:** clue, code, indicator, answer

kickback *n.* **BRIBE:** grease, payback, payola, tribute; **BACKLASH:** backfire, reaction, recoil

kickoff *adj.* start, opening, beginning, launching

kid *n.* child, son, daughter, tot, boy, girl

kid *v.* mock, tease

kidnap *v.* abduct, capture, shanghai

kill *v.* **SLAY:** slaughter, murder, assassinate, massacre, butcher, dispatch, execute, liquidate, finish; **CANCEL:** annul, nullify, counteract; **VETO:** cancel, prohibit, refuse, forbid

killer *n.* murderer, gangster, assassin, cutthroat

killjoy *n.* grouch, sourpuss, spoilsport

kiln *n.* dryer, oast, oven

kind *adj.* accommodating, agreeable, charitable, compassionate, considerate, generous, kindhearted, loving, obliging, sensitive, tactful, tender

kind *n.* **CLASS:** classification, species, genus; **TYPE:** sort, variety, description, denomination, designation

kindhearted *adj.* amiable, generous, good, humane

kindle *v.* fire, excite, light, ignite

kindly *adj.* generous, helpful, good, humane, kind

kindness *n.* **TENDERNESS:** consideration, thoughtfulness, humanity, understanding, compassion, graciousness, kindheartedness; **SERVICE:** benevolence, philanthropy, lift, boost, help

kindred *adj.* alike, kin, connected, related, similar

kingdom *n.* realm, domain, country, empire, principality, dominions, territory

kink *n.* bend, obstacle, hitch

kinship *n.* affiliation, relationship, connection, alliance, family

kit *n.* **EQUIPMENT:** material, tools, outfit; **PACK:** poke, knapsack, satchel, bag, container

knack *n.* dexterity, trick, skill, faculty, ability

knapsack *n.* sack, bag, pack, kit, rucksack

knead *v.* work, shape, twist, press

kneel *v.* genuflect, bend, stoop, bow, curtsey

knickknack *n.* bric–a–brac, curio, ornament, trifle, bauble, trinket, showpiece, gewgaw

knife *n.* blade, dagger, stiletto, lancet, machete, scalpel, dirk

knit *v.* unite, join, intermingle, affiliate

knob *n.* **PROJECTION:** bulge, protuberance, bulge, node, bump; **HANDLE:** doorknob, latch

knock *v.* rap, strike, thump, whack, beat, tap, hit

knoll *n.* mound, hill, hillock

knot *n.* **FASTENING:** bond, tie, cinch, hitch, splice; **CLUSTER:** group; **SNARL:** snag tangle twist

know *v.* **UNDERSTAND:** comprehend, apprehend; **RECOGNIZE:** perceive, discern, acknowledge

knowing *adj.* **SHREWD:** acute, clever, intelligent, reasonable, sharp; **DELIBERATE:** conscious, intentional

knowledge *n.* information, learning, lore, wisdom, enlightenment, expertise, awareness, insight

label *n.* tag, marker, insignia, identification, name

label *v.* identify, mark, name, specify

labor *n.* **TASK:** work, activity, toil, operation, employment, undertaking, job; **EXERTION:** energy, industry, diligence, strain, stress, effort

labor *v.* work, toil, strive

laborious *adj.* arduous, difficult, exhausting, onerous

lace *v.* fasten, tie, adorn, strap, bind, close

lacerate *v.* tear, wound

lacing *n.* bond, hitch, tie, fastener, knot

lack *n.* **ABSENCE:** deficiency, scarcity, insufficiency, inadequacy; **WANT:** need, privation, poverty, distress

lack *v.* need, want, require

lackadaisical *adj.* halfhearted, indifferent, languid

lackey *n.* **MENIAL:** servant; **FLUNKY:** toady, underling

laconic *adj.* concise, curt, succinct, terse

lad *n.* fellow, youth, stripling, boy, child

ladle *n.* spoon, skimmer, scoop

lady *n.* woman, female, matron, gentlewoman

ladylike *adj.* cultured, well–bred, polite, refined

lag *v.* tarry, straggle, falter, delay

laggard *n.* loiterer, idler

lair *n.* den, cave, home, pen

lame *adj.* halt, impaired, handicapped, limping

lament *v.* grieve, deplore

lamentation *n.* dirge, mourning, tears, wailing

lampoon *v.* satirize, burlesque

lance *v.* foil, point, spear

land *n.* **PROPERTY:** estate, tract, ranch, farm, lot; **COUNTRY:** province, region, nation

landing *n.* **ARRIVING:** docking, anchoring, arrival; **DOCK:** marina, pier, wharf

landlord *n.* innkeeper, landowner, lessor, owner

landscape *n.* countryside, scenery, panorama, view

lane *n.* way, alley, passage, path, road

language *n.* expression, tongue, word, sign, signal, gesture, vocabulary, diction, dialect, idiom, patois, vernacular, speech, jargon

languid *adj.* spiritless, sluggish

languish *v.* weaken, decline

lank *adj.* angular, bony, gaunt. lean, slender, spare

lanky *adj.* lean, rangy

lantern *n.* light, torch, lamp

lap *n.* **EXTENSION:** fold, flap, projection; **RACECOURSE:** circuit, round, course, distance

lapidary *n.* jeweler, engraver

lapse *v.* pass, void, slip, deteriorate, decline, weaken

larceny *n.* theft, burglary, thievery, robbery, crime

large *adj.* huge, wide, grand, great, considerable, substantial, vast, massive, immense, spacious, bulky, extensive

largely *adv.* **MOSTLY:** mainly, chiefly, principally; **EXTENSIVELY:** abundantly, comprehensively, widely

lariat *n.* lasso, riata, tether, line, rope

lascivious *adj.* bawdy, carnal, immoral, lewd, licentious, lurid, sensual, sexual

lash *n.* whip, stroke

lash *v.* strike, flog, thrash, scourge, beat, hit

lass *n.* girl, woman, lady, damsel, maiden

lassitude *adj.* weariness, listlessness

lasso *n.* rope, lariat, tether, noose

lasso *v.* rope, catch

last *adj.* **FINAL:** ultimate, concluding, ending, terminal, decisive, crowning, climactic, closing; **RECENT:** latest, newest, freshest

last *v.* **ENDURE:** continue, maintain, persist, remain, stay, survive, sustain; **SUFFICE:** do, satisfy, serve
lasting *adj.* enduring, abiding, constant, permanent
latch *n.* catch, hasp, hook, bar, fastener, lock
latch *v.* fasten, lock, cinch, close
late *adj.* **OVERDUE:** tardy, lagging, delayed; **DEFUNCT:** deceased, departed, dead; **RECENT:** new, fresh
latent *adj.* potential, undeveloped, dormant
lather *n.* foam, froth, suds, bubbles
lather *v.* foam, froth, soap
latitude *n.* freedom, degree, measure
latter *adj.* after, following, late, last, recent
lattice *n.* arbor, framework, trellis
laud *v.* glorify, honor, praise
laugh *v.* chuckle, snicker, titter, chortle, cackle, guffaw, giggle, roar
launch *v.* initiate, originate, start, begin
launder *v.* cleanse, wash, clean
lavatory *n.* basin, privy, bathroom, washroom, toilet
lave *v.* clean, wash
lavish *adj.* profuse, extravagant, generous, unstinted, unsparing, plentiful
lawful *adj.* **LEGAL:** legitimate, decreed, permitted, constitutional; **LEGISLATED:** enacted, official, enforced, protected, legitimized, established
lawless *adj.* **WILD:** untamed, uncivilized, savage, barbarous, disordered, uncontrolled; **UNRESTRAINED:** riotous, insubordinate, disobedient, unruly
lawsuit *n.* action, suit, case, prosecution, claim, trial
lawyer *n.* attorney, solicitor, jurist, defender, prosecuting, counsel, solicitor, barrister, advocate
lax *adj.* slack, loose, remiss, soft, careless, indifferent

laxity, laxness *n.* slackness, negligence

layer *n.* stratum, thickness, fold, lap, floor, story, tier

layman *n.* nonprofessional, novice, dilettante, amateur, recruit

layout *n.* arrangement, design, organization, plan

lazy *adj.* indolent, idle, sluggish, apathetic, loafing, flagging, slothful, lethargic

lead *n.* **GUIDANCE:** leadership, direction; **CLUE:** evidence, trace, hint, proof, sign; **ROLE:** part, character

lead *v.* **CONDUCT:** steer, pilot, show, guide; **DIRECT:** manage, supervise

leaden *adj.* heavy, burdensome, oppressive, weighty

leader *n.* **GUIDE:** conductor, pilot; **DIRECTOR:** manager, officer, captain, master, ruler, boss, brains

leading *adj.* foremost, chief, dominating, best

leaflet *n.* brochure, handbill, circular, pamphlet

league *n.* union, alliance, group, unit, organization

leak *n.* **HOLE:** puncture, chink, crevice; **WASTE:** loss, leakage, seepage, expenditure, decrease; **NEWS:** exposé, slip

leak *v.* **ESCAPE:** drip, ooze, drool, flow

lean *v.* **INCLINE:** slant, sag, list, tip, veer, droop, pitch, tilt; **TEND:** favor, prefer

lean *adj.* **THIN:** lank, meager, slim, skinny; **FIBROUS:** muscular, sinewy

leaning *n.* inclination, preference, tendency

lean–to *n.* shelter, shanty, hut, hovel

leap *v.* jump, bound, spring, vault, bounce

learn *v.* acquire, read, master, ascertain, determine, unearth, hear, memorize, study

learned *adj.* scholarly, erudite, accomplished, well–informed, professorial, cultured, educated

learning *n.* lore, training, education, knowledge
lease *v.* let, rent, charter
least *adj.* SMALLEST: tiniest; TRIVIAL: piddling, unimportant; MINIMAL: bottom, lowest
leave *n.* PARTING: departure, farewell; PERMISSION: consent, dispensation, indulgence, authorization, consent; LIBERTY: furlough, vacation
leave *v.* ABANDON: forsake, desert; DEPART: withdraw, part, defect, flee, embark, emigrate, scram, split, vacate, go; BEQUEATH: transmit, will, give, dower; OMIT: drop, forget, neglect
leaving *n.* departure, exodus
lecher *n.* debaucher, rake
lecture *n.* INSTRUCTION: address, discourse, lesson, oration, speech, talk; REPROOF: dressing–down, rebuke, reprimand
lecture *v.* INSTRUCT: address, instruct, talk, teach; REPROVE: rebuke, reprimand
ledge *n.* shelf, mantle, bar, step, ridge, rim
ledger *n.* accounts, books, records, journal
leech *n.* PARASITE: tapeworm, hookworm, bloodsucker; DEPENDENT: hanger–on, sponger, weakling
leer *n.* glance, grin, look, smirk
leery *adj.* distrustful, doubting, suspicious, wary
leeway *n.* space, margin, latitude, extent
left *adj.* REMAINING: staying, continuing, over, extra; RADICAL: left–wing, liberal, progressive, revolutionary; DEPARTED: gone, absent, lacking
legacy *n.* bequest, inheritance
legal *adj.* lawful, constitutional, permissible, allowable, legalized, sanctioned, legitimate, authorized
legality *n.* legitimacy, lawfulness, authority, law

legalize *v.* authorize, sanction, approve
legate *n.* ambassador, envoy
legation *n.* delegation, embassy
legend *n.* story, myth, saga, fable; inscription
legendary *adj.* fabulous, mythical, fanciful, allegorical
legerdemain *n.* deception, trickery
legible *adj.* readable, distinct, plain, sharp, clear
legion *n.* multitude, horde, throng, crowd
legislate *v.* enact, pass, constitute
legislation *n.* bill, enactment, act, law
legislature *n.* lawmakers, congress, parliament, senate, house, representatives
legitimate *adj.* **LICIT:** statutory, authorized, lawful, legal, honorable; **LOGICAL:** reasonable, probable, consistent, understandable; **AUTHENTIC:** real, verifiable, valid, reliable, genuine
leisure *n.* relaxation, recreation, holiday, vacation
leisurely *adj.* unhurried, lazily, calmly, listlessly
lend *v.* loan, advance, furnish, entrust, accommodate
length *n.* **DISTANCE:** measure, span, range, longitude, magnitude, dimension; **DURATION:** period, interval
lengthen *v.* extend, stretch, protract, increase;
lengthy *adj.* tedious, long, dull
lenient *adj.* mild, merciful, tolerant, kind
lesion *n.* abrasion, injury, tumor, wound
less *adj.* fewer, smaller, reduced, declined, inferior, secondary, subordinate, diminished, shortened
lessen *v.* diminish, dwindle, decline, decrease; reduce
lesser *adj.* inferior, minor, secondary, subordinate
lesson *n.* learning, precept, assignment
let *v.* **PERMIT:** approve, authorize, consent, tolerate, allow; **LEASE:** rent, hire, sublet

letdown *n.* frustration, setback, disillusionment, disappointment

lethal *adj.* deadly, fatal, mortal, malignant, harmful

lethargic *adj.* apathetic, listless, sluggish

lethargy *n.* stupor, dullness, drowsiness

letter *n.* MESSAGE: memo, note, memorandum, epistle, missive, line, mail; SYMBOL: character, type

letter *v.* inscribe, write

letup *n.* reduction, slowdown, pause, interval, respite

levee *n.* embankment, dike

level *adj.* SMOOTH: planed, even, flat; REGULAR: uniform, flush, straight, trim, precise, exact, matched, unbroken, aligned, continuous

level *v.* STRAIGHTEN: flatten, surface, bulldoze, smooth; DEMOLISH: destroy, ruin, wreck, raze

lever *n.* bar, fulcrum, pry, crowbar

leverage *n.* power, purchase; lift, hold, support

leviathan *n.* monster, beast

levity *n.* flippancy, frivolity

levy *n.* collection, seizure, toll, duty, custom, tax

levy *v.* collect, assess

lewd *adj.* RIBALD: smutty, indecent, sensual; LUSTFUL: wanton, lascivious, licentious, lecherous, dissolute, debauched, corrupt, depraved, vulgar

lexicon *n.* dictionary, vocabulary, glossary

liability *n.* obligation, responsibility, debt, indebtedness, responsibility

liable *adj.* RESPONSIBLE: accountable, answerable, exposed, obliged; APT: inclined, likely, tending

liaison *n.* LINK: agent, connection, emissary, proxy; AFFAIR: intrigue, romance, tryst

liar *n.* prevaricator, deceiver, perjurer, falsifier, fibber

libel *v.* defame, slander, smear, vilify

libelous *adj.* defamatory, derogatory, slanderous

liberal *adj.* **PROGRESSIVE:** broad–minded, nonconformist, permissive, radical, tolerant; **GENEROUS:** indulgent, lavish, magnanimous

liberate *v.* free, loose, release

liberation *n.* rescue, freedom, deliverance

libertine *n.* lecher, pervert, rake, roué

liberty *n.* **DELIVERANCE:** emancipation, enfranchisement, rescue, freedom; **LEAVE:** relaxation, rest, leisure, recreation; **PRIVILEGE:** permission, decision, selection; **RIGHTS:** freedom, independence

libretto *n.* lyric, words

license *n.* **CONSENT:** authorization, permission, sanction; **DOCUMENT:** permit, certificate, registration; **FREEDOM:** looseness, excess, immoderation, latitude

license *v.* grant, authorize, permit, allow

licit *adj.* authorized, lawful, sanctioned

lick *v.* beat, thrash, whip, defeat, overcome, vanquish, frustrate, conquer

lid *n.* cover, cap, top, roof, hood

lie *n.* falsehood, untruth, misrepresentation, prevarication, falsification, fabrication, distortion

lie *v.* **FIB:** falsify, prevaricate, deceive, misinform, exaggerate, distort, concoct, misrepresent, dissemble, delude; **PROSTRATE:** recline, retire, rest, sleep; **ABIDE:** remain, exist

lieu *n.* place, stead

life *n.* **BEING:** entity, presence, consciousness, vitality; **BIOGRAPHY:** story, memoir; **DURATION:** lifetime, span, career, generation, season, cycle; **SPIRIT:** animation, excitement, zeal

lifeless *adj.* **INERT:** inanimate, departed, dead; **LACKING SPIRIT:** lackluster, listless, heavy, dull, slow

lifetime *n.* existence, endurance, continuance

lift *v.* **ELEVATE:** raise, hoist; **STEAL:** filch, pilfer, swipe; **RESCIND:** repeal, reverse, revoke

light *adj.* **ILLUMINATED:** radiant, luminous, bright; **VIVID:** colorful, rich, clear; **SUPERFICIAL:** slight, frivolous, trivial, unimportant; **LIVELY:** spirited, animated, active; **ETHEREAL:** airy, fluffy, downy, dainty, thin, sheer, insubstantial, graceful

light *v.* **ILLUMINATE:** illumine, lighten, brighten; **IGNITE:** inflame, spark, kindle, burn; **REST:** stop, arrive

lighten *v.* unburden, lessen, uplift, alleviate, reduce, shift, change, unload

light–headed *adj.* **GIDDY:** inane, fickle, frivolous, silly; **FAINT:** tired, delirious, dizzy, weak

light–hearted *adj.* gay, joyous, cheerful, happy

lightly *adj.* delicately, airily, daintily, gently, subtly, softly, tenderly

like *adj.* similar, resembling, close, matching, related, analogous, corresponding, comparable

like *v.* **ENJOY:** relish, savor, fancy; **ADMIRE:** esteem, approve; **PREFER:** choose, desire, fancy

likelihood *n.* possibility, probability

likely *adj.* probable, conceivable, rational, plausible, apt, tending, prone, liable

likeness *n.* **SIMILARITY:** resemblance, correspondence; **REPRESENTATION:** image, effigy, portrait, picture

liking *n.* desire, fondness, devotion, affection, love

limb *n.* **BRANCH:** arm, bough, offshoot; **APPENDAGE:** arm, leg, part, wing, pinion, fin, flipper

limber *adj.* flexible, pliant, supple, nimble

limit

limit *n.* boundary, frontier, border, extent, extremity

limit *v.* confine, bound, curb, restrict

limitation *n.* **RESTRICTION:** restraint, control; **CONDITION:** qualification, stricture, inhibition, constraint; **SHORTCOMING:** inadequacy, deficiency, weakness, failing, frailty, flaw

limp *adj.* weak, pliant, flaccid, flabby, pliable, slack, loose, flimsy

limp *n.* hitch, hobble

limp *v.* halt, stumble, shuffle, stagger, totter, falter

line *n.* **BORDER:** limit, boundary, edge, boundary; **ROW:** rank, file, order, arrangement, sequence, column, groove, thread; **JOB:** profession, career, vocation; **ROPE:** cord, filament; **DESCENT:** pedigree, lineage, family, heredity; **WARES:** goods, merchandise, produce, material; **TALK:** speech, patter

line *v.* **ARRANGE:** align, order, dress, array, fix, place; **BORDER:** edge, bound, fringe; **PROTECT:** face, back, bind, trim, pad; **TRACE:** delineate, outline, draw

linear *adj.* successive, direct, straight

linger *v.* remain, loiter, tarry, lag, delay, dawdle, wait

lingerie *n.* underwear, dainties, unmentionables

linguist *n.* lexicographer, translator, grammarian

liniment *n.* ointment, lotion, balm, medicine

lining *n.* interlining, filling, quilting, stuffing, padding

link *n.* **LOOP:** ring, coupling; **CONNECTION:** seam, weld, intersection, fastening, splice, articulation, joint

link *v.* connect, associate, combine, join

lint *n.* fluff, raveling, fiber, dust

liquid *adj.* **WATERY:** molten, moist, aqueous, liquefied, dissolved, melted, thawed, wet; **FLOWING:** running, splashing, thin, moving, viscous, fluid, juicy

liquidate *v.* **CHANGE:** sell, convert, exchange; **DESTROY:** eliminate, kill, annul, cancel

list *n.* roll, record, agenda, slate, inventory, account, tally, roster, muster, menu, docket

list *v.* **ARRANGE:** catalogue, register, tally, inventory, index; **LEAN:** pitch, slant, incline

listen *v.* hear, heed, attend, overhear

listless *adj.* languid, sluggish, indolent, indifferent

litany *n.* form, ritual

literacy *n.* scholarship, education, knowledge

literal *adj.* precise, exact, verbatim, accurate

literally *adj.* actually, exactly, strictly, verbatim

literary *adj.* scholarly, learned, bookish, literate

literate *adj.* lettered, learned, scholarly, educated

lithograph *n.* print, copy

lithograph *v.* engrave, print

litter *n.* **DEBRIS:** mess, jumble, hodgepodge, trash, clutter; **BROOD:** piglets, puppies, kittens, offspring

litter *v.* scatter, confuse, jumble

little *adj.* **SMALL:** diminutive, tiny, wee, slight, miniature, puny; **INADEQUATE:** inconsiderable, insufficient; **TRIFLING:** shallow, petty, superficial, frivolous, paltry, trivial; **BASE:** weak, shallow, mean, petty

livable *adj.* **HABITABLE:** inhabitable, comfortable; **BEARABLE:** acceptable, adequate, tolerable

live *adj.* **ACTIVE:** energetic, vital, vivid; **AWARE:** conscious, existing

live *v.* **EXIST:** subsist, survive, breathe, be; **RELISH:** savor, experience; **DWELL:** inhabit, abide; **CONTINUE:** remain, survive, endure, last

livelihood *n.* job, career, means, subsistence

lively *adj.* active, animated, brisk, energetic, spirited, vigorous, vivacious

living *adj.* **ALIVE:** active, live, existing, breathing, being; **VIGOROUS:** awake, brisk, alert, active

living *n.* means, sustenance, maintenance, subsistence, work, vocation, business

load *n.* **BURDEN:** cargo, lading, payload, shipment, capacity, bundle; **RESPONSIBILITY:** charge, obligation, trust, duty

loaf *v.* loiter, idle, lounge, relax, shirk, dream

loafer *n.* malingerer, slacker, goldbrick, deadbeat

loan *v.* lend, provide, advance

loath *adj.* disinclined, unwilling

loathe *v.* detest, dislike

lobby *n.* **ENTRYWAY:** antechamber, foyer, hall, vestibule; **INFLUENCE:** pressure

lobby *v.* influence, promote

local *adj.* **LIMITED:** confined, restricted, bounded; **INDIGENOUS:** native, territorial, provincial, regional

locale *n.* vicinity, territory, district, area, region

locality *n.* district, section, sector, region, location, site, neighborhood, block, vicinity

locate *v.* **DISCOVER:** find, establish, determine, place; **SETTLE:** inhabit, dwell

lock *n.* **HOOK:** catch, latch, bolt, bar, hasp, bond; **TRESS:** tuft, ringlet, curl

lock *v.* fasten, unite, bolt, bar

locker *n.* cabinet, wardrobe, cupboard, closet

locket *n.* case, pendant, jewelry, necklace

lodge *n.* **RETREAT:** inn, hostel, chalet, hotel, motel, resort, cabin, cottage; **SOCIETY:** club, fraternity

lodge *v.* **SHELTER:** board, harbor, quarter; **PLACE:** fix, leave, deposit, embed

lodging *n.* accommodation, refuge, shelter, residence, home, hotel, motel, resort

lofty *adj.* HIGH: elevated, tall, towering, raised; EXALTED: arrogant, commanding, haughty, proud

log *n.* WOOD: limb, timber, stick JOURNAL: account, register, ledger, diary, record

logic *n.* reasoning, deduction, induction, thought

logical *adj.* coherent, consistent, probable, sound, congruent, reasonable

logistics *n.* procurement, distribution, management

logy *adj.* lethargic, sluggish

loiter *v.* linger, dawdle, idle, loll, tarry, wait

lone *adj.* solitary, deserted, alone

lonely *adj.* abandoned, homesick, forlorn, deserted, lonesome, solitary, secluded

lonesome *adj.* forlorn, alone, homesick, lonely

long *adj.* ELONGATED: extended, lengthy, outstretched; PROLONGED: protracted, meandering, lengthy, sustained; TEDIOUS: dull

long *v.* desire, yearn, wish, want

longing *n.* craving, yearning, pining, desire, wish

long-lived *adj.* perpetual, enduring, permanent

look *n.* SIGHT: glance, survey, glimpse, peek, peep, leer, stare; APPEARANCE: presence, mien, expression, looks, manner, aspect

look *v.* EYE: view, gaze, behold, contemplate, scrutinize, regard, inspect, observe, examine, watch; SEEM: resemble, appear

lookout *n.* VIEW: panorama, scene, observatory, station; WATCHMAN: watcher, sentinel, scout

loom *v.* APPEAR: rise, emerge; MENACE: threaten, hulk, hover, approach

loop

loop *v.* curve, encircle, connect, bend
loophole *n.* escape, omission, avoidance
loose *adj.* SLACK: free, careless; LICENTIOUS: wanton, unrestrained, dissolute; UNBOUND: unattached, disconnected, baggy, free; VAGUE: random, obscure
loose *v.* FREE: release, liberate; RELAX: slack ease
loosen *v.* extricate, untie, undo, disentangle, free
loot *n.* plunder, spoils, take, booty
loot *v.* plunder, steal, thieve, rifle, rob
lop *v.* cut, trip, prune, chop
lope *v.* jog, run, trot
lopsided *adj.* uneven, unbalanced, tipped, irregular
lordly *adj.* grand, dignified, honorable, noble
lore *n.* enlightenment, wisdom, learning, knowledge
loss *n.* RUIN: destruction, calamity, disaster; DEPRIVATION: bereavement, destitution
lost *adj.* MISPLACED: mislaid, obscured, strayed, vanished; BEWILDERED: perplexed, puzzled; DESTROYED: demolished, wasted, ruined
lot *n.* FATE: destiny, fortune, doom, chance; PORTION: cluster, array, bunch, group; LAND: tract, parcel, division, patch, field; LOAD: consignment; ABUNDANCE: plenty, loads, oodles
lotion *n.* cream, balm, salve, unguent, cosmetic
loud *adj.* CLAMOROUS: noisy, vociferous, boisterous, cacophonous, raucous, harsh; BRASH: offensive, loud-mouthed, rude, vulgar; GARISH: gaudy, flashy, tawdry, ornate
lounge *n.* SOFA: couch, divan; ROOM: bar, lobby, parlor, salon
lounge *v.* recline, ease, idle, repose, loaf, rest
lovable *adj.* winning, winsome, lovely, friendly

love *n.* **DEVOTION:** attachment, infatuation, rapture, ardor; **ESTEEM:** respect, regard, admiration

love *v.* adore, idolize, prize, treasure, cherish

lovely *adj.* beautiful, attractive, comely, fair, handsome, engaging, enchanting, captivating, pleasing

lover *n.* suitor, sweetheart, admirer, escort, paramour, fiancé, boyfriend, girlfriend, steady

loving *adj.* devoted, thoughtful, passionate, amorous, affectionate, caring, considerate

low *adj.* **SQUAT:** flat, prostrate, crouched, sunken; **FAINT:** muffled, hushed, quiet; **SAD:** dejected, moody, blue; **VULGAR:** base, mean, coarse; **ECONOMICAL:** moderate, inexpensive, cheap

lower *adj.* inferior, beneath, under

lower *v.* diminish, fall, sink, depress, decrease, drop

lowering *adj.* threatening, dark, gloomy

lowly *adj.* unpretentious, meek, humble, unassuming

loyal *adj.* faithful, true, dependable, firm, faithful

loyalty *n.* fidelity, allegiance, faithfulness, constancy, attachment, support, devotion

lucid *adj.* **CLEAR:** obvious, unmistakable; **SHINING:** bright, luminous; **SANE:** rational, normal

luck *n.* **FORTUNE:** prosperity, wealth, windfall, blessings; **CHANCE:** fate, opportunity, break, accident

lucky *adj.* **BLESSED:** wealthy, favored, successful, prosperous, fortunate; **AUSPICIOUS:** providential, propitious, magic

lucrative *adj.* profitable, fruitful, productive, gainful

ludicrous *adj.* absurd, ridiculous, laughable, farcical, incongruous

lug *v.* carry, tug, lift, draw

luggage *n.* baggage, trunks, bags, valises

lukewarm *adj.* cool, tepid, chilly
lull *n.* pause, hiatus, stillness, hush, silence
lull *v.* soothe, quiet, calm
lumber *v.* slog, plod
luminescence *n.* fluorescence, fire, radiance, light
luminous *adj.* lighted, glowing, radiant, bright
lump *n.* mass, clump, block, chunk, hunk
lunacy *n.* **INSANITY:** madness, dementia, mania; **FOOLISHNESS:** silliness
lunatic *adj.* **INSANE:** demented, deranged, psychotic; **FOOLISH:** irrational, idiotic, daft, stupid
lunge *v.* thrust, surge, bound, jump
lurch *v.* roll, stagger, weave, sway, totter
lure *n.* bait, decoy, trick
lure *v.* entice, enchant, bewitch, allure
lurid *adj.* ghastly, gruesome, sensational
lurk *v.* skulk, slink, prowl, wait, crouch, conceal, hide
luscious *adj.* toothsome, palatable, delicious
lush *adj.* **GREEN:** verdant, dense, grassy; **DELICIOUS:** rich, juicy, succulent; **ELABORATE:** extravagant, luxurious, ornamental, ornate
lust *n.* desire, appetite, passion, sensuality
luster *n.* brightness, radiance, glow, brilliance, light
lusty *adj.* hearty, boisterous, robust, vigorous
luxuriant *adj.* exuberant, overabundant
luxuriate *v.* indulge, bask, revel
luxurious *adj.* comfortable, affluent, expensive, rich
luxury *n.* indulgence, idleness, leisure, lavishness, extravagance, excess
lying *adj.* **FRAUDULENT:** deceitful, double–dealing, dishonest; **FALSIFYING:** prevaricating, misrepresenting; **UNRELIABLE:** unsound, tricky, treacherous, false

lynch *v.* punish, hang, murder
lyrical *adj.* melodious, sweet, rhythmical, poetic
machination *n.* conspiracy, plot
machine *n.* contrivance, device, implement
machinist *n.* operator, engineer, workman
macrocosm *n.* universe, world
mad *adj.* INSANE: demented, deranged, psychotic; ANGRY: provoked, enraged, exasperated
madden *v.* craze, infuriate, enrage, anger
maddening *adj.* annoying, infuriating, disturbing
made *adj.* fashioned, built, formed, manufactured
made-up *adj.* invented, concocted, devised, fictitious
madhouse *n.* bedlam, confusion
madman *n.* lunatic, maniac, screwball, oddball
magazine *n.* periodical, journal, publication
magic *adj.* enchanting, mystic, enchanting
magic *n.* occultism, legerdemain, wizardry, sorcery, divination, witchcraft, voodooism, soothsaying
magical *adj.* occult, enchanting, mystic, mysterious
magician *n.* conjurer, sorcerer, wizard, shaman
magnanimous *adj.* charitable, noble, unselfish, forgiving, generous
magnate *n.* tycoon, mogul
magnetic *adj.* alluring, appealing, attractive, irresistible, captivating, fascinating, charming
magnetism *n.* attraction, lure, attraction
magnetize *v.* fascinate, attract
magnificence *n.* grandeur, majesty, stateliness, glory, radiance, luxuriousness, greatness, lavishness, brilliance, splendor, richness, pomp
magnificent *adj.* splendid, grand, exalted, majestic
magnify *v.* amplify, expand, increase, enlarge

magnitude *n.* SIZE: extent, quantity; IMPORTANCE: greatness, consequence, significance

maid *n.* GIRL: maiden, woman; SERVANT: nursemaid, housemaid, chambermaid

mail *v.* post, send, drop

maim *v.* disfigure, mutilate, disable, damage, hurt

main *adj.* principal, chief, leading, dominant, foremost

main *n.* conduit, channel, duct, pipe

mainly *adv.* chiefly, largely, essentially, predominantly, principally

maintain *v.* UPHOLD: support, sustain, affirm, defend; ASSERT: state, attest, declare, say; PRESERVE: keep, conserve, reserve, save, manage

majestic *adj.* stately, dignified, exalted, grand, noble

majesty *n.* grandeur, nobility, greatness

major *adj.* important, significant, main, principal

make *v.* MANUFACTURE: construct, fabricate, assemble, fashion, produce, build, form; CREATE: originate, generate, devise, conceive, invent; FORCE: constrain, compel, coerce; WAGE: conduct, engage, act; PREPARE: ready, arrange, adjust, cook; OBTAIN: earn, gain; ATTAIN: reach, arrive

makeshift *adj.* temporary, expedient, stopgap

make–up *n.* COSMETICS: paint, mascara, liner, powder; COMPENSATION: atonement, conciliation, payment; COMPOSITION: structure, arrangement, formation

maladroit *adj.* awkward, bungling, clumsy, inept

malady *n.* affliction, ailment, disease, sickness

malformation *n.* deformity, distortion

malfunction *n.* breakdown, slip, failure

malice *n.* hatred, spite, animosity, resentment

malicious *adj.* hateful, spiteful, bad

malign *v.* vilify, defame, slander
malignant *adj.* lethal, poisonous, deadly, harmful, destructive, deleterious, corrupt, dangerous
malinger *v.* lounge, loll
mall *n.* market, shop
malnutrition *n.* starvation, hunger
malodorous *adj.* stinking, fetid
malpractice *n.* negligence, neglect, carelessness
mammoth *adj.* huge, large
manacle *v.* chain, handcuff, shackle
manage *v.* **DIRECT:** control, lead, oversee, mastermind, engineer, handle, supervise; **CONTRIVE:** accomplish, effect, achieve; **ENDURE:** survive
manageable *adj.* docile, compliant, tractable, obedient, submissive, yielding
manager *n.* supervisor, administrator, director, superintendent, executive
managerial *adj.* executive, administrative
mandate *v.* decree, require
mandatory *adj.* imperative, compulsory, obligatory
mane *n.* hair, ruff, fur
maneuver *v.* plot, scheme, contrive, design, conspire
manger *n.* trough, tub
manhandle *v.* damage, maul, mistreat, abuse, beat
mania *n.* craze, lunacy, madness, desire, obsession
maniac *n.* madman, lunatic
manifest *adj.* apparent, clear, evident, obvious
manifest *v.* show, prove
manifestation *n.* evidence, indication, sign
manipulate *v.* control, shape, mold, form manage
mankind *n.* humanity, society, man
mannequin *n.* model, dummy, display

manner *n.* **CONDUCT:** deportment, demeanor, behavior; **CUSTOM:** habit, use, way, practice
mannerism *n.* peculiarity, idiosyncrasy, quirk
mannerly *adj.* polished, considerate, charming
mansion *n.* house, villa, hall, estate, home
mantel *n.* shelf, ledge
mantle *n.* cloak, blanket
manual *n.* handbook, guidebook, reference
manufacture *v.* make, fabricate, produce, build
manuscript *n.* book, paper, document, composition
many *adj.* numerous, multiple, innumerable, several
map *n.* chart, graph, drawing, portrayal, draft, plan
mar *v.* damage, spoil, disfigure, harm, scratch, deface
maraud *v.* raid, pillage
march *v.* parade, tramp, advance, proceed
margin *n.* edge, border, lip, shore, boundary
marina *n.* dock, mooring
marine *adj.* nautical, maritime, oceanic
maritime *adj.* nautical, marine, seafaring, aquatic
mark *n.* **STAMP:** imprint, impression
mark *v.* **BRAND:** imprint, label, identify, earmark; **SIGNIFY:** denote mean characterize, qualify
marker *n.* ticket, trademark, seal, brand, stamp, pencil, pen, boundary, inscription, label
market *v.* sell, trade, vend, exchange, barter
marquee *n.* awning, canopy
marry *v.* **WED:** espouse; **JOIN:** unite, combine
marsh *n.* swamp, morass, bog, quagmire
marshal *v.* arrange, gather, lead
martial *adj.* warlike, combative, aggressive
martyr *n.* saint, victim, sufferer, offering, scapegoat
marvel *v.* wonder, awe, stare

marvelous *adj.* fabulous, astonishing, spectacular

mash *v.* crush, bruise, squash, pulverize press

mask *v.* disguise, cloak, conceal, veil, hide

mass *n.* **MATTER:** piece, portion, wad, hunk, lump; **HEAP:** volume quantity; **SIZE:** magnitude, extent

massacre *v.* slaughter, kill, exterminate, annihilate

massage *v.* rub, knead, stimulate, caress

massive *adj.* weighty, bulky, huge, cumbersome, large

master *n.* lord, teacher, mentor, genius, maestro

master *v.* **CONQUER:** subdue, humble, succeed, overcome; **LEARN:** understand, comprehend

masterful *adj.* commanding, skillful, excellent

mastery *n.* **CONTROL:** dominance, sovereignty, superiority; **SKILL:** capacity, proficiency, ability

match *n.* **EQUAL:** peer, equivalent, counterpart, approximation; **CONTEST:** race, rivalry, competition

match *v.* equalize, liken, coordinate, even, balance

material *adj.* physical, real, tangible; essential

materialize *v.* form, become, actualize

maternal *adj.* motherly, protective

mathematics *n.* arithmetic, geometry, algebra, computation, trigonometry, calculus, logarithms

matrimony *n.* marriage, wedlock, union

matrix *n.* mold, die

matron *n.* dame, dowager, lady, wife, mother, woman

matter *n.* **SUBSTANCE:** material, constituents, object, thing, element; **SUBJECT:** interest, focus, theme; **AFFAIR:** undertaking, circumstance, concern

mature *adj.* developed, ripe, grown, cultured

maturity *n.* competence, development, cultivation; adulthood, majority

maudlin *adj.* tearful, sentimental

maxim

maxim *n.* saying, proverb, aphorism, adage, epithet
maximum *adj.* greatest, supreme, highest, best
maybe *adv.* perhaps, possibly, conceivable
mayhem *n.* crime, violence
maze *n.* labyrinth, tangle, convolution, intricacy
meadow *n.* grass, pasture, field
meager *adj.* lean, scanty, spare, wanting
meal *n.* **FOOD:** repast, feast, chow, spread, banquet
tea; **GRAIN:** fodder, provender, forage, feed
mean *adj.* **HUMBLE:** servile, pitiful, shabby; **VICIOUS:**
contemptible, despicable, degenerate, knavish, unscrupulous; **BASE:** low, vulgar, common
mean *v.* **SIGNIFY:** denote, symbolize, imply, suggest,
designate, intimate; **INTEND:** propose, expect
meander *v.* wander, wind, roam, flow, ramble
meaning *n.* sense, import, definition, implication, intent, connotation, context, significance
meaningful *adj.* significant, essential, important
means *n.* **INSTRUMENTALITY:** machinery, method, system, agency; **WEALTH:** resources, substance, property
measure *n.* **EXTENT:** degree, dimension, capacity,
weight, volume, distance, quantity, area, mass;
STANDARD: rule, test, example, norm, criterion
measured *adj.* steady, systematic, deliberate, regular
mechanical *adj.* **AUTOMATED:** programmed, automatic;
PERFUNCTORY: stereotyped, unchanging, monotonous
mechanism *n.* machine, device, process, tool
medal *n.* badge, award, commemoration, decoration
meddle *v.* interfere, interlope, intervene, encroach
meddlesome *adj.* intrusive, prying, snoopy, nosy
mediate *v.* arbitrate, negotiate
medication *n.* remedy, pill, vaccination

mediocre *adj.* middling, average, common, ordinary
meditation *n.* contemplation, reflection, thought
medium *n.* **MEANS:** mechanism, tool, agency, device; **SPIRITUALIST:** seer, oracle, prophet
medley *n.* mixture, conglomeration, variety
meek *adj.* humble, unassuming, passive, docile
meet *v.* **ENCOUNTER:** engage, battle, match, face; **TOUCH:** coincide, join, intersect; **CONVENE:** assemble, gather, converge, congregate; **SATISFY:** fulfill, suffice
melancholy *adj.* gloomy, depressed, dispirited, sad
mellow *v.* ripen, mature, age
melodramatic *adj.* artificial, sensational, exaggerated
melody *n.* song, tune, air, lyric, strain
melt *v.* **DISSOLVE:** liquefy, thaw, soften, **DWINDLE:** vanish, go, pass; **RELENT:** forgive, yield
member *n.* **LIMB:** organ, arm, leg; **ASSOCIATE:** constituent, affiliate; **PART:** segment, fragment, division
memento *n.* keepsake, reminder, souvenir
memoir *n.* biography, autobiography, account
memorabilia *n.* memento, souvenir
memorable *adj.* unforgettable, notable, significant, monumental, eventful, exceptional, singular
memorial *n.* monument, tablet, tombstone, mausoleum, statue; celebration, ceremony
memorize *v.* retain, learn, remember
memory *n.* recollection, retrospection, reminiscence
menace *v.* threaten, intimidate, portend
mend *v.* repair, patch, fix, aid, remedy, cure, correct
menial *n.* servant, domestic, maid, lackey
mental *adj.* thoughtful, rational, intellectual, subconscious, telepathic, psychic, clairvoyant
mentality *n.* intellect, comprehension, reasoning

mention *v.* remark, comment, infer, intimate, suggest
merchandise *n.* goods, wares, commodities, stock
merchandise *v.* advertise, sell
merchant *n.* trader, shopkeeper, dealer, jobber
merciful adj. lenient, softhearted, mild tolerant
mercurial *adj.* changeable, volatile
mere *adj.* minor, insignificant, little
merge *v.* combine, fuse, join, blend, mix, unite
merit *n.* worth, excellence, honor, character, virtue
merit *v.* earn, warrant, justify, deserve
merriment *n.* mirth, joy, gaiety, happiness, humor
mesh *v.* engage, coincide, suit, agree, fit
mess *n.* confusion, disorder, jumble, clutter
message *n.* communication, tidings, information
messenger *n.* courier, envoy, minister, herald, runner, emissary, angel, prophet
metamorphosis *n.* transformation, change
metaphorical *adj.* figurative, symbolical, allegorical
method *n.* procedure, process, technique, system
meticulous *adj.* mindful, cautious
metropolitan *adj.* cosmopolitan, modern, urban
mettlesome *adj.* spirited, active
middle *adj.* median, mean, midway, equidistant, central, halfway, intermediate
middleman *n.* wholesaler, jobber
miff *v.* offend, annoy
might *n.* power, ability, strength, force, sway
mighty *adj.* powerful, great, imposing, impressive
migrate *v.* move, emigrate, leave
migration *n.* voyage, departure, journey, movement
mild *adj.* moderate, gentle, meek, temperate
militant *adj.* aggressive, warlike, belligerent

millinery *n.* hats, bonnets
mimic *v.* **IMITATE:** copy, simulate, impersonate; **MOCK:** burlesque, caricature, ridicule
mind *n.* **MENTALITY:** perception, judgment, wisdom, intellect; **INTENTION:** inclination, determination
mind *v.* **OBEY:** heed, behave, attend, regard; **OBJECT:** complain, deplore, dislike
mindless *adj.* **CARELESS:** inattentive, oblivious, neglectful, indifferent; **FOOLISH:** senseless, rash
miniature *adj.* small, tiny, little, minute
minimize *v.* reduce, lessen, depreciate, decrease
minister *n.* clergyman, ambassador
minister *v.* attend, tend, help
ministration *n.* assistance, comfort, relief
minor *adj.* inferior, secondary, lesser, trivial
minor *n.* adolescent, child, infant, youth
minute *adj.* **SMALL:** microscopic, tiny; **TRIVIAL:** paltry, immaterial; **EXACT:** particular, detailed
minutiae *n.* particulars, details
miracle *n.* marvel, revelation, wonder
miraculous *adj.* supernatural, wonderful, marvelous, phenomenal, mysterious
mirage *n.* illusion, phantasm, hallucination, fantasy
mirth *n.* gaiety, laughter, frolic, jollity, fun
misbehave *v.* sin, trespass, err
miscalculate *v.* blunder, miscount, err, mistake
miscellaneous *adj.* **DIVERSE:** unmatched, unlike; **MIXED:** muddled, scattered, confused, disordered
mischievous *adj.* playful, roguish, naughty
misconduct *n.* misbehavior, wrongdoing, mischief
miser *n.* niggard, skinflint, money–grubber
miserable *adj.* wretched, distressed, troubled

misery *n.* PAIN: distress, suffering, agony; DESPAIR: depression, sadness; TROUBLE: grief, anxiety

misfortune *n.* calamity, adversity, unpleasantness

misgiving *n.* mistrust, doubt, uncertainty

misguided *adj.* misled, deceived, confused

misjudge *v.* miscalculate, overestimate, underestimate, mistake

mislead *v.* delude, trick, beguile, dupe, misrepresent

mismatched *adj.* incompatible, discordant, unfit

misrepresent *v.* distort, falsify, deceive, lie, mislead

miss *n.* FAILURE: slip blunder mishap mistake deviation WOMAN: lass maid female girl

mission *n.* purpose, charge, commission

missionary *n.* apostle, evangelist, messenger

mist *n.* vapor, cloud, rain, haze, fog

mistake *n.* BLUNDER: error, slip, omission, goof; MISUNDERSTANDING: confusion, misinterpretation

mistake *v.* err, blunder, misjudge, botch, bungle

mistreat *v.* harm, injure, wrong, abuse

mistrust *v.* suspect, distrust, doubt

misunderstanding *n.* MISAPPREHENSION: misinterpretation; DISAGREEMENT: quarrel, dispute

mix *v.* BLEND: combine, mingle, stir, unite; CONFUSE: jumble, tangle; ASSOCIATE: fraternize

mixture *n.* combination, blend, compound, amalgam, medley, potpourri, incorporation, hodgepodge

mix–up *n.* chaos, commotion, confusion, disorder

moan *v.* groan, wail, whine

mob *n.* throng, crowd, rabble, multitude, horde

mob *v.* attack, crowd, swarm, press, overwhelm

mobile *adj.* movable, loose, free

mock *adj.* imitation, counterfeit, sham

mock *v.* deride, taunt, mimic, caricature, imitate
mockery *n.* disparagement, ridicule
mode *n.* manner, fashion
model *n.* **EXAMPLE:** prototype, ideal; **PATTERN:** design, standard; **POSER:** sitter, mannequin, nude
model *v.* **FORM:** shape, fashion; **SIT:** pose; **DEMONSTRATE:** show, wear, display
moderate *adj.* **INEXPENSIVE:** cheap, economical; **MODEST:** temperate, calm, reserved; **TOLERANT:** restrained, cautious; **PLEASANT:** temperate, mild
moderate *v.* abate, decline, decrease
moderation *n.* restraint, temperance, balance
modern *adj.* **STYLISH:** chic, smart, fashionable; **CONTEMPORARY:** new, current, renovated, improved
modest *adj.* **HUMBLE:** unassuming, meek, diffident; **UNPRETENTIOUS:** plain, seemly, tasteful, unadorned, unaffected; **MODERATE:** reasonable, inexpensive, economical; **PROPER:** pure, chaste, seemly, decent; **LOWLY:** simple, unaffected
modify *v.* change, vary, alter
moist *adj.* wet, humid, dank, moistened, damp
mold *n.* **FORM:** matrix shape frame, pattern, die, cast; **GROWTH:** rust, parasite, fungus, lichen, decay
molest *v.* disturb, bother, annoy, irritate, badger
mollify *v.* assuage, pacify
molten *adj.* melted, liquefied
moment *n.* **TIME:** instant, jiffy; **IMPORTANCE:** significance, note, consequence
momentary *adj.* fleeting, passing, transient, cursory
momentum *n.* impetus, impulse, force, drive, energy
monetary *adj.* pecuniary, financial, fiscal
money *n.* currency, cash, notes, specie, funds

monologue *n.* speech, talk, discourse, address
monopolize *v.* dominate, engross, corner
monopoly *n.* trust, syndicate, cartel
monotonous *adj.* tiresome, tedious, wearying, dull
monster *n.* **MONSTROSITY:** chimera, werewolf; **FREAK:** abnormality; **BRUTE:** criminal, rascal, savage
monstrous *adj.* **HUGE:** stupendous, prodigious, enormous, large; **UNNATURAL:** abnormal, unusual
monument *n.* memorial, shrine, statue, monolith
monumental *adj.* lofty, impressive, majestic, grand
mood *n.* state, condition, temper, humor, disposition
moody *adj.* downcast, pensive, unhappy, sad
moot *adj.* disputable, arguable
mope *v.* fret, pine, sorrow, brood, sulk
moral *adj.* virtuous, proper, scrupulous, honorable, aboveboard, principled, chaste, noble
morale *n.* assurance, resolve, spirit, confidence
morality *n.* righteousness, uprightness, virtue
morals *n.* ethics, ideals, standards, mores, principles
moratorium *n.* delay, halt, suspension
morbid *adj.* **DISEASED:** sickly, unhealthy, ailing; **PATHOLOGICAL:** gloomy, melancholic, depressed
morning *n.* dawn, morn, daybreak, cockcrow, sun–up
morose *adj.* surly, downcast, gloomy
morsel *n.* piece, bite, chunk, bit, part
mortal *adj.* **FATAL:** malignant, lethal, deadly; **TEMPORAL:** human, transient, perishable, temporary
mostly *adv.* **FREQUENTLY:** often, regularly; **LARGELY:** chiefly, essentially, principally
motel *n.* hotel, cabin, inn, resort
motherly *adj.* maternal, devoted, protective, loving
motif *n.* theme, melody

motion *n.* **MOVEMENT:** change, act, action, passage; **PROPOSAL:** suggestion, proposition, plan

motivate *v.* inspire, stimulate, incite, spur, goad

motive *n.* cause, purpose, idea, reason

motto *n.* maxim, adage, saw, aphorism, sentiment, slogan, catchword, axiom, proverb, saying

mound *n.* pile, heap, knoll, hill

mount *v.* **RISE:** ascend; **CLIMB:** scale, clamber

mountainous *adj.* steep, lofty, craggy, rugged

mourn *v.* grieve, sorrow, bemoan, languish, pine

mournful *adj.* sorrowful, unhappy, sad

movable *adj.* portable, mobile, detachable, free

move *v.* **EXCITE:** arouse, stir, stimulate; **PROPEL:** impel, actuate; **PROPOSE:** introduce, submit; **ADVANCE:** go, walk, run, travel, progress, proceed, traverse

movement *n.* **CHANGE:** migration, evolution, transition, progression; **TREND:** drift, tendency, inclination

mow *v.* cut, scythe, reap, harvest

mud *n.* muck, mire, slush, silt, ooze

muddle *v.* confuse, disarrange, mix, jumble, snarl

muddy *adj.* **MURKY:** dull, cloudy, indistinct, obscure; **SWAMPY:** soggy, sodden, slushy, boggy

muffle *v.* deaden, mute, stifle, decrease, soften

muffler *n.* scarf, neckpiece, choker

mug *n.* vessel, stein, flagon, cup

muggy *adj.* damp, humid, moist

multitude *n.* throng, mob, crowd, gathering, people

mumble *v.* mutter, utter, murmur

munch *v.* chew, masticate, crunch, bite, eat

mundane *adj.* normal, ordinary, everyday

municipality *n.* community, district, village, town

murder *n.* homicide, carnage, slaying, butchery

murder *v.* kill, slay, assassinate, butcher
murky *adj.* gloomy, dark, dim, dusky, dingy, dirty
muscular *adj.* brawny, powerful, husky, strong
museum *n.* collection, archives, treasury, depository
music *n.* melody, harmony, tune, air, strain
musical *adj.* tuneful, sweet, pleasing, lyrical
musty *adj.* moldy, sour, stale, crumbling
mutation *n.* change, modification, deviation
mute *adj.* speechless, silent, bewildered, unspoken
mutilate *v.* maim, damage, injure, deface, disfigure
mutiny *n.* insurrection, revolt, resistance, revolution
mutter *v.* mumble, murmur, grumble, complain
mutual *adj.* reciprocal, common, joint, shared
muzzle *v.* gag, muffle, silence, suppress, hush, quiet
myriad *n.* variable, innumerable, endless, multiple
mysterious *adj.* PUZZLING: enigmatic, strange, unnatural; SECRET: veiled, obscure, hidden, ambiguous
mystical *adj.* occult, spiritual, mysterious, secret
mystify *v.* puzzle, perplex, hoodwink, deceive
myth *n.* legend, fable, lore, saga, parable, tale, story
mythological *adj.* whimsical, fantastic, imaginary
nab *v.* grab, take, snatch, seize
nag *v.* scold, vex, annoy, pester, bother
naïve *adj.* unaffected, artless, innocent, unsophisticated, gullible, credulous, trusting, inexperienced
naïveté *n.* inexperience, innocence
naked *adj.* uncovered, unclad, bare, exposed
name *n.* REPUTATION: renown, fame; TITLE: designation; STAR: hero, lion, celebrity
name *v.* appoint, nominate, select, delegate, designate
nameless *adj.* undistinguished, obscure, unknown
namely *adv.* specifically, particularly

nap *n.* REST: sleep, siesta, doze; PILE: shag, texture

napkin *n.* serviette, linen, towel

narrate *v.* tell, recite, describe, reveal, report

narrow *adj.* CRAMPED: close, confined; DOGMATIC: intolerant, prejudiced; CLOSE: precarious, dangerous

nasty *adj.* OFFENSIVE: foul, gross, vulgar; INDECENT: immodest, smutty, lewd; UNKIND: sarcastic, mean

nation *n.* PEOPLE: populace, community, society; STATE: realm, country, domain

nationalism *n.* chauvinism, jingoism, loyalty

native *adj.* NATURAL: innate, inborn, hereditary; INDIGENOUS: aboriginal, primeval, domestic, local

natty *adj.* trim, spruce

natural *adj.* INTRINSIC: original, fundamental, inherited, native; TYPICAL: characteristic, usual, customary; UNSTUDIED: ingenuous, artless, spontaneous; REAL: actual, tangible, physical

naughty *adj.* bad, mischievous, wayward, roguish

nausea *n.* sickness, queasiness, vomiting, illness

nauseate *v.* sicken, repulse, bother, disgust, disturb

nauseous *adj.* ill, queasy, squeamish, sick

navigable *adj.* passable, open, safe

near, nearby *adj., adv.* BORDERING: adjacent, adjoining, neighboring; EXPECTED: approaching, coming

neat *adj.* TIDY: trim, prim, spruce, dapper, orderly, precise; CLEVER: dexterous, skillful, agile

nebulous *adj.* vague, cloudy, hazy

necessary *adj.* essential, important, requisite, required, imperative, compulsory, mandatory

necessitate *v.* compel, constrain, oblige, force

necessity *n.* requirement, need, requisite

nectar *n.* drink, juice, fluid

need *n.* **POVERTY:** indigence, penury; **LACK:** shortage, inadequacy; **REQUIREMENT:** necessity

needy *adj.* destitute, indigent, penniless, poor

nefarious *adj.* vile, wicked

negate *v.* repeal, retract, neutralize, cancel, nullify

negative *n.* **REFUSAL:** contradiction, disavowal, refutation, denial; **PICTURE:** film, image, plate

neglect *v.* **SLIGHT:** disregard, disdain, affront, ignore, spurn; **EVADE:** defer, procrastinate, postpone

negligent *adj.* careless, indifferent, inattentive

negotiate *v.* bargain, mediate, conciliate, arbitrate

negotiation *n.* compromise, intervention, mediation

neighborhood *n.* vicinity, environs, locality

neophyte *n.* convert, novice, apprentice

nerve *n.* **COURAGE:** resolution, mettle, boldness; **IMPUDENCE:** temerity, audacity, effrontery, rudeness

nervous *adj.* **EXCITABLE:** impatient, restless, uneasy, unstable; **EXCITED:** fidgety, jittery, agitated, bothered

nestle *v.* snuggle, cuddle, huddle

neurosis *n.* compulsion, nervousness, obsession

neurotic *adj.* disturbed, unstable, troubled

neutral *adj.* **UNBIASED:** impartial; **DULL:** drab, vague

new *adj.* **RECENT:** current, late; **MODERN:** contemporary, fashionable; **NOVEL:** unique, original, unusual; **INEXPERIENCED:** unseasoned, unskilled, incompetent

newcomer *n.* outsider, alien, stranger

newfangled *adj.* novel, unique, fashionable, modern

news *n.* information, tidings, report, account

next *adj., adv.* **FOLLOWING:** succeeding, subsequent; **ADJACENT:** beside, adjoining, neighboring, touching

nibble *v.* nip, gnaw, snack, bite, eat

nice *adj.* likable, pleasant, agreeable, amiable

niche *n.* recess, cranny, corner, cubbyhole
nick *v.* indent, notch, slit, cut, dent
night *n.* evening, nightfall, twilight, bedtime
nimble *adj.* **AGILE:** light, quick, spry, active, graceful;
　ALERT: bright, clever, intelligent
noble *adj.* **EXALTED:** courtly, lordly, dignified, distin-
　guished; **MERITORIOUS:** virtuous, refined, chivalrous;
　TITLED: aristocratic, patrician; **GRAND:** stately, im-
　pressive, imposing
nobody *n.* nonentity, upstart, cipher
nod *v.* **SIGNAL:** bow, acknowledge; **NAP:** drowse, sleep
noise *n.* sound, clamor, racket, fracas, din, uproar
noisome *adj.* unhealthy, disgusting
noisy *adj.* clamorous, vociferous, boisterous, loud
nomad *n.* wanderer, migrant, vagabond, traveler
nominate *v.* name, appoint, propose, designate
nonchalant *adj.* **CASUAL:** unconcerned, impassive,
　detached, indifferent; **CARELESS:** negligent, trifling
nonconformist *n.* radical, rebel, eccentric, maverick
nonprofit *adj.* charitable, altruistic, humane
nonsense *n.* **INANITY:** trash, senselessness, bun-
　combe; **FUN:** jest, absurdity
nonviolent *adj.* passive, calm, quiet
nook *n.* niche, cubbyhole, cranny, hole
noose *n.* loop, hitch, lasso, rope
normal *adj.* **USUAL:** ordinary, typical, common
　REGULAR: routine, orderly, methodical; **SANE:** lucid,
　rational, reasonable; **HEALTHY:** whole, sound
nostalgia *n.* longing, homesickness, wistfulness
nosy *adj.* snoopy, curious, inquisitive, interested
notable *adj.* remarkable, distinguished, striking
notch *n.* nick, indent, cut, dent, groove

note *n.* memo, reminder, memorandum
note *v.* **NOTICE:** perceive, see; **RECORD:** transcribe
noted *adj.* well–known, celebrated, notorious, famous
notice *n.* warning, notification, announcement
noticeable *adj.* appreciable, conspicuous, obvious
notion *n.* whim, fancy, idea, assumption
notorious *adj.* infamous, known, disreputable
notwithstanding *adv.* despite, although, but
nourish *v.* feed, encourage, sustain
nourishing *adj.* healthy, nutritious
novel *adj.* new, strange, odd, unique, unusual
novelist *n.* writer, narrator, author
novelty *n.* fad, innovation, creation
novice *n.* beginner, neophyte, amateur
now *adv.* momentarily, promptly, instantly
noxious *adj.* injurious, harmful
nuance *n.* subtlety, distinction, difference
nucleus *n.* essence, core, kernel, center, hub, focus
nudge *v.* poke, bump, tap, push, touch
nugget *n.* lump, ingot, chunk, rock
nuisance *n.* **BOTHER:** annoyance, vexation, trouble; **CRIME:** breach, infraction, affront
null *adj.* void, invalid, vain, unsanctioned
numb *adj.* deadened, unfeeling, senseless
numb *v.* deaden, stupefy, paralyze, stun, dull
numerous *adj.* many, copious, diverse, infinite
nuptials *n.* wedding, marriage, matrimony
nurse *v.* tend, minister, aid, treat
nurture *v.* nourish, feed, sustain
nutriment *n.* food, nourishment, provisions, victuals
nutritious *adj.* nourishing, wholesome, healthful
nuzzle *v.* caress, cuddle, snuggle, nestle

oasis *n.* refuge, retreat

oath *n.* **PROMISE:** vow, pledge; **PROFANITY:** curse, swearword, blasphemy

obdurate *n.* stubborn, hardhearted

obedient *adj.* **DUTIFUL:** loyal, devoted, deferential, faithful; **DOCILE:** submissive, compliant

obese *adj.* fat, corpulent, plump, stout

obey *v.* yield, conform, submit, serve comply

object *n.* **THING:** article, gadget; **GOAL:** aim, objective

object *v.* disapprove, protest, dispute, complain

objective *adj.* impartial, impersonal

objective *n.* goal, aim, target, mission, destination

obligate *v.* bind, restrict, constrain, force

obligatory *adj.* required, essential, binding, necessary

oblige *v.* **ACCOMMODATE:** assist, aid, contribute, help; **REQUIRE:** constrain, bind, force, compel, coerce

obliging *adj.* amiable, accommodating, helpful, kind

oblivion *n.* obscurity, void, emptiness, nothing

oblivious *adj.* distracted, preoccupied, absorbed

obnoxious *adj.* offensive, annoying, disagreeable

obscene *adj.* indecent, lewd, wanton, lascivious

obscure *adj.* vague, indistinct, unclear, hazy, arcane

obscure *v.* **DIM:** cloud, screen; **CONCEAL:** cover, veil

observable *adj.* perceptible, noticeable, discernible

observance *n.* **CUSTOM:** ritual, practice, rite; **AWARENESS:** observation, notice

observant *adj.* alert, discerning, perceptive, bright

observe *v.* **WATCH:** scrutinize, see, notice; **COMMENT:** remark, note, mention; **COMMEMORATE:** dedicate, solemnize; **ABIDE BY:** comply, follow, obey

obsessed *adj.* haunted, beset, controlled, troubled

obsession *n.* fixation, fascination, passion, mania

obsessive *adj.* compulsive, preoccupied
obsolete *adj.* antiquated, archaic, out–of–date
obstacle *n.* hindrance, restriction, obstruction
obstinate *adj.* stubborn, headstrong, opinionated
obstreperous *adj.* noisy, unruly
obstruct *v.* block, interfere, bar, hinder, prevent
obtain *v.* get, take, acquire, seize, procure
obtuse *adj.* blunt, stupid
obvious *adj.* apparent, perceptible, open, clear, intelligible, comprehensible, understandable
occasion *n.* event, occurrence, incident, happening
occasional *adj.* sporadic, random, infrequent
occult *adj.* hidden, mysterious, supernatural, secret
occupancy *n.* possession, occupation
occupation *n.* vocation, employment, job, profession
occupy *v.* SEIZE: conquer, invade; FILL:, pervade, permeate; ENGAGE: absorb, engross, involve, fascinate
occur *v.* happen, transpire, befall
oceanic *adj.* marine, aquatic, maritime, nautical
odd *adj.* UNUSUAL: unique, strange; SINGLE: sole, unpaired, unmatched, lone
odious *adj.* hateful, offensive, repulsive
odor *n.* smell, perfume, fragrance, bouquet
offal *n.* refuse, rubbish
offend *v.* displease, annoy, affront, outrage, bother
offense *n.* MISDEED: transgression; ATTACK: assault, aggression; RESENTMENT: pique, indignation, anger
offensive *adj.* AGGRESSIVE: assaulting, attacking, invading; REVOLTING: disgusting, repulsive, detestable
offer *v.* present, proffer, tender, propose, submit
offering *n.* contribution, donation, present, gift
offhand *adj.* impromptu, informal, improvised

officer *n.* executive, manager, director, president
official *adj.* **FORMAL:** proper, accepted; **AUTHORIZED:** endorsed, sanctioned; **RELIABLE:** authentic, genuine
official *n.* **ADMINISTRATOR:** comptroller, director, executive; **UMPIRE:** referee, linesman
offspring *n.* child, progeny, issue, descendant, heir
ointment *n.* salve, unguent, lotion, cream, balm
old *adj.* **AGED:** venerable, seasoned, enfeebled; **WORN:** thin, faded; **ANCIENT:** archaic, prehistoric, antique
ombudsman *n.* investigator, mediator
omen *n.* warning, portent, augury, indication, sign
ominous *adj.* threatening, forbidding, menacing
omission *n.* exclusion, lack, need, want
omit *v.* exclude, ignore, slight, overlook, disregard
omnipotent *adj.* all–powerful, almighty
omnipresent *adj.* universal, pervasive
once *adj., adv.* formerly, previously, earlier
oncoming *adj.* impending, imminent, approaching
only *adj.* **SOLELY:** exclusively, entirely, totally; **MERELY:** simply, barely, hardly; **SOLE:** single, isolated, unique
onset *n.* beginning, opening, start, origin
ooze *v.* leak, seep, exude, flow
opaque *adj.* dim, dusky, darkened, murky, gloomy
open *adj.* **CLEAR:** divulged, revealed, unobstructed; **UNRESTRICTED:** free, public; **UNGUARDED:** accessible; **UNDECIDED:** debatable, questionable; **FRANK:** plain, candid, straightforward
open *v.* **BEGIN:** inaugurate, initiate; **UNLOCK:** undo, unbolt; **BREACH:** penetrate, pierce; **EXPOSE:** reveal
openly *adv.* **FRANKLY:** candidly, honestly, sincerely; **SHAMELESSLY:** immodestly, flagrantly, wantonly
operate *v.* **FUNCTION:** work, serve, run, percolate;

   MANAGE: manipulate, conduct, administer
operation *n.* ACTION: act, deed, undertaking, work;
  METHOD: process, formula, procedure
operative *adj.* effective, functioning
opinion *n.* belief, view, sentiment, conception
opinionated *adj.* obstinate, bigoted, stubborn, unyielding, prejudiced
opponent *n.* rival, competitor, adversary, antagonist
opportunity *n.* chance, circumstance, moment
oppose *v.* CONTRADICT: dispute, defy, confront, resist;
  FIGHT: compete, encounter, assail, storm, clash
opposite *n.* opposition, antithesis, counterpart
opposition *n.* CONFLICT; hostility, resistance; DISLIKE:
  antagonism, defiance, antipathy, abhorrence
oppress *v.* harass, maltreat, abuse, bother
oppression *n.* tyranny, domination, persecution
opprobrium *n.* disgrace, shame
optimal *adj.* favorable, desirable, optimum
optimism *n.* faith, cheerfulness, confidence, enthusiasm, expectation, certainty
option *n.* choice, selection, alternative
optional *adj.* discretionary, elective, voluntary
opulence *n.* riches, wealth
oracle *n.* prophet, seer, sage, fortuneteller
oral *adj.* spoken, vocal, verbal, uttered, voiced
orbit *v.* revolve, encircle, encompass
ordain *v.* ESTABLISH: install, appoint; DESTINE: foreor-
  dain, intend; CONSECRATE: invest, bless
ordeal *n.* trial, test, distress, calamity, difficulty
order *n.* ARRANGEMENT: plan, system; ORGANIZATION:
  fraternity, society; COMMAND: stipulation mandate,
  injunction; CLASS: kind, hierarchy, classification;

SEQUENCE: progression, succession, series
order *v.* **ARRANGE:** classify, organize; **COMMAND:** direct, instruct, require; **BUY:** secure, reserve, request
orderly *adj.* **NEAT:** tidy, arranged; **METHODICAL:** systematic, thorough, precise, careful
orderly *n.* aide, assistant
ordinance *n.* law, direction, mandate
ordinarily *adv.* usually, generally, habitually
ordinary *adj.* **USUAL:** normal, common; **AVERAGE:** mediocre, accepted, typical, characteristic
ordination *n.* investment, investiture, induction
organization *n.* **SYSTEM:** arrangement, classification; **ASSOCIATION:** federation, institute, alliance
organize *v.* **ARRANGE:** systematize, coordinate, classify; **ESTABLISH:** build, found, plan, formulate
orientation *n.* familiarization, introduction
origin *n.* birth, start, foundation, beginning, source
original *adj.* **FIRST:** fundamental; **CREATIVE:** imaginative, inventive; **GENUINE:** authentic, real
originate *v.* introduce, found, start, begin
ornament *n.* decoration, embellishment, adornment, beautification
ornate *adj.* showy, gaudy, adorned, embellished
orphan *n.* foundling, waif, stray
ostensible *adj.* professed, apparent
other *adj.* separate, distinct, opposite, extra
oust *v.* eject, expel, discharge, evict, dislodge
out *n.* escape, excuse, explanation
outbreak *n.* **ERUPTION:** explosion, outburst, commotion, tumult; **VIOLENCE:** mutiny, revolution
outburst *n.* discharge, eruption, outbreak
outcast *n.* exile, fugitive, pariah, refugee

outcome *n.* upshot, consequence, result
outcry *n.* complaint, clamor, objection
outdated *adj.* outmoded, antiquated, old
outdo *v.* surpass, best, beat, exceed
outfit *v.* supply, equip, provide
outflank *v.* surround, outmaneuver, defeat
outgrowth *adj.* end, result, outcome, effect, result
outing *n.* excursion, airing, drive, vacation
outlandish *adj.* **STRANGE:** foreign; **BARBARIC:** rude
outlast *v.* outlive, outwear, endure, survive
outlaw *v.* forbid, ban, banish, condemn
outline *n.* **PLAN:** framework, draft; **CONTOUR:** boundary, frame; **SILHOUETTE:** profile, shape, formation
outlook *n.* **VIEWPOINT:** scope, vision; **PROSPECT:** likelihood, possibility, opportunity, probability
outlying *adj.* exterior, frontier, distant
outnumbered *v.* exceeded, bested, overcome, beaten
outrage *v.* offend, wrong, affront, insult
outrageous *adj.* shameless, disgraceful, scandalous, flagrant, contemptible, ignoble, atrocious
outright *adj.* unmitigated, unconditional, obvious
outside *adj.* outermost, external, outer
outsider *n.* foreigner, stranger, refugee, alien
outskirts *n.* suburbs, limits, boundary, edge
outspoken *adj.* blunt, candid, artless, frank
outstanding *adj.* distinguished, conspicuous, notable
outwit *v.* trick, bewilder, confuse, deceive
ovation *n.* outburst, applause
over *adj.* **ABOVE:** overhead, higher; **AGAIN:** afresh; **BEYOND:** past, farther; **DONE:** accomplished, finished
overbearing *adj.* domineering, tyrannical, dictatorial
overcast *adj.* cloudy, gloomy, dark

overcome v. conquer, overwhelm, best, vanquish
overconfident n. reckless, impudent, heedless, rash
overdo v. MAGNIFY: amplify, overreach, exaggerate, enhance; WEARY: tire, fatigue, exhaust, overtax
overdue adj. late, delayed, belated, tardy
overestimate v. overvalue, overrate, exaggerate
overflow v. SPILL OVER: waste, cascade, spout, gush, surge; FLOOD: inundate
overhaul v. recondition, modernize, fix, renew, repair
overpower v. overwhelm, master, subjugate, defeat
overrate v. overvalue, magnify, exaggerate
overrule v. invalidate, override, cancel, revoke, reject
overrun v. DEFEAT: overwhelm, invade, occupy; INFEST: ravage, invade, overwhelm
oversee v. superintend, supervise, manage
oversight n. failure, overlooking, mistake, error
overt adj. apparent, open
overtake v. catch, exceed, overhaul, reach
overthrow v. upset, overcome, overrun, overpower
overtone n. inference, hint, suggestion
overture n. SUGGESTION: advance, tender, negotiations; PRELUDE: prologue, preface, introduction
overturn v. subvert, ruin, overthrow, reverse, overthrow, upset
overwhelm v. DEFEAT: overcome, overthrow, conquer; ASTONISH: bewilder, confound, confuse, surprise
overwrought adj. excited, overexcited
owed adj. owing, due, indebted, unpaid
own v. ACKNOWLEDGE: grant, admit, declare; POSSESS: hold, have, enjoy, retain, keep
owner n. proprietor, landlord, landlady, partner
ownership n. possession, claim, deed, title, control

pace *n.* step, gait, movement, speed
pacify *v.* calm, soothe, conciliate, appease, placate
package *n.* bundle, parcel, packet, box, carton
pact *n.* contract, agreement, bargain, treaty
pad *n.* **TABLET:** stationery, notebook; **STUFFING:** cushion, wadding, waste, filling
pad *v.* **STUFF:** pack, fill, **INCREASE:** inflate, increase
padding *n.* stuffing, wadding, waste, filling
paddle *v.* spank, thrash, rap, punish
padlock *n.* lock, latch, fastener, catch
pagan *adj.* heathen, unchristian, idolatrous
pagan *n.* heathen, gentile, unbeliever, infidel
page *n.* leaf, sheet, folio, side, surface, recto, verso
page *v.* call, summon
pageant *n.* parade, celebration, pomp
pail *n.* vessel, bucket, pot, receptacle, jug, container
pain *n.* **SUFFERING:** anguish, distress, misery, wretchedness, torment; **HURT:** ache, spasm, cramp, agony, sting, burn; **GRIEF:** despondency, worry, anxiety, depression, sadness
pain *v.* distress, hurt, grieve, trouble
painful *adj.* **SORE:** raw, throbbing, burning, hurtful, piercing, smarting, sensitive, tender
paint *v.* **PORTRAY:** sketch, picture, depict; **COAT:** brush, swab, daub, cover, spread
pair *n.* set, two, brace, couple
pair *v.* join, couple, combine, match, balance
palace *n.* manor, mansion, castle
pale *adj.* wan, pallid, sickly, anemic, cadaverous, haggard, deathlike, ghostly
palpitate *v.* tremble, quiver, pulsate
paltry *adj.* worthless, small, insignificant, trifling

pamper *v.* overindulge, spoil, indulge, pet, humor, gratify, coddle, please

pamphlet *n.* booklet, leaflet, brochure, bulletin, circular, broadside, handbill, announcement

pan *n.* vessel, kettle, pail, bucket, container

pandemonium *n.* noise, disorder, uproar, anarchy, riot, confusion

pane *n.* panel, window, glass

panel *n.* ornament, tablet, inset, decoration

pang *n.* pain, throb, sting, bite

panhandle *v.* solicit, ask, bum, beg

panic *n.* dread, alarm, fright, fear

panorama *n.* view, spectacle, scenery, prospect

pant *v.* gasp, desire, wheeze, throb, palpitate

pantomime *n.* sign, charade, mime

pantry *n.* storage, provisions, storeroom, larder, cupboard, closet, room

pants *n.* trousers, breeches, slacks, jeans, overalls, cords, shorts, corduroys, pantaloons, chaps, knickers, bloomers, rompers

paper *n.* DOCUMENT: record, abstract, affidavit, bill, certificate, contract, credentials, deed, diploma; NEWSPAPER: journal, daily; ESSAY: article, theme

par *n.* equality, standard, level, norm, model

parable *n.* fable, allegory, moral, story, tale

parade *n.* PROCESSION: spectacle, ceremony, demonstration, review, pageant, ritual

parade *v.* march, demonstrate, display, exhibit

paradox *n.* mystery, enigma, ambiguity, puzzle

paragon *n.* model, example, ideal, perfection, best

parallel *n.* match, correspond, correlate, equal

paraphernalia *n.* trappings, equipment, gear

parasite *n.* dependent, sponger, hanger–on, toady
parcel *n.* package, bundle, packet, carton
parch *v.* scorch, dry, shrivel, desiccate, dehydrate
pardon *v.* exonerate, clear, absolve, reprieve, acquit, liberate, discharge, free, release, forgive, condone, overlook, exculpate, excuse
pare *v.* cut, diminish, shave, skin
parentage *n.* birth, descent, parenthood
parental *adj.* paternal, maternal, familial, genetic
park *n.* plaza, square, lawn, green, promenade, boulevard, tract, grounds, woodland, meadow
parochial *adj.* limited, restricted, narrow, provincial, insular, sectional, local, regional
parody *v.* mimic, copy, caricature, imitate, joke
parole *v.* release, discharge, pardon, liberate, free
parson *n.* clergyman, cleric, preacher, minister
part *n.* PORTION: piece, fragment, fraction, section, sector, segment, particle, component, share; ROLE: character, hero, heroine, constituent
part *v.* DIVIDE: separate, sever; DEPART: withdraw
partial *adj.* INCOMPLETE: unfinished; PREJUDICED: unfair, influenced, biased, inclined
partiality *n.* fondness, inclination, preference
participate *v.* compete, play, strive, engage
particle *n.* jot, scrap, atom, molecule, fragment, piece, shred, bit, part
particular *adj.* SPECIFIC: distinct, singular, appropriate, special; ACCURATE: precise, minute, exact
particularly *adj.* expressly, especially
partisan *n.* adherent, supporter, disciple, follower
partition *n.* DIVISION: apportionment, distribution, BARRIER: separation, wall, obstruction

partly *adj.* partially, somewhat

partner *n.* associate, co–worker, ally, comrade

partnership *n.* alliance, union, brotherhood, society

party *n.* **AFFAIR:** social, reception, gathering, function; **GROUP:** company, crowd, assembly; **ORGANIZATION:** bloc, faction; **PERSON:** someone, somebody

pass *v.* **ELAPSE:** transpire; **TRANSFER:** relinquish, give; **ENACT:** legislate, establish; **EXCEED:** excel, transcend; **PROCEED:** progress, advance; **THROW:** toss, fling

passable *adj.* open, navigable, accessible

passage *n.* **JOURNEY:** voyage, crossing, trek; **PASSAGEWAY:** entrance, hall; **READING:** excerpt, section, portion, paragraph, quote

passenger *n.* traveler, commuter

passion *n.* feeling, craving, desire, emotion

passionate *adj.* excitable, tempestuous, impassioned, fervent, moving, inspiring, dramatic, stirring, eloquent, spirited, intense

passive *adj.* complacent, inert, lifeless, idle

passport *n.* pass, permit, visa, identification

password *n.* countersign, watchword, identification

past *adj.* former, preceding, foregoing, earlier

past *n.* antiquity, history

paste *n.* adhesive, cement, glue, mucilage

paste *v.* fasten, affix, patch, stick

pastime *n.* amusement, recreation, sport, hobby

pastor *n.* priest, rector, clergyman, minister

pastry *n.* dessert, delicacy

pasture *n.* grass, grazing, meadow, field

pat *v.* tap, touch, stroke, pet, rub

patch *n.* piece, bit, scrap, spot

patch *v.* repair, darn, mend

path *n.* trail, way, track, byway
pathetic *adj.* sad, touching, affecting, moving, pitiful
pathos *n.* pity, sorrow, grief
patience *n.* forbearance, fortitude, composure, endurance, perseverance, persistence
patient *adj.* submissive, forbearing, unruffled, imperturbable, passive, persevering, calm
patio *n.* porch, courtyard, square, yard
patriarch *n.* ruler, master, ancestor, chief
patriot *n.* statesman, nationalist, loyalist, chauvinist
patrol *v.* watch, walk, inspect, guard
patron *n.* protector, sponsor, benefactor, backer
patronize *v.* condescend, stoop, snub
pattern *n.* model, original, guide, copy
pause *n.* delay, respite, suspension, hiatus, interim, lapse, cessation, interval
pause *v.* STOP: halt, cease, interrupt, suspend; REFLECT: deliberate
pawn *v.* deposit, pledge, hock, sell
pay *n.* PROCEEDS: return, recompense, indemnity, reparation, settlement, reimbursement; WAGES: compensation, salary, remuneration, earnings
pay *v.* COMPENSATE: recompense, remunerate, repay, reimburse; RETURN: yield, profit, pay, dividends
payment *n.* REIMBURSEMENT: restitution, refund, reparation; INSTALLMENT: portion, part
peace *n.* ARMISTICE: pacification, conciliation, agreement; CALM: tranquillity, harmony, silence, stillness; COMPOSURE: contentment
peaceful *adj.* quiet, tranquil, serene, calm
peak *n.* summit, top, crown, zenith, height, summit
peasant *n.* laborer, farmer, worker, workman

peculiar *adj.* **UNUSUAL:** wonderful, singular, outlandish, strange; **UNIQUE:** characteristic, eccentric
peddle *v.* hawk, vend, trade, sell
pedestal *n.* base, stand, foundation, support
pedestrian *adj.* common, ordinary
peek *n.* sight, glimpse, glance, look
peek *v.* glance, peep, glimpse
peel *n.* skin, rind, husk, bark, shell
peel *v.* strip, skin, pare, flay, uncover
peep *v.* **CHIRP:** cheep; **PEEK:** glimpse, glance
peer *n.* equal, match, rival, companion
peer *v.* gaze, inspect, scrutinize
peeve *v.* irritate, annoy, anger, bother
peevish *adj.* cross, fretful, angry
pen *n.* cage, coop, sty, enclosure
pen *v.* **ENCLOSE:** confine; **WRITE:** compose
penalize *v.* chasten, castigate, punish
penalty *n.* punishment, fine, discipline
penance *n.* repentance, atonement, reparation
penchant *n.* inclination, taste, bias
pencil *v.* write, sketch, mark,
pendant *n.* locket, lavaliere, decoration, jewelry
pending *adj.* continuing, awaiting, ominous
penetrable *adj.* permeable, open, accessible, porous
penetrate *v.* pierce, perforate, puncture
penetrating *adj.* keen, astute, shrewd, sharp, intelligent, perceptive
penitentiary *n.* prison, reformatory, pen, jail
pension *n.* annuity, payment, allowance, retirement
perceive *v.* **OBSERVE:** note, look, notice; **UNDERSTAND:** comprehend, sense, grasp
perceptible *adj.* discernible, recognizable, obvious

perception *n.* judgment, understanding, apprehension, discernment, insight, observation
perceptive *adj.* alert, incisive, keen, observant
perch *v.* roost, land, rest, sit
peremptory *adj.* decisive, final, imperious, dictatorial
perfect *adj.* COMPLETE: absolute, whole; FAULTLESS: impeccable, immaculate, untainted, ideal, sublime, excellent; EXACT: precise, sharp, distinct, accurate
perfect *v.* finish, fulfill, realize, achieve, complete
perfectly *adj.* flawlessly, faultlessly, ideally
perforate *v.* bore, pierce, drill, slit, stab, penetrate
perforation *n.* break, aperture, slit, hole
perform *v.* ACCOMPLISH: do, achieve, fulfill, discharge, effect, complete, finish, realize; PRESENT: enact, show, exhibit, display, dramatize, execute
performance *n.* exhibition, appearance, offering, representation, revue, play, concert, drama
perfume *n.* scent, fragrance, aroma, odor
perhaps *adj.* maybe, possibly, conceivably, reasonably
perilous *adj.* precarious, unsafe, dangerous
perimeter *n.* boundary, margin, outline, border, edge
period *n.* EPOCH: era, age; END: limit, conclusion
periodical *adj.* rhythmic, regular, recurrent
periodical *n.* publication, magazine, newspaper
periphery *n.* circumference, perimeter, border
perish *v.* die, pass, depart
perjure *v.* prevaricate, falsify, lie
permanence *n.* continuity, durability, stability
permanent *adj.* fixed, enduring, abiding, continuing, lasting, imperishable, persevering, constant
permeate *v.* penetrate, pervade, saturate, fill
permissible *adj.* allowable, sanctioned, permitted

permission *n.* liberty, consent, license, authorization, approval, sanction, endorsement, affirmation

permit *n.* permission, warrant, license, grant

permit *v.* consent, sanction, tolerate, let, allow

perpetrate *v.* perform, commit, act, do

perpetual *adj.* **UNENDING:** continual, unceasing, constant, endless; **REPETITIOUS:** repeating, recurrent

perplex *v.* puzzle, confound, bewilder, confuse

perplexed *adj.* troubled, uncertain, bewildered

persecute *v.* oppress, harass, victimize, abuse

persecution *n.* torture, torment, teasing, provoking

perseverance *n.* grit, resolution, pluck, determination

persevere *v.* persist, remain, pursue, endure

persist *v.* persevere, pursue, strive, continue, endure

person *n.* individual, being, character, personage

personable *adj.* agreeable, pleasant, charming

personage *n.* someone, individual, person

personal *adj.* **PRIVATE:** secret, confidential; **INDIVIDUAL:** peculiar, particular, individual, special

personality *n.* **CHARACTER:** disposition, nature, temper, individuality; **CELEBRITY:** star, luminary

personify *v.* represent, symbolize, exemplify

personnel *n.* employees, workers, group, staff

perspective *n.* view, vista, aspect, attitude, outlook

persuade *v.* influence, induce, convince, cajole

persuasion *n.* **INFLUENCE:** inducing, enticing; **BELIEF:** creed, tenet, religion, faith

persuasive *adj.* convincing, influential, winning, enticing, compelling, potent, powerful, forceful, plausible

pertain *v.* belong, relate, refer, concern

pertinent *adj.* relevant, pertaining, related

perturb *v.* disturb, pester, worry, irritate, bother

pervade *v.* penetrate, spread, suffuse, permeate
perverse *adj.* deviant, wayward, delinquent, bad
perversion *n.* DISTORTION: deception, lie; CORRUPTION: depravity, wickedness, vice
pervert *v.* corrupt, ruin, vitiate, divert
pessimism *n.* unhappiness, gloom, sadness
pessimistic *adj.* DISCOURAGING: worrisome, troubling, dismal; CYNICAL: hopeless, gloomy, sad
pester *v.* annoy, harass, provoke, bother
pestilence *n.* disease, epidemic, sickness, illness
pet *n.* darling, lover, favorite, idol, adored
pet *v.* caress, fondle, cuddle, touch embrace
petition *n.* request, prayer, supplication, appeal
petrified *adj.* stone, hardened, mineralized, firm
petty *adj.* small, contemptible, insignificant, frivolous, trivial, unimportant
phantasm *n.* vision, illusion, specter
phenomenal *adj.* extraordinary, unique, remarkable
philanthropic *adj.* benevolent, humanitarian, kind
philosophic *adj.* thoughtful, reflective, cogitative, rational, profound, erudite, deep, learned
philosophy *n.* STUDY: wisdom, theory, explanation; PRINCIPLE: truth, axiom, conception, basis; BELIEF: outlook, view, position, opinion, viewpoint
phlegmatic *adj.* calm, sluggish, indifferent
phobia *n.* avoidance, aversion, hatred, resentment
phony *adj.* affected, imitation, artificial, false
photograph *n.* print, portrait, likeness, snapshot
photographic *adj.* accurate, detailed, exact, graphic
physical *adj.* material, corporeal, visible, tangible, palpable, substantial, real
physician *n.* healer, practitioner, surgeon, doctor

physique *n.* structure, build, constitution, body
pick *v.* **CHOOSE:** select, separate; **GATHER:** pluck, pull
picket *n.* **STAKE:** pole, post; **WATCHMAN:** guard, sentry
picket *v.* strike, blockade, boycott, protest
picture *n.* **REPRESENTATION:** view, photograph, image, portrait; **DESCRIPTION:** depiction, portrayal
picture *v.* **DEPICT:** sketch, portray, draw, paint, represent, describe; **IMAGINE:** create, conceive
picturesque *adj.* charming, pictorial, scenic, graphic, striking, arresting, quaint
piece *n.* part, portion, share, section
pierce *v.* penetrate, stab
piety *n.* reverence, devotion, devoutness, veneration
pigment *n.* coloring, paint, dye, color
pile *n.* heap, collection, mass, quantity
pile *v.* amass, stack, gather, accumulate, store
pilgrim *n.* traveler, wayfarer, wanderer, sojourner
pill *n.* tablet, capsule, pellet, medicine, drug
pillage *v.* plunder, loot, rob, destroy, steal
pillar *n.* **COLUMN:** pedestal, mast, shaft, post; **SUPPORT:** mainstay, prop
pillow *n.* cushion, pad, support, headrest
pilot *v.* guide, conduct, manage, lead
pin *v.* close, clasp, bind, fasten
pinnacle *n.* apex, zenith, crest, summit, climax
pious *adj.* reverent, devout, divine, holy, religious
pipe *n.* tube, conduit, culvert, duct
piracy *n.* robbery, theft, pillage, holdup
pirate *n.* plunderer, marauder, privateer, buccaneer
pit *n.* hole, abyss, cavity, depression
pitch *n.* **SLOPE:** slant, incline, angle, grade; **THROW:** toss, hurl, cast; **FREQUENCY:** tone, sound

pitfall *n.* snare, mesh, deadfall, trap
pith *n.* center, essence, heart, core
pitiful *adj.* sorry, mean, despicable, miserable, distressed, pathetic, pitiable, depressing
pity *n.* compassion, charity, tenderness, kindliness, benevolence, clemency, humanity, sympathy
pity *v.* **COMMISERATE:** sympathize, console, grieve, weep, comfort; **FORGIVE:** pardon, reprieve, spare
pivot *v.* turn, whirl, swivel, rotate
place *n.* **POSITION:** point, spot; **LOCALITY:** locus, site, area, region; **RANK:** status, position
place *v.* **PUT:** locate, deposit; **ARRANGE:** fix, order
placement *n.* situation, position, arrangement
plague *n.* pestilence, illness, epidemic
plague *v.* afflict, vex, disturb, trouble, irk, bother
plain *adj.* **OBVIOUS:** open, manifest, clear, understandable; **SIMPLE:** unadorned, unpretentious, modest; **ORDINARY:** everyday, commonplace; **BLUNT:** outspoken, candid, impolite, rude
plan *n.* **DRAFT:** diagram, design, schematic, drawing; **SCHEME:** project, idea, undertaking, plot, conspiracy, strategy; **ARRANGEMENT:** layout, disposition, order,
plan *v.* **SCHEME:** plot, devise, contrive, intrigue, conspire, calculate; **OUTLINE:** draft, sketch, map; **INTEND:** propose, think, expect
plane *n.* level, horizontal, flat
plane *v.* finish, smooth, level, flatten
planned *adj.* projected, budgeted, programmed
plantation *n.* farm, acreage, estate, ranch
plateau *n.* tableland, mesa, elevation, hill
platform *n.* **STAGE:** dais, rostrum, stand, terrace; **PROGRAM:** principles, policies

plausible *adj.* convincing, probable, credible, likely

play *n.* **AMUSEMENT:** enjoyment, diversion; **RECREATION:** games, sports; **THEATER:** drama, musical

play *v.* revel, carouse, gambol, cavort, participate

player *n.* athlete, contestant, actor, performer

playful *adj.* joking, whimsical, comical, funny

playmate *n.* comrade, neighbor, companion, friend

playwright *n.* writer, author, tragedian

plea *n.* appeal, request, supplication, pleading

plead *v.* **BEG:** implore, beseech, solicit, ask; **ARGUE:** present, allege, cite, declare

pleasant *adj.* affable, agreeable, obliging, charming, gracious, amiable, polite, civil, cordial, sociable

please *v.* gratify, delight, satisfy

pleasing *adj.* charming, agreeable, delightful, pleasant

pleasure *n.* enjoyment, delight, happiness, amusement, preference, desire

pledge *n.* security, surety, guarantee, agreement

pledge *v.* promise, swear, vow, vouch

plentiful *adj.* bountiful, prolific, profuse, lavish, extravagant, copious, abundant, abounding

plenty *n.* abundance, lavishness, deluge, torrent, bounty, profusion, flood, avalanche

pliable, pliant *adj.* flexible, limber, supple, plastic

plight *n.* condition, dilemma, state

plod *v.* trudge, hike, walk

plot *v.* **INTRIGUE:** frame, contrive, scheme, conspire; **PLAN:** sketch, outline, draft

plump *adj.* obese, stout, fleshy, fat

plunder *v.* seize, burn, steal, raid, ravage

plunge *v.* cast, fall, rush, dive, jump

plus *adj.* increase, additionally, surplus, extra

poach *v.* steal, filch, pilfer, smuggle
pocket *n.* CAVITY: hollow; POUCH: poke, sac
pocket *v.* take, conceal, hide, enclose, steal
poetic *adj.* lyrical, romantic, imaginative
poetry *n.* verse, rhythm, rhyme, poesy
poignant *adj.* penetrating, moving, touching
point *n.* POSITION: location, locality; PURPOSE: aim, object, intent; MEANING: force, drift, import
point *v.* INDICATE: show, name, denote; DIRECT: guide, steer, influence, lead
pointer *n.* INDICATOR: dial, gauge; HINT: clue, tip
pointless *adj.* DULL: prosaic, trivial, unnecessary; INEFFECTIVE: useless, impotent, incompetent, weak
poise *n.* carriage, bearing, grace, composure, dignity
poisonous *adj.* noxious, venomous, toxic, harmful
poke *v.* jab, punch, crowd, push,
policy *n.* principle, doctrine, scheme, design
polish *v.* smooth, burnish, finish, shine
polite *adj.* polished, mannerly, amiable, gracious, cordial, diplomatic, civil, sociable, respectful
politeness *n.* refinement, culture, civility, courtesy
poll *v.* sample, canvass, question, register, enroll, list
pollute *v.* soil, defile, stain, dirty
pollution *n.* dirt, grime, smog, sewage, garbage, waste, exhaust, pesticides, smoke
poltergeist *n.* ghost, spirit, apparition, specter, spook
pomp *n.* pageantry, magnificence, splendor
pompous *adj.* pretentious, arrogant, haughty, proud
ponder *v.* meditate, think, deliberate, consider
ponderous *adj.* weighty, dull, lifeless, heavy
pool *n.* WATER: puddle; STAKES: ante, pot, kitty
pool *v.* merge, unite, consolidate, combine, blend, join

poor *adj.* **INSOLVENT:** indigent, penniless, destitute, needy, starved, beggared, broke, **WEAK:** puny, feeble, infirm; **INFERIOR:** mediocre, trashy, shoddy, deficient, cheap, flimsy

pop *n.* **SODA:** beverage, seltzer, cola; **NOISE:** report, burst, shot, crack, detonation

poppycock *n.* drivel, nonsense, gibberish

populace *n.* people, multitudes, masses, people

popular *adj.* liked, favorite, beloved, celebrated, admired, famous, widespread

popularity *n.* acceptance, notoriety, prevalence

populated *adj.* inhabited, occupied, peopled, urban

population *n.* inhabitants, citizenry, populace, society

porous *adj.* absorbent, pervious, permeable

port *n.* harbor, haven, refuge, anchorage, dock

portable *adj.* movable, transportable, transferable

portal *n.* entrance, archway, gateway, opening

portend *v.* foretell, predict, herald

porter *n.* doorkeeper, custodian, caretaker

portfolio *n.* **CASE:** briefcase, folder; **ASSETS:** holdings, stocks, bonds

portion *n.* **PART:** scrap, fragment, piece; **ALLOTMENT:** share, quota

portrait *n.* likeness, painting, picture

portray *v.* draw, describe, depict, characterize

portrayal *n.* description, replica, likeness

pose *n.* position, attitude, affectation, pretense

pose *v.* **MODEL:** sit; **PRETEND:** profess, feign, act:

posh *adj.* rich, smart, comfortable

position *n.* **LOCATION:** whereabouts, bearings; **OPINION:** view, belief; **PROFESSION:** job, office, occupation; **STATION:** status, rank; **POSTURE:** carriage, bearing

positive *adj.* decisive, clear, emphatic, assertive, resolute, certain, confident, sure

possess *v.* have, hold, own, occupy, control, maintain

possessions *n.* belongings, effects, estate, property

possessor *n.* owner, holder, proprietor, occupant

possibility *n.* plausibility, feasibility, chance, hazard, hope, prospect

possible *adj.* likely, conceivable, imaginable

possibly *adv.* likely, maybe, perhaps, potentially

post *n.* column, pillar, pedestal, upright, mast

poster *n.* advertisement, sign, card, note

posterior *adj.* **SUBSEQUENT:** coming, after, succeeding, next, following, later; **BEHIND:** back

posterity *n.* eternity, descendants, children, offspring

postpone *v.* defer, table, delay, suspend, retard, withhold, shelve, adjourn, pause

postscript *n.* appendix, addition, supplement

posture *n.* **STANCE:** pose, carriage, aspect, presence; **ATTITUDE:** feeling, sentiment, disposition

pot *n.* **KITTY:** jackpot, ante; **CONTAINER:** vessel, kettle, pan, crock, receptacle, urn, bowl

potable *adj.* clean, fresh, unpolluted

potency *n.* **STRENGTH:** power, energy, vigor; **AUTHORITY:** influence, control, dominion, command

potential *adj.* possible, latent, implied, likely

pouch *n.* bag, sack, receptacle, container

pounce *v.* seize, spring, attack, bound, surge, jump

pound *v.* beat, crush, pulverize, strike, crush, hit

pour *v.* **FLOW:** discharge, emit, issue, drain, rush; **EMPTY:** spill, splash; **RAIN:** stream, flood, drench

poverty *n.* **DESTITUTION:** indigence, want, privation, insolvency; **LACK:** shortage, inadequacy, scarcity

power *n.* STRENGTH: vigor, stamina; AUTHORITY: jurisdiction, dominion, dominance, control, sway, sovereignty, supremacy; FORCE: compulsion, coercion, duress; ENERGY: horsepower, potential, dynamism

powerful *adj.* mighty, omnipotent, influential, authoritative, potent, forceful, compelling

powerless *adj.* helpless, feeble, weak, impotent, infirm

practical *adj.* useful, feasible, workable, rational, utilitarian, serviceable, efficient, effective

practically *adv.* effectively, virtually, nearly, almost

practice *n.* CUSTOM: usage; METHOD: mode, manner, fashion; REPETITION: exercise, rehearsal

practice *v.* drill, train, exercise, rehearse

practiced *adj.* skilled, able, experienced, trained

pragmatic *adj.* logical, sensible, practical, realistic

praise *v.* commend, applaud, acclaim, endorse, eulogize, compliment, celebrate, honor, glorify, extol

prance *v.* strut, caper, cavort, frisk, gambol, dance

prank *n.* trick, antic, game, escapade, caper, joke

pray *v.* ask, petition, plead, beseech, beg, implore

prayer *n.* appeal, request, petition, plea, entreaty,

preach *v.* lecture, teach, sermonize, discourse, exhort, moralize, talk, harangue, inform, address

preacher *n.* missionary, parson, evangelist, minister

preamble *n.* preface, prelude, introduction

precarious *adj.* uncertain, unsafe, risky, doubtful, dubious, dangerous, unstable

precaution *n.* care, prudence, anticipation, forethought, regard, foresight

precede *v.* lead, antedate, preface, introduce, herald

precedence *n.* superiority, preference, priority

preceding *adj.* foregoing, former, previous, earlier

precious *adj.* **VALUABLE:** costly, expensive; **BELOVED:** cherished, prized; **REFINED:** delicate, fragile, dainty

precipice *n.* cliff, crag, bluff, hill, mountain

precipitate *v.* cause, accelerate, press, hasten, speed

precipitous *adj.* sheer, steep, sharp, abrupt

precise *adj.* exact, accurate, definite, careful

precision *n.* exactness, correctness, accuracy

preconception *n.* prejudice, bias, assumption

predecessor *n.* forerunner, antecedent, ancestor

predicament *n.* difficulty, strait, plight, scrape, circumstance, mess, pinch, crisis

predict *v.* foretell, prophesy, prognosticate, divine

predominance *n.* dominance, supremacy, control

predominant *adj.* **SUPREME:** almighty, powerful; **FIRST:** transcendent, surpassing, superlative, principal

preeminent *adj.* distinguished, eminent, outstanding

preface *v.* introduce, commence, precede, begin

preference *n.* choice, election, option, selection, pick

preferred *adj.* chosen, selected, favored

prehistoric *adj.* ancient, primitive, antiquated, old

prejudice *n.* bias, inclination, partiality

prejudiced *adj.* predisposed, opinionated, partisan, narrow, intolerant, parochial, provincial

preliminary *adj.* preparatory, preceding, introductory

prelude *n.* introduction, preamble, prologue, preface

premature *adj.* rash, precipitate, untimely, early

premise *n.* supposition, assumption, proposition

premium *adj.* excellent, select, prime, superior

premium *n.* reward, prize, remuneration, bonus

premonition *n.* foreboding, portent, sign, warning

preoccupied *adj.* distracted, absorbed, engrossed, disturbed, troubled,

preparation *n.* **READYING:** rehearsal, anticipation, build-up; **PREPAREDNESS:** readiness, fitness, training, education; **MIXTURE:** compound, medicine, poultice

prepare *v.* **READY:** fix, fabricate, devise, anticipate, plan, arrange, make; **OUTFIT:** equip; **COOK:** concoct

prepossessing *adj.* winning, captivating, charming

prerequisite *n.* requirement, necessity, essential

prerogative *n.* privilege, advantage, exemption, right

prescription *n.* remedy, formula, medicine

presence *n.* **ATTENDANCE:** occupancy, residence, inhabitancy; **PROXIMITY:** nearness, closeness; **DEMEANOR:** appearance, behavior, carriage

present *adj.* now, existing, contemporary, immediate, instant, today, nowadays, already, current

present *n.* gift, grant, donation, offering

present *v.* **EXHIBIT:** do, act, perform; **BESTOW:** give, grant, confer donate, proffer, offer

presentable *adj.* proper, satisfactory, attractive

presently, *adv.* soon, directly, shortly, immediately

preservation *n.* protection, conservation, keeping, storage, curing, refrigeration

preserve *v.* **GUARD:** protect, shield; **KEEP:** process, cure

preside *v.* superintend, direct, lead, control, manage

press *n.* haste, urgency, rush, confusion, strain

pressing *adj.* important, urgent, demanding

pressure *n.* **TENSION:** burden, stress, squeeze; **PERSUASION:** compulsion, coercion

pressure *v.* press, compel, constrain, urge, persuade

prestige *n.* influence, reputation, fame, esteem

presume *v.* believe, consider, suppose, assume

presumption *n.* **ASSUMPTION:** conjecture, supposition; **IMPUDENCE:** arrogance, audacity, effrontery

pretend *v.* feign, affect, imitate, simulate, represent

pretense *n.* simulation, fabrication, imitation; deception, affectation, subterfuge, pretext

pretentious *adj.* presumptuous, arrogant, pompous

pretty *adj.* **ATTRACTIVE:** comely, lovely, beautiful; **PLEASANT:** delightful, cheerful, pleasing

prevalent *adj.* prevailing, common, widespread

prevent *v.* preclude, block, stop, thwart, halt, impede, check, frustrate, obstruct, inhibit, restrain, hinder

previous *adj.* former, antecedent, prior, preceding

prey *v.* hunt, spoil, pillage, loot, victimize

price *n.* expense, cost, worth, payment

price *v.* appraise, assess, rate, value

priceless *adj.* invaluable, inestimable, valuable

prick *v.* pierce, stick, cut, hurt, puncture

prickly *adj.* thorny, pointed, spiny, sharp

pride *n.* egotism, haughtiness, disdain, condescension

prim *adj.* exact, stiff, formal, demure, decorous, polite

primary *adj.* **EARLIEST:** primitive, first, original; **FUNDAMENTAL:** elemental, basic; **PRINCIPAL:** chief, prime, main

primitive *adj.* **SIMPLE:** rough, rude, fundamental; **ANCIENT:** primeval, old, beginning, uncivilized

primp *v.* dress, prepare, paint, powder

princely *adj.* lavish, sumptuous, luxurious, expensive, handsome, rich

principal *adj.* chief, leading, first, main, foremost, preeminent, dominant, prevailing

principle *n.* **FUNDAMENTAL:** law, origin, source, postulate; **BELIEF:** opinion, teaching, faith

prior *adj.* before, antecedent, foregoing, preceding

priority *n.* preference, precedence, advantage

prisoner *n.* captive, convict, detainee, hostage

privacy *n.* seclusion, solitude, isolation, aloofness, separation, concealment, secrecy

private *adj.* personal, separate, secluded, clandestine

privilege *n.* right, perquisite, prerogative, concession

prize *n.* reward, premium, bonus, booty, plunder, loot, award, medal, trophy, crown

probable *adj.* likely, seeming, presumable, feasible

problem *n.* DIFFICULTY: dilemma, quandary, obstacle; QUESTION: query, intricacy, enigma, puzzle

procedure *n.* fashion, mode, method, system, order

proceed *v.* move, progress, continue, advance

proceeding *n.* performance, undertaking, venture, happening, operation, procedure, exercise

proceeds *n.* gain, interest, yield, return

process *n.* operations, means, manner, method

process *v.* treat, ready, concoct, prepare

prod *v.* provoke, crowd, shove, push

produce *v.* CREATE: originate, conceive, design, devise, compose, invent; CAUSE: effect, occasion; MAKE: assemble, build, construct, manufacture;

product *n.* result, output, outcome

productive *adj.* rich, fruitful, prolific, fertile

profanity *n.* irreverence, abuse, cursing, swearing

profession *n.* CAREER: occupation, calling, avocation, vocation, position; DECLARATION: avowal, vow, oath

professional *adj.* skillful, expert, adept, able, qualified

professor *n.* teacher, educator, instructor, lecturer

proficiency *n.* learning, skill, knowledge, ability

proficient *adj.* adept, expert, skilled, skillful, able

profit *n.* gain, return, proceeds, remuneration

profitable *adj.* lucrative, beneficial, advantageous

profound *adj.* SCHOLARLY: learned, sagacious, intellectual; HEARTFELT: great, intense

program *n.* SCHEDULE: agenda, calendar, curriculum, plan, outline; ENTERTAINMENT: performance, show

progress *n.* headway, impetus, motion, improvement, advancement, development, growth

progressive *adj.* tolerant, lenient, open–minded

prohibit *v.* forbid, interdict, obstruct, prevent, ban

project *n.* plan, scheme, outline, design

projection *n.* BULGE: prominence, protuberance; FORECAST: prognostication, prediction, guess

prolong *v.* extend, lengthen, continue, increase

prominent *adj.* FAMOUS: notable, leading, distinguished; CONSPICUOUS: striking, noticeable

promiscuous *adj.* indiscriminate, unrestricted, lewd

promise *n.* agreement, pact, covenant, contract

promise *v.* pledge, declare, vow, swear, profess, guarantee, warrant, insure, underwrite, subscribe

promising *adj.* likely, encouraging, hopeful

promote *v.* further, encourage, help, aid, assist, support, back, champion, advocate, bolster, nourish, nurture, subsidize, boost, advance

prompt *adj.* timely, precise, punctual

prompt *v.* instigate, arouse, inspire, incite, urge

prone *adj.* disposed, inclined, predisposed, likely

pronounced *adj.* noticeable, clear, definite, obvious

pronouncement *n.* report, declaration, statement

proof *n.* verification, confirmation, substantiation, corroboration, testimony

propensity *n.* talent, capacity, ability, inclination

proper *adj.* decent, conventional, decorous, prudish: prim, precise, strait–laced

property *n.* possessions, belongings, assets, holdings
prophecy *n.* prediction, forecast, prognostication
prophesy *v.* foretell, predict, divine
prophet *n.* seer, oracle, soothsayer, astrologer
propitious *adj.* auspicious, encouraging, promising
proponent *n.* defender, advocate, champion, protector
proposal *n.* **OFFER:** overture, proposition, suggestion,
   PLAN: scheme, program, prospectus
propose *v.* offer, recommend, submit, volunteer
proposition *n.* offer, scheme, project, plan
propriety *n.* accordance, compatibility, congruity,
   modesty, dignity, pleasantness
prospect *n.* expectation, promise, outlook, possibility
prospective *adj.* promised, planned, proposed
prosper *v.* thrive, flourish, flower, succeed
protect *v.* shelter, shield, guard, preserve, defend
protection *n.* shield, screen, shelter, defense, safeguard, security, guaranty
protector *n.* champion, defender, patron, sponsor,
   benefactor, supporter, advocate
protest *n.* meeting, rally, demonstration, dissent
protest *v.* object, demur, disagree, oppose
proud *adj.* **DIGNIFIED:** stately, lordly; **EGOTISTICAL:**
   vain, vainglorious, haughty, arrogant
prove *v.* demonstrate, substantiate, authenticate, corroborate, validate, confirm, establish
provide *v.* furnish, equip, outfit, stock, supply
provincial *adj.* narrow, backward, rude, unpolished
provision *v.* requirement, stipulation, prerequisite
provisional *adj.* transient, passing, temporary
provoke *v.* **VEX:** irritate, aggravate, bother; **INCITE:**
   stir, rouse, arouse; **CAUSE:** make, produce, begin

prowl *v.* slink, lurk, rove, sneak

proxy *n.* agent, broker, representative, delegate

prudent *adj.* CAREFUL: cautious, circumspect, wary, discreet; PRACTICAL: sensible, wise, discerning

pry *v.* snoop, spy, nose, inquire, meddle

pseudo *adj.* imitation, quasi, sham, false

publication *n.* broadcasting, announcement, advisement, disclosure

publicize *n.* announce, broadcast, promulgate

publish *v.* DISTRIBUTE: print, issue; ADVERTISE: announce, promulgate, proclaim

pudgy *adj.* fat, chubby, chunky, stout

pull *n.* TOW: drag, haul; INFLUENCE: power, authority

pulpy *adj.* soft, smooth, thick, fleshy

pulse *n.* beating, pulsation, vibration, throb, beat

pun *n.* witticism, quip, joke

punch *v.* HIT: thrust, blow, strike, knock; PERFORATE: pierce, puncture, bore, penetrate, prick

punctual *adj.* prompt, precise, exact, meticulous

puncture *v.* pierce, prick, perforate, penetrate

punish *v.* correct, discipline, chasten, reprove, penalize, fine, incarcerate, chastise

puny *adj.* small, feeble, inferior, diminutive, weak

purchase *v.* obtain, acquire, buy

pure *adj.* UNMIXED: unadulterated, simple, clear, undiluted; CLEAN: immaculate, germ–free, sterilized, sanitary, refined; CHASTE: virginal, continent, celibate; ABSOLUTE: sheer, utter, complete

purge *v.* cleanse, evacuate, eliminate

purpose *n.* aim, intention, end, goal, mission, objective, expectation, intent, aspiration

pursue *v.* chase, seek, hound, track, stalk

push *n.* shove, force, bearing, propulsion, drive, exertion, weight, straining, inducement, reserve, impact, blow, pressure

push *v.* **PRESS:** thrust, shove, ram, jostle, elbow; **PROMOTE:** advance, launch, start, sell

put *v.* **PLACE:** set, plant, lodge, situate, deposit

putrid *adj.* rotten, corrupt, putrefied, decayed

puzzle *v.* **PERPLEX:** obscure, bewilder, complicate, confuse; **WONDER:** marvel, surprise, astonish

puzzling *adj.* **OBSCURE:** uncertain, ambiguous, mystifying; **DIFFICULT:** perplexing, abstruse, hard

quaint *adj.* odd, strange, fanciful, cute, whimsical

quake *v.* tremble, shrink, cower, shake

qualified *adj.* **LIMITED:** conditional, confined, restricted; **COMPETENT:** adequate, equipped, able

quality *n.* **ATTRIBUTE:** trait, endowment, condition, property; **CHARACTER:** nature, essence; **GRADE:** class, merit, worth, excellence, variety, rank

qualm *n.* scruple, suspicion, doubt, uncertainty

quantity *n.* amount, number, measure

quarantined *adj.* isolated, restrained, separated,

quarrel *v.* dispute, wrangle, contend, squabble, clash, bicker, contest, disagree, argue, feud, oppose

quarrelsome *adj.* factious, irritable, pugnacious, unruly, contentious, churlish, cantankerous

queasy *adj.* squeamish, sick, uneasy, uncomfortable

queer *adj.* odd, peculiar, strange, curious

question *v.* **ASK:** inquire, interrogate, petition, solicit, quiz, probe, investigate; **DOUBT:** challenge, dispute

questionable *adj.* **CONTROVERSIAL:** vague, unsettled, debatable, ambiguous, indefinite; **DUBIOUS:** disreputable, notorious, suspicious

quick *adj.* **RAPID:** swift, fleet, fast; **IMMEDIATE:** instantaneous, prompt; **HASTY:** impetuous, quick–tempered, rash; **ALERT:** ready, sharp, vigorous, active

quicken *v.* **HASTEN:** speed, hurry, accelerate, move, **EXPEDITE:** urge, promote

quiet *adj.* silent, calm, peaceful, hushed, muffled, noiseless, still, reserved, reticent

quiet *n.* **REST:** calm, tranquillity, relaxation, peace, repose; **SILENCE:** hush, stillness

quip *n.* retort, remark, jest, repartee, banter, language

quirk *n.* whim, caprice, fancy, peculiarity

quit *v.* **ABANDON:** surrender, renounce, relinquish; **CEASE:** discontinue, halt, desist, stop; **LEAVE:** go, depart, vacate, resign

quiver *v.* vibrate, shudder, wave, shiver, tremble

quiz *v.* question, examine, test, cross–examine, query

quote *v.* **EXCERPT:** extract, say, repeat; **PRICE:** request, demand, value

rabble *n.* crowd, mob, masses, riffraff, people

rabid *adj.* **FANATICAL:** obsessed, zealous; **INSANE:** raging, deranged, mad;

race *v.* hurry, run, tear, bustle, fly, dash, sprint

racket *n.* **UPROAR:** clatter, din, disturbance, noise, **CONSPIRACY:** scheme, corruption, crime, theft

racketeer *n.* criminal, extortionist, trickster

radial *adj.* branched, outspread, spreading

radiant *adj.* shining, luminous, radiating, bright

radiate *v.* spread, diffuse, disperse, disseminate

radiation *n.* fallout, pollution, radioactivity, heat

radical *adj.* **FUNDAMENTAL:** original, primitive, native, organic; **EXTREME:** progressive, militant, seditious, riotous, rebellious, revolutionary, heretical

raffle *n.* lottery, sweepstakes, pool

raft *n.* flatboat, barge, float, catamaran, boat

rag *n.* cloth, remnant, wiper, shred

rage *n.* **FURY:** frenzy, tantrum, uproar, storm, outburst; **FAD:** fashion, style, mode, vogue, craze, mania

rage *v.* rave, splutter, scream, bluster, storm, rant

ragged *adj.* tattered, frayed, frazzled, threadbare

raid *n.* attack, invasion, foray, assault, roundup

rain *v.* pour, drizzle, shower, sprinkle, mist, storm

raise *v.* **LIFT:** elevate, hoist, boost; **REAR:** breed, cultivate, produce; **ERECT:** construct, build

rake *n.* **RASCAL:** lecher, drunkard, scoundrel

rally *n.* gathering, meeting, celebration, session

ram *v.* butt, bump, collide, thrust, drive

ramble *v.* **SAUNTER:** stroll, roam, wander; **DRIFT:** stray, diverge, meander, digress

ramp *n.* incline, slope, grade, hill, inclination

rampant *adj.* raging, uncontrolled, violent, turbulent, tumultuous, unruly, unrestrained

rancid *adj.* unpleasant, tainted, stale, bad, rotten

random *adj.* aimless, haphazard, casual, unpredictable, irregular

range *n.* **SCOPE:** extent, area, expanse; **MOUNTAINS:** highlands; **DISTANCE:** reach, span, projection

range *v.* **VARY:** differ, fluctuate, diverge; **TRAVERSE:** wander, ramble, explore, traverse

rank *adj.* foul, smelly, fetid, putrid, stinking, rancid, offensive, noxious, gamy, disgusting, malodorous

rank *n.* **ROW:** column, file, string, line; **EMINENCE:** position, distinction, standing, status, ancestry

rank *v.* **ARRANGE:** assign, order; **EVALUATE:** judge, fix, valuate, classify

ransack v. SEARCH: rummage, scour, seek; LOOT: pillage, plunder, ravish, strip, rifle

rant v. rave, fume, rail, rage, yell

rap n. knock, thump, slap, blow

rapid adj. swift, speedy, accelerated, hurried, fast

rapt adj. awed, transported, entranced, enchanted

rapture n. delight, ecstasy, pleasure, satisfaction

rare adj. UNCOMMON: exceptional, singular, extraordinary, unusual; SCARCE: expensive, precious; CHOICE: select, superlative, excellent

rascal n. scoundrel, rogue, rake, knave, shyster, cad, scalawag, reprobate, miscreant

rash adj. hasty, impetuous, impulsive, foolish, heedless, foolhardy, brash

rasping adj. hoarse, grating, grinding, harsh

rate v. rank, judge, evaluate, grade

ratify v. substantiate, endorse, approve, sanction

rating n. grade, class, degree, rank

ration n. allowance, allotment, portion, quota, share

rational adj. LOGICAL: stable, thoughtful, sensible, impartial, objective, sober; REASONABLE: intelligent, sensible, wise; SANE: normal, lucid, responsible

rattle v. disconcert, bother, unnerve, confuse, disturb, embarrass

raucous adj. hoarse, harsh, loud, gruff, rough

ravage v. pillage, devastate, despoil, plunder, sack

rave v. TALK: babble, gabble, jabber; RAGE: storm, splutter, rail, rant

ravel v. untwist, disentangle, unsnarl, free, loosen

ravenous adj. voracious, starved, hungry

ravine n. hollow, gully, gorge, canyon, gulch, valley, gap, chasm, abyss, break, crevice, crevasse

raw *adj.* **UNFINISHED:** natural, crude, rough; **UN-TRAINED:** immature, inexperienced; **COLD:** biting, windy, bleak; **SCRAPED:** chafed, bruised

reach *n.* compass, range, scope, grasp, stretch, extension, orbit, horizon, gamut, ability, limit, extent

reach *v.* **EXTEND:** span, encompass, overtake; **STRETCH:** lunge, strain, seize; **ARRIVE:** gain, enter

react *v.* respond, reciprocate, behave, answer

reaction *n.* response, rejoinder, repercussion

read *v.* **UNDERSTAND:** comprehend, perceive, apprehend, grasp, learn; **INTERPRET:** decipher, explain, expound, construe

readable *adj.* **LEGIBLE:** distinct, comprehensible, decipherable; **INTERESTING:** absorbing, fascinating, engrossing, entertaining, engaging, stimulating

readily *adv.* quickly, promptly, eagerly, willingly

reading *n.* **INTERPRETATION:** commentary, translation; **EXCERPT:** passage, section, quotation

ready *adj.* **PREPARED:** alert, handy, expectant, available; **ENTHUSIASTIC:** eager, willing, ardent, zealous

real *adj.* **GENUINE:** authentic, original; **EXISTING:** actual, substantive, tangible

realism *n.* authenticity, naturalness, actuality, reality

realization *n.* understanding, comprehension, consciousness, awareness

realize *v.* **FULFILL:** complete, accomplish; **UNDERSTAND:** recognize, apprehend, discern; **OBTAIN:** receive get

realm *n.* kingdom, province, domain, sphere

rear *n.* back, hindmost, tail, posterior, rump, butt

reason *n.* **JUDGMENT:** intelligence, sanity; **LOGIC:** speculation, rationalism, analysis; **MOTIVE:** end, rationale, aim, intent; **MIND:** brain, mentality, intellect

reason v. THINK: reflect, deliberate, contemplate; ASSUME: suppose, gather, conclude; DISCUSS: persuade, argue, contend, debate

reasonable adj. RATIONAL: sane, conscious, sensible, unbiased; JUST: fair, right, honest; LIKELY: feasible, sound, plausible; MODERATE: inexpensive, fair, cheap

reassure v. console, comfort, encourage, guarantee

rebel n. revolutionary, agitator, insurgent, seditionist, malcontent, dissenter, renegade, radical

rebel v. rise, revolt, resist, mutiny, riot, oppose

rebellion n. insurrection, revolt, revolution

rebound v. recoil, reflect, ricochet, bounce

rebuke v. chide, reprove, condemn, reprimand

recede v. retreat, shrink, ebb, lower, abate, decline, drop, lessen, decrease, fall

receipt n. ACQUISITION: receiving, acceptance, arrival; VOUCHER: acknowledgment, notice, stub

receive v. ACCEPT: admit, inherit, acquire, obtain, secure; EXPERIENCE: undergo, suffer; WELCOME: accommodate, accept, greet

recent adj. modern, fresh, novel, contemporary, late

receptacle n. repository, holder, container

reception n. gathering, party, soiree, entertainment

receptive adj. alert, sensitive, perceptive, observant

recess n. ALCOVE: nook, cell, cubicle; SUSPENSION: intermission, interlude

recipe n. formula, compound, instructions, directions

recipient n. receiver, legatee, heir

recite v. render, enact, dramatize, interpret, soliloquize, narrate, recount, portray

reckless adj. heedless, thoughtless, wild, rash

reckon v. account, consider, evaluate, judge, estimate

reclaim *v.* recover, redeem, regain, mend, improve

recognition *n.* acknowledgment, verification, appreciation, esteem, attention, regard, honor

recognize *v.* DISTINGUISH: place, recall, remember, perceive;, ACKNOWLEDGE: appreciate, realize

recoil *v.* shrink, retreat, bounce, spring

recommend *v.* commend, praise, endorse, suggest, prescribe, urge, advise

reconcile *v.* ADJUST: adapt, arrange, regulate; HARMONIZE: pacify, mitigate, mediate, intercede

reconciliation *n.* conciliation, adjustment, agreement

record *n.* DOCUMENT: manuscript, account, history, deed; RECORDING: disk, phonograph, record, cut

record *v.* write, transcribe, catalogue, tabulate, chronicle, preserve

recover *v.* SALVAGE: redeem, rescue, reclaim; RALLY: convalesce, heal, mend, revive, recuperate

recreation *n.* pastime, amusement, relaxation

recuperate *v.* recover, convalesce, heal

recur *v.* return, reappear, happen, repeat

redecorate *v.* refurbish, refresh, restore, recondition, remodel, renovate, revamp

redeem *v.* RECOVER: repay, purchase, atone, compensate; SAVE: liberate, free, deliver, rescue

redemption *n.* regeneration, salvation, rebirth, rescue

redress *n.* compensation, payment, reparation

reduce *v.* LESSEN: dilute, diminish, decrease, lower; DEFEAT: conquer, overcome, subdue; HUMBLE: degrade, demote, abase, humiliate

redundant *adj.* superfluous, wordy, verbose, dull

referee *n.* arbitrator, umpire, conciliator, judge

reference *n.* allusion, mention, relation, implication

refine *v.* **PURIFY:** rarefy, strain, filter, clean, separate; **IMPROVE:** better, clarify, explain

refined *adj.* genteel, cultivated, polished, elegant, gracious, mannerly, courteous, polite

refinement *n.* **CULTURE:** cultivation, sophistication, breeding, enlightenment, scholarship, learning; **POLITENESS:** polish, manners, tact, civility, affability

reflect *v.* ponder, contemplate, concentrate, weigh, consider, think

reflection *n.* thought, consideration, contemplation, rumination, speculation, deliberation, meditation

reform *n.* reformation, betterment, improvement

reform *v.* revise, redeem, rectify, rehabilitate, remedy, restore, rebuild, reclaim, regenerate, amend, correct

refrain *v.* avoid, cease, forbear, abstain

refresh *v.* invigorate, animate, exhilarate, renew, replenish, restore

refuge *n.* shelter, sanctuary, retreat, haven

refugee *n.* exile, expatriate, fugitive, renegade, derelict, foundling, alien, outcast

refund *n.* return, reimbursement, repayment, remuneration, compensation, rebate, settlement

refuse *n.* rubbish, leavings, remains, residue, trash

refuse *v.* reject, decline, rebuff, spurn, deny

refute *v.* disprove, answer, deny

regain *v.* recapture, retrieve, reacquire, recover

regard *n.* **LOOK:** gaze, glance; **OPINION:** estimation, appreciation, affection, admiration

regard *v.* **OBSERVE:** notice, mark; **CONSIDER;** view, think; **RESPECT:** esteem, value, admire

regimentation *n.* organization, regulation, uniformity

region *n.* territory, area, realm, locale, domain, sphere

regress *v.* backslide, relapse, revert, retreat, sink

regret *n.* REMORSE: compunction, repentance, misgiving, qualm; GRIEF: pain, anxiety, sorrow

regret *v.* MOURN: lament, rue, repent, grieve, sorrow

regular *adj.* CUSTOMARY: conventional, usual; ORDERLY: methodical, precise, systematic, organized, consistent, rhythmic, periodic, measured

regularly *adv.* customarily, habitually, usually, commonly, ordinarily, normally

regulate *v.* CONTROL: rule, legislate, direct, govern, manage; ADJUST: adapt, standardize, rectify, correct

regulation *n.* rule, law, statute, ordinance, command

rehabilitate *v.* restore, reinstate, change, reestablish

reign *v.* rule, govern, manage

reimburse *v.* repay, compensate, refund

reinforce *v.* buttress, strengthen, support

reject *v.* REFUSE: repudiate, decline, renounce, deny; DISCARD: expel, eliminate

rejoice *v.* exult, enjoy, revel, celebrate

rejoinder *n.* answer, reply, rebuttal, refutation

rejuvenate *v.* reinvigorate, refresh, strengthen

relapse *v.* backslide, revert, regress, deteriorate, degenerate, weaken, sink

relate *v.* TELL: recount, recite, retell, describe, report; CONNECT: associate, correlate, compare

related *adj.* associated, linked, affiliated, akin, parallel, correlated, similar

relax *v.* slacken, repose, recline, unbend, rest

relaxed *adj.* untroubled, carefree, comfortable

relay *n.* communicate, transmit, deliver, carry, send

release *v.* liberate, acquit, loose, free

relent *v.* soften, comply, relax, yield

relentless *adj.* unmerciful, vindictive, hard, ruthless

relevance *n.* connection, pertinence, importance

relevant *adj.* pertinent, pertaining, applicable, related, concerning, connected

reliable *adj.* unimpeachable, trustworthy, reputable, irrefutable, incontestable, dependable, unfailing

reliance *n.* confidence, hope, faith, trust, dependence

relic *n.* vestige, trace, heirloom, antique, keepsake, memento, curiosity, token

relief *n.* **SOFTENING:** alleviation, comforting; **AID:** assistance, support, help, succor; **RELAXATION:** comfort, contentment, restfulness

relieve *v.* **REPLACE:** discharge, dismiss; **LESSEN:** ease, alleviate, allay, lighten, mitigate

religion *n.* **FAITH:** belief, persuasion, theology, doctrine, communion, piety

religious *adj.* **DEVOUT:** pious, sanctimonious, reverential; **SCRUPULOUS:** methodical, thorough, careful

relish *v.* fancy, like, enjoy

reluctance *n.* unwillingness, disinclination, qualm, hesitation, doubt

remain *v.* **STAY:** inhabit, stop, settle; **ENDURE:** prevail, continue; **SURVIVE:** outlive, outlast

remainder *n.* residue, remains, remnant, dregs, surplus, leavings, excess, scrap, fragment, salvage

remark *v.* say, state, speak, mention, observe

remarkable *adj.* exceptional, extraordinary, unusual

remedy *v.* help, aid, heal, counteract, repair, cure

remember *v.* **RECALL:** recollect, reminisce; **MEMORIZE:** learn, master, retain

remembrance *n.* **MEMORY:** recollection, recognition, reminder; **GIFT:** reward, token, keepsake

remind *v.* hint, caution, mention, prompt, prod, stress, emphasize, note, warn

remit *v.* transmit, pay, tender, forward

remnant *n.* remainder, residue, leavings, dregs

remodel *v.* renovate, refurbish, redecorate, modernize

remorse *n.* anguish, guilt, compunction, contrition, grief, regret

remote *adj.* **DISTANT:** removed, secluded, isolated; **ANCIENT:** aged, old; **SEPARATED:** unrelated, irrelevant

removal *n.* dismissal, discharge, expulsion, exile, deportation, banishment, elimination, ejection

rend *v.* tear, burst, rip, sever, sunder, break

rendition *n.* interpretation, translation, version

renew *v.* refresh, regenerate, rehabilitate, invigorate, restore, freshen, stimulate

renounce *v.* disown, disavow, deny, discard

renovate *v.* remake, rehabilitate, renew

rent *n.* **LEASE:** lend, sublet; **HIRE:** charter, engage

reorganize *v.* renovate, regenerate, reconstruct

repair *v.* restore, fix, correct, refurbish, mend

reparation *n.* amends, compensation, indemnity, retribution, payment

repay *v.* **REIMBURSE:** recompense, refund, indemnify, compensate; **RETALIATE:** reciprocate, revenge

repeal *v.* revoke, abrogate, annul, abolish, cancel

repeat *v.* iterate, echo, recite, recapitulate

repel *v.* **REBUFF:** resist, oppose, repulse; **OFFEND:** revolt, disgust; **REJECT:** disown, dismiss, refuse

repentance *n.* sorrow, remorse, self–reproach, regret

repentant *adj.* penitent, regretful, contrite, sorry

repetition *n.* recurrence, duplication, renewal, reiteration, wordiness

repetitious *adj.* boring, wordy, repeating, dull
replace *v.* substitute, supplant, restore, reinstate
replenish *v.* refill, restock, renew
replica *n.* copy, likeness, model, duplicate, imitation
reply *v.* answer, retort, rejoin, return
report *v.* narrate, recount, inform, advise, relate, tell
reporter *n.* journalist, newsman, correspondent
represent *v.* DEPICT: render, portray, enact, symbolize, describe; IMITATE: substitute, impersonate
representative *n.* emissary, deputy, agent, delegate, congressman, deputy, diplomat
repress *v.* check, restrain, control, curb, hinder
reprieve *n.* delay, respite, suspension
reprimand *v.* reprove, rebuke, chide, reproach, denounce, criticize, scold
reproach *v.* censure, upbraid, condemn, scold, blame
reproduce *v.* COPY: duplicate, mimeograph; REPEAT: recreate, re–enact, relive, mirror, echo; MULTIPLY: procreate, breed, propagate
reproduction *n.* copy, imitation, print, blowup
repudiate *v.* reject, retract, repeal, revoke, abandon
repulse *v.* resist, repel, rebuff, spurn, snub
repulsive *adj.* offensive, disgusting: odious, forbidding, horrid
reputable *adj.* distinguished, celebrated, honorable, trustworthy, honest, worthy, brave, noble
reputation *n.* character, honor, standing, prestige, prominence, eminence, notoriety
request *v.* ask, solicit, beseech, entreat, sue, beg
require *v.* NEED: want; DEMAND: exact, expect
requirement *n.* PREREQUISITE: condition, provision, stipulation, qualification; NEED: necessity, demand

rescue *v.* **SAVE:** recover, redeem, salvage, retrieve; **FREE:** deliver, liberate, release

research *n.* search, investigation, analysis, experimentation, examination, study

resemblance *n.* likeness, correspondence, coincidence, similarity

resentment *n.* annoyance, irritation, anger

reserve *n.* **SECURITY:** savings, insurance, resources, provisions, assets, hoard; **CALM:** caution, restraint, reticence, inhibition, demureness

reserve *v.* retain, keep, possess, have, hold, own

reserved *adj.* **BOOKED:** saved, claimed, held; **WITHHELD:** preserved, conserved; **RESTRAINED:** composed, sedate, collected, serene, placid

reservoir *n.* supply, store, reserve, pool, cistern

reside *v.* dwell, live, stay, lodge, occupy

residence *n.* habitation, quarters, apartment, home

residue *n.* remainder, leavings, scraps, shavings

resign *v.* **RELINQUISH:** yield, surrender, capitulate, abandon, submit; **QUIT:** retire, leave

resigned *adj.* quiet, peaceable, docile, submissive, yielding, relinquishing, obedient, passive

resilient *adj.* rebounding, elastic, springy, flexible

resist *v.* oppose, endure, bear, persist, suffer, abide, persevere, last, repel

resolute *adj.* constant, determined, steadfast, firm

resolution *n.* **DETERMINATION:** fortitude, perseverance, resolve; **PROPOSAL:** recommendation, declaration

resolve *v.* decide, determine, conclude, decree

resource *n.* reserve, support, means, stratagem

resourceful *adj.* ingenious, capable, active, intelligent

resources *n.* means, money, riches, assets, capital,

property, reserve, wealth

respect *n.* regard, relation, esteem, honor, admiration

respectable *adj.* presentable, tolerable, passable, virtuous, honorable

respectful *adj.* deferential, courteous, reverent, attending, venerating, deferring, polite

respite *n.* delay, postponement, reprieve, pause, delay

respond *v.* reply, rejoin, acknowledge, answer

response *n.* reply, rejoinder, acknowledgment, answer

responsibility *n.* STABILITY: loyalty, faithfulness, competence, honesty; DUTY: obligation, trust

responsible *adj.* ACCOUNTABLE: liable, obligated, obliged, pledged, bound, answerable; ABLE: reliable, capable, dutiful, dependable, competent

rest *n.* REPOSE: quiet, slumber, peacefulness, relaxation, doze, nap, respite; REMAINDER: residue, surplus, remnant, balance; CESSATION: intermission, interval, inactivity, pause, recess

restful *adj.* tranquil, calm, peaceful, quiet, serene, soothing, relaxing, refreshing

restitution *n.* restoration, amends, compensation

restless *adj.* fidgety, jumpy, nervous, uneasy, agitated, unsettled, restive, impatient, jittery

restore *v.* RETURN: replace; RECREATE: revive, recover, renew; REBUILD: reconstruct, rehabilitate, repair; HEAL: refresh, cure

restrain *v.* curb, bridle, rein, regulate, muzzle, inhibit, deter, hamper, restrict, gag, limit, contain, check

restraint *n.* SELF—CONTROL: reserve, reticence, forbearance, abstinence, abstention; LIMITATION: hindrance, restriction, impediment

restrict *v.* limit, circumscribe, contract, shorten

restricted *adj.* limited, confined, hampered, bridled, blocked, barred, decreased, diminished, reduced

result *n.* consequence, outcome, aftermath, upshot, settlement, determination, payoff, end

resurrection *n.* transformation, rebirth, renewal

retain *v.* **HOLD:** grasp, clutch; **EMPLOY:** maintain, engage, hire; **REMEMBER:** recall, recollect, recognize

retaliate *v.* repay, requite, return, revenge

retard *v.* hinder, postpone, delay, impede

retire *v.* **LEAVE:** withdraw, part, retreat; **REST:** sleep; **RESIGN:** relinquish

retort *n.* reply, counter, repartee, response, answer

retort *v.* reply, rejoin, answer

retraction *n.* denial, revocation, cancellation

retreat *n.* refuge, sanctuary, port, haven, resort

retreat *v.* withdraw, depart, reverse, backtrack, leave

retribution *n.* punishment, reprisal, retaliation

retrieve *v.* recover, regain, reclaim

return *n.* **HOMECOMING:** arrival, reappearance; **RESTORATION:** restitution, recompense; **PROCEEDS:** profit, income, results, gain, revenue, yield, interest

return *v.* **REAPPEAR:** recur, repeat, revive, rebound; **REINSTATE:** restore, replace; **ANSWER:** reply, respond, retort; **REPAY:** reimburse, recompense, refund; **YIELD:** interest, profit

reveal *v.* disclose, publish, betray, announce, declare

revelation *n.* **DISCLOSURE:** discovery, announcement, betrayal; **WORD:** truth, apocalypse, doctrine, faith

revenge *n.* retaliation, reprisal, retribution

revenue *n.* income, return, earnings, yield, receipts, proceeds, profits

reverence *n.* veneration, respect, admiration, regard,

esteem, adoration, praise

reverse *n.* **OPPOSITE:** converse, contrary; **DEFEAT:** vanquishment, downfall, annihilation

review *v.* **CORRECT:** criticize, revise; **INSPECT:** examine, analyze, check

revise *v.* improve, correct, reconsider, rewrite, edit

revival *n.* renewal, rebirth, resurrection, restoration, freshening, awakening

revive *v.* enliven, refresh, renew, resuscitate, invigorate; freshen, rouse, arouse, strengthen

revoke *v.* annul, reverse, recall, retract, cancel

revolt *n.* rebellion, uprising, mutiny, revolution

revolting *adj.* awful, loathsome, repulsive, offensive

revolutionary *adj.* **REBELLIOUS:** mutinous, insurgent, subversive; **NOVEL:** new, unusual, advanced, forward

revolve *v.* roll, spin, rotate, twirl, turn

reward *n.* **PAYMENT:** compensation, remuneration, pay, recompense; **PRIZE:** premium, bonus, award

rhythmic *adj.* measured, balanced, regular

rich *adj.* **WEALTHY:** moneyed, affluent; **SUMPTUOUS:** luxurious, magnificent, resplendent, lavish, ornate, splendid, elegant; **FERTILE:** lush, fruitful, luxuriant

riches *n.* wealth, fortune, possessions, money

rickety *adj.* infirm, shaky, fragile, weal

ricochet *v.* carom, rebound, reflect, bounce

rid *v.* clear, relieve, shed, free

riddle *n.* enigma, puzzle, dilemma, complexity

ride *n.* excursion, drive, trip, transportation, journey

rider *n.* addition, codicil, addendum, amendment, appendix, supplement

ridicule *v.* mock, gibe, scoff, sneer, taunt, mimic, deride, scorn, caricature, satirize

ridiculous *adj.* absurd, ludicrous, preposterous, funny, unusual

rig *n.* tackle, apparatus, gear, equipment

right *adj.* **CORRECT:** precise, accurate, exact, factual, true, valid; **JUST:** lawful, legitimate, honest, fair

right *n.* **PREROGATIVE:** immunity, exemption, license; **JUSTICE:** equity, fairness

right *v.* correct, repair, restore, remedy, rectify, mend

righteous *adj.* **VIRTUOUS:** just, honorable, exemplary, noble, trustworthy, ethical, impartial; **RELIGIOUS:** devout, pious, saintly, angelic, devoted, reverent, spiritual, holy

rightful *adj.* proper, just, honest, fair, legal

rigid *adj.* **STIFF:** unyielding, inflexible, solid, firm; **STRICT:** exact, rigorous, severe; **FIXED:** set, unmoving, definite, determined

rigorous *adj.* harsh, austere, uncompromising, severe

rim *n.* margin, edge, border, verge, brim, lip, brink

rind *n.* covering, skin, peel, hull, shell

ring *n.* **CIRCLE:** circlet, girdle, rim; **JEWELRY:** band, signet, bracelet; **GROUP:** party, bloc, faction, group, gang, band; **SOUND:** clangor, jangle

rinse *v.* cleanse, clean, flush, dip, soak, wash

riot *n.* uproar, tumult, confusion, disorder, disturbance, protest

rip *v.* divide, tear, cut, rend, split, cleave, rive, shred

ripe *adj.* matured, grown, developed

ripen *v.* develop, evolve, advance, grow

rise *v.* **ASCEND:** mount, climb, scale; **HEIGHTEN:** grow, enlarge, extend, raise; **BEGIN:** spring, emanate, issue; **IMPROVE:** prosper, flourish, thrive; **SWELL:** inflate, billow, bulge

risk *n.* **DANGER:** hazard, peril, jeopardy; **CHANCE:** contingency, prospect, uncertainty

risky *adj.* perilous, precarious, hazardous, dangerous

rite *n.* ceremony, observance, service, ritual, custom

rival *n.* competitor, antagonist, opponent

rival *v.* approach, match, equal

rivalry *n.* competition, contention, opposition, dispute

roam *v.* ramble, range, meander, saunter, traipse

rob *v.* burglarize, plunder, defraud, cheat, pilfer, purloin, filch, embezzle, pillage, sack, loot

robbery *n.* burglary, larceny, thievery

robust *adj.* vigorous, husky, hale, hearty, sound

rock *v.* totter, sway, reel, quake, convulse, tremble

rogue *n.* knave, outlaw, miscreant, criminal

roll *n.* **LIST:** register, index, record; **BREAD:** pastry, bun; **ROTATION:** turn, revolution

roll *v.* rotate, circle, turn, revolve, spin

romantic *adj.* poetic, fanciful, chivalrous, courtly

romp *v.* play, skip, gambol, celebrate, frolic

room *n.* **SPACE:** vastness, sweep, extent; **OPENING:** place, vacancy; **QUARTERS:** lodgings, apartment

roomer *n.* lodger, occupant, dweller, renter, tenant

rooted *adj.* grounded, based, fixed, firm

rosy *adj.* promising, optimistic, favorable, cheerful

rot *n.* **DECAY:** decomposition, corruption, disintegration, **NONSENSE:** trash, silliness, foolishness

rotate *v.* turn, twist, wheel, revolve, move

rotation *n.* turn, circumrotation, circle, revolution

rotten *adj.* **SPOILED:** putrefying, decaying, rancid; **UNSOUND:** defective, impaired, weak; **CORRUPT:** contaminated, polluted, tainted, defiled, dirty

rough *adj.* **UNEVEN:** irregular, bumpy, jagged, coarse;

SEVERE: harsh, strict, stern; **CRUDE:** boorish, uncivil, uncultivated, rude; **TURBULENT:** buffeting, stormy, tumultuous; **UNFINISHED:** incomplete, imperfect; **APPROXIMATE:** inexact, unprecise, uncertain

round *adj.* **SPHERICAL:** circular, globular, cylindrical; **CURVED:** arched, rounded, bowed, curled

rouse *v.* **WAKEN:** arouse, raise, awaken; **STIMULATE:** urge, stir, provoke, animate, excite

routine *adj.* usual, customary, conventional, habitual

rove *v.* walk, meander, wander, roam

row *n.* line, series, order, file

rowdy *adj.* noisy, rebellious, mischievous, unruly

royal *adj.* **REGAL:** imperial, sovereign, supreme, noble; **STATELY:** dignified, majestic, courtly, aristocratic, lordly, imposing, resplendent

rub *v.* stroke, smooth, scrape, scour, polish

rubbish *n.* waste, debris, nonsense, litter, trash

rude *adj.* **BOORISH:** loutish, brutish, uncouth, vulgar, ribald; **HARSH:** gruff, abusive, brazen, audacious, hostile, insensitive, rough, violent; **COARSE:** rough, unrefined, unpolished, crude; **PRIMITIVE:** ignorant, uncivilized, barbarous

ruffle *v.* **DISARRANGE:** rumple, tousle; **ANGER:** irritate, fret, bother, agitate

rug *n.* mat, carpet, carpeting, linoleum

rugged *adj.* **ROUGH:** uneven, hilly, broken, mountainous; **STRONG:** vigorous, hale, sturdy, hardy, healthy

ruin *v.* **DESTROY:** demolish, wreck, ravage; **BANKRUPT:** impoverish, beggar

ruins *n.* remains, debris, wreckage, destruction

rule *v.* govern, control, dictate, manage, regulate

ruling *n.* order, decision, precept, law

rumble *n.* reverberation, resounding, roll, noise
rumor *n.* report, gossip, tidings, hearsay, tale
rumple *v.* wrinkle, crumple, crush, fold
run *n.* **SPRINT:** pace, bound, flow, amble, gallop, canter, lope, spring, trot, dart, rush, dash, flight, escape, break, charge, swoop, race, scamper, tear, whisk, fall, drop, **SERIES:** continuity, succession, sequence, **SCORE:** record, tally, point, **AVERAGE:** par, norm, **COURSE:** way, route, field, track
run *v.* **FLOW:** pour, tumble, drop, melt; **RUSH:** hurry, scurry, scramble, dash, speed, scamper, scuttle; **FUNCTION:** move, work, go; **MANAGE:** control, govern; **CONTINUE:** last, persevere
runoff *n.* drainage, surplus, flow, water
rupture *v.* break, burst, crack, tear
rural *adj.* country, rustic, agrarian, suburban
rush *n.* haste, dash, charge, hurry
rut *n.* **GROOVE:** hollow, trench, furrow, track; **HABIT:** custom, course, routine, practice
ruthless *adj.* cruel, savage, brutal, merciless, fiendish, unmerciful, ferocious, vengeful, barbarous
sabotage *v.* subvert, undermine, attack, destroy
sack *v.* plunder, ravage
sacrifice *n.* **OFFERING:** tribute, atonement; **LOSS:** discount, deduction, reduction
sacrifice *v.* forfeit, forgo, relinquish, yield, renounce
sad *adj.* **UNHAPPY:** downcast, gloomy, sorrowful, glum, dispirited, depressed, melancholy, blue; **PITIABLE:** disheartening, discouraging, dreary, disquieting
safe *adj.* **SECURE:** protected, guarded, shielded, sheltered; **INNOCENT:** innocuous, harmless; **RELIABLE:** trustworthy, dependable, competent

safe *n.* chest, strongbox, coffer, repository, vault, case

sag *v.* sink, settle, stoop, bend, lean

saint *n.* paragon, martyr, altruist, believer

salary *n.* wages, recompense, payroll, pay

sale *n.* **COMMERCE:** traffic, exchange, barter, trade; **DEAL:** transaction, purchase, auction, disposal; **CLEARANCE:** bargain, reduction, unloading

salute *v.* greet, recognize, praise

salvage *v.* save, retrieve, recover, regain

salvation *n.* deliverance, liberation, emancipation, rescue, safeguard, assurance

same *adj.* equivalent, identical, corresponding, equal

sample *v.* try, examine, taste, test, experiment

sanction *v.* approve, confirm, authorize, countenance

sanctuary *n.* **CHURCH:** shrine, temple; **SHELTER:** refuge, asylum, resort, haven

sane *adj.* rational, normal, lucid, sober, sound, balanced, sensible, reasonable, wise

sanitary *adj.* hygienic, wholesome, sterile, healthful

sap *n.* **FLUID:** secretion, essence, liquid; **DUPE:** dolt, gull, simpleton, fool

sarcastic *adj.* scornful, mocking, ironical, satirical, taunting, derisive, sneering, snickering, cynical

satire *n.* irony, sarcasm, mockery, ridicule, caricature

satisfaction *n.* **GRATIFICATION:** fulfillment, achievement; **COMFORT:** pleasure, contentment, serenity

satisfy *v.* please, delight, amuse, entertain, gladden, gratify, indulge, humor, fascinate, fill

saturate *v.* soak, overfill, drench, steep, immerse

savage *adj.* **PRIMITIVE:** crude, simple; **CRUEL:** barbarous, inhuman, brutal; **WILD:** untamed, uncivilized, uncultured, uncontrolled

save *v.* DELIVER: rescue, extricate, liberate, ransom, redeem; HOARD: collect, store, accumulate, gather; PRESERVE: conserve, keep

savor *v.* partake, enjoy, relish, appreciate, like

say *v.* utter, speak, state, announce, declare, assert

saying *n.* aphorism, maxim, proverb, adage

scaffold *n.* platform, gallows, framework, structure

scald *v.* burn, steam, char, blanch, parboil

scale *v.* MOUNT: climb, ascend, surmount; MEASURE: compare, balance, compute

scamper *v.* hasten, speed, haste, hurry, run

scan *v.* examine, scrutinize, browse, consider, look

scandal *n.* gossip, slander, defamation, gossip

scanty *adj.* scarce, meager, small, inadequate, thin, skimpy, sparse, diminutive

scarcity *n.* deficiency, inadequacy, insufficiency, lack

scare *v.* panic, terrify, alarm, frighten

scatter *v.* DISPERSE: disband, spread; DIFFUSE: dispel, dissipate, strew, distribute; WASTE: dissipate, spend

scene *n.* occurrence, spectacle, view, display

scenic *adj.* beautiful, spectacular, dramatic

scent *v.* smell, perfume, odor, fragrance, redolence

scheme *v.* plan, contrive, intrigue, devise

scholarly *adj.* erudite, cultured, studious, learned

schooling *n.* education, learning, nurture, discipline

scientific *adj.* ACCURATE: precise, exact, clear, objective; LOGICAL: deductive, methodical, sound

scoff *v.* mock, deride, jeer, ridicule

scold *v.* chide, admonish, rebuke, censure, reprove, reprimand, criticize, denounce, chasten

scoot *v.* run, dart, speed, rush, hasten, hurry

scope *n.* range, reach, field, extent

scorching *adj.* fiery, searing, sweltering, burning, hot
score *n.* tally, reckoning, account, summary
score *v.* **COMPOSE:** orchestrate, arrange, adapt; **PURCHASE:** get, procure, secure, buy
scorn *v.* refuse, despise, disdain
scornful *adj.* contemptuous, disdainful, haughty
scoundrel *n.* rogue, scamp, villain, rascal
scour *v.* scrub, cleanse, rub, clean, wash
scowl *v.* frown, glower, disapprove, grimace
scramble *v.* **MIX:** combine, blend, beat; **CLIMB:** clamber, push, struggle
scrap *n.* **TRASH:** junk, waste, cuttings, chips; **BIT:** fragment, particle, piece, morsel; **FIGHT:** quarrel, brawl, squabble
scrape *v.* rub, abrade, scour, rasp
scratch *v.* wound, hurt, cut, mark, injure, scar
scrawl *v.* write, scribble, scratch, doodle
scrawny *adj.* lean, lanky, gaunt, thin
scream *v.* shriek, screech, squeal, cry, yell
screen *v.* **HIDE:** veil, conceal, mask, shelter; **CHOOSE:** select, eliminate
screwy *adj.* odd, crazy, inappropriate, insane, wrong
scribble *n.* scrawl, scrabble, scratch, handwriting
scrub *v.* rub, cleanse, scour, clean, wash
scrupulous *adj.* exact, punctilious, strict, careful
scrutinize *v.* examine, view, study, stare, watch
scrutiny *n.* analysis, inspection, examination
scuffle *n.* struggle, shuffle, strife, fight
sealed *adj.* secured, fixed, firm, tight
seam *n.* joint, union, stitching, closure, suture
sear *v.* dry, scorch, brown, toast, cook
search *v.* seek, examine, rummage, hunt, quest

seasonal *adj.* periodically, biennial, annual, yearly

seasoned *adj.* **SPICY:** tangy, sharp, aromatic; **EXPERIENCED:** established, settled, mature, able

seated *adj.* situated, located, established, rooted, set

secede *v.* withdraw, retract, leave, retreat

seclude *v.* screen, conceal, cover, hide

seclusion *n.* solitude, aloofness, privacy, retirement

secondary *adj.* **DERIVED:** dependent, subsequent, subsidiary, subordinate; **MINOR:** inconsiderable, petty, small, trivial, unimportant

secondhand *adj.* used, reclaimed, borrowed, derived

secrecy *n.* concealment, hiding, seclusion, privacy, mystery, dark, darkness, isolation, reticence, stealth

secret *adj.* unknown, mysterious, arcane, cryptic, occult, mystical, veiled, obscure, shrouded, hidden, concealed, clandestine, underhanded, stealthy

secretary *n.* **ASSISTANT:** clerk, typist, stenographer, correspondent; **OFFICER:** director, executive

secrete *v.* **HIDE:** conceal, cover, disguise; **EMIT:** discharge, produce, exude

secretive *adj.* reticent, taciturn, undercover, reserved

sector *n.* section, district, quarter, area, division

secure *adj.* **SAFE:** guarded, defended; **SELF–CONFIDENT:** assured, determined, confident

secure *v.* **FASTEN:** bind, tighten; **OBTAIN:** achieve, acquire, grasp, get

security *n.* guarantee, token, pawn, pledge, collateral, bail, warranty, convenant, agreement, hostage

sediment *n.* dregs, silt, grounds, residue

see *v.* **PERCEIVE:** observe, regard, view, gaze, detect, notice, contemplate; **UNDERSTAND:** comprehend, discern, recognize; **WITNESS:** observe, regard

seek *v.* search, delve, dig, ransack, look, sniff, prowl
seem *v.* appear, look, resemble, show
seep *v.* percolate, trickle, leak, flow, drain
seethe *v.* boil, simmer, stew
segment *n.* part, portion, section, fragment, division
segregate *v.* separate, isolate, sever, divide
seize *v.* **GRASP:** take, catch, grip, grab, clutch, snatch; **CAPTURE:** conquer, overwhelm, apprehend, arrest; **UNDERSTAND:** comprehend, perceive
seizure *n.* spasm, spell, convulsion, breakdown, fit
seldom *adv.* rarely, infrequently, occasionally, uncommonly, scarcely, hardly
select *v.* pick, decide, elect, choose
selective *adj.* discriminating, judicious, particular
self–conscious *n.* unsure, uncertain, shy, doubtful
self–control *n.* poise, restraint, reserve, discretion, stability, dignity, constraint
self–esteem *n.* pride, vanity, haughtiness, egotism
self–evident *n.* obvious, plain, visible, apparent
self–restraint *n.* patience, endurance, control
sell *v.* market, vend, barter, exchange, trade, bargain, peddle, retail, wholesale, contract, retail
seller *n.* dealer, tradesman, salesman, retailer, agent, vender, merchant, auctioneer, shopkeeper, peddler, trader, marketer, storekeeper
sellout *n.* betrayal, deception, deal, trick
semblance *n.* resemblance, aspect, appearance
send *v.* **DISPATCH:** convey, ship, post, convey; **BROADCAST:** transmit, relay
senile *adj.* aged, infirm, feeble, old, sick
senior *adj.* older, elder, higher, superior
seniority *n.* standing, ranking, station

sensation *n.* consciousness, perception, feeling

sensational *adj.* **FASCINATING:** exciting, marvelous, incredible, impressive; **MELODRAMATIC:** exaggerated, excessive, emotional

sense *n.* **SENSATION:** feeling, touch, sight, hearing, taste, smell; **INTELLECT:** perception, reason, cleverness, knowledge, thought; **REASONABLENESS:** judgment, discretion, fairness; **INSIGHT:** tact, understanding, discernmen

senseless *adj.* ridiculous, silly, foolish, illogical, stupid

sensible *adj.* reasonable, prudent, perceptive, careful, aware, capable, rational, intelligent

sensitive *adj.* **TENDER:** delicate, sore, painful; **TOUCHY:** tense, nervous, irritable, unstable

sensitivity *n.* awareness, delicacy, feelings, sympathy

sensuality *n.* appetite, ardor, desire, emotion, love

sensuous *adj.* passionate, physical, exciting, sensual

sentence *n.* judgment, decree, punishment, verdict

sentiment *n.* feeling, emotion, opinion, thought

sentimental *adj.* emotional, tender, romantic, idealistic, visionary, affected

sentry *n.* sentinel, watch, protector, watchmen

separate *v.* **ISOLATE:** divide, seclude; **DEPART:** leave

separated *adj.* apart, disconnected, disjointed, removed, scattered, severed

sequel *n.* continuation, progression, sequence, series

sequence *n.* **SUCCESSION:** order, continuity, progression, flow; **ARRANGEMENT:** distribution, classification; **SERIES:** chain, string, array

serene *adj.* calm, unruffled, tranquil, composed, sedate, placid

series *n.* rank, file, line, row, set, range, string, order, sequence, succession, array, gradation

serious *adj.* **GRAVE:** solemn, pressing, important; **THOUGHTFUL:** earnest, somber, reflecting, sincere

sermon *n.* discourse, lesson, doctrine, lecture

serve *v.* help, aid, assist, attend

service *v.* maintain, sustain, repair

session *n.* sitting, assembly, gathering

set *adj.* **FIRM:** stable, settled, fixed, rigid; **DETERMINED:** steadfast, decided

set *n.* **GROUP:** clique, circle, faction; **COLLECTION:** assemblage, assortment

set *v.* **PLACE:** put, plant, situate, deposit; **ESTABLISH:** anchor, fix, install; **JELL:** solidify, congeal, harden

setback *n.* hindrance, check, delay, difficulty

setting *n.* environment, surroundings, mounting, backdrop, frame, background, context

settle *v.* **PROVE:** establish, verify; **FINISH:** end, achieve; **LOCATE:** reside, dwell, colonize

settlement *n.* **AGREEMENT:** covenant, compact, contract; **COMPENSATION:** remuneration, reimbursement

setup *n.* composition, plan, order, organization

sever *v.* separate, part, split, cleave, cut, divide

several *adj.* some, sundry, various, numerous, many

severe *adj.* exacting, inflexible, harsh, cruel, oppressive, rigid, rigorous, difficult, oppressive, relentless

sew *v.* join, fasten, stitch, tack, bind, piece, baste

sewage *n.* refuse, excrement, offal, waste, residue

shabby *adj.* threadbare, worn, ragged, faded, dilapidated, deteriorated, seedy

shade *n.* **DARKNESS:** blackness, shadow; **TINT:** color, brilliance, saturation, hue; **VARIATION:** difference, hint, suggestion; **SCREEN:** shelter, covering, curtain

shake *n.* tremble, shiver, pulsation, movement
shaken *adj.* unnerved, upset, overcome, excited
shaky *adj.* **INFIRM:** trembling, unsteady, tottering, unstable; **UNRELIABLE:** uncertain, questionable
shallow *adj.* **SLIGHT:** inconsiderable, superficial; **SILLY:** trifling, inane, frivolous, petty, foolish
sham *adj.* pretended, false, misleading, untrue
shame *v.* humiliate, mortify, dishonor, disgrace
shameful *adj.* **IMMODEST:** immoral, debauched, degraded, indecent, lewd, vulgar; **DISHONORABLE:** scandalous, infamous, outrageous, disreputable
shameless *adj.* brazen, bold, forward, rude, lewd
shape *v.* **CAST:** mold, form, fashion, **DEVELOP:** adapt, regulate, become, grow
shape *n.* **FORM:** contour, configuration; **PATTERN:** frame, mold; **CONDITION:** fitness, health
shapely *adj.* symmetrical, comely, proportioned, trim
share *v.* **DIVIDE:** allot, apportion; **PARTAKE:** participate, receive; **GIVE:** yield, bestow, accord
sharp *adj.* **EDGED:** honed, cutting, keen; **CLEVER:** astute, bright, intelligent; **DISTINCT:** explicit, clear, definite; **INTENSE:** piercing, shrill; **STYLISH:** dressy, chic, fashionable
shatter *v.* break, sliver, split, burst
shears *n.* clippers, cutters, snips, scissors
sheath *n.* scabbard, case, covering
shed *n.* shelter, hut, outbuilding, lean–to, woodshed
shed *v.* drop, molt, slough, discard, exude, emit
sheer *adj.* **ABRUPT:** steep, precipitous, perpendicular; **THIN:** transparent, delicate, fine
shelter *n.* protection, refuge, haven, sanctuary
shelter *v.* cover, defend, screen, hide, conceal, harbor,

protect, shield, safeguard, surround, enclose

shine *v.* **RADIATE:** glitter, sparkle, twinkle, glimmer, glow, blaze; **REFLECT:** glisten, gleam, mirror; **POLISH:** scour, brush, burnish, wax

ship *v.* transport, send, consign

shirk *v.* avoid, elude, malinger, evade

shiver *v.* shake, tremble, vibrate, quiver

shock *v.* **STARTLE:** astound, disturb; **OFFEND:** disgust, outrage, horrify, abash, dismay; **JAR:** rock, jolt

shocking *adj.* repulsive, revolting, offensive

shoddy *adj.* cheap, flimsy, tacky, inferior, poor

shore *n.* **COAST:** beach, seaside, bank; **SUPPORT:** prop, buttress, strut

short *adj.* **CONCISE:** brief, condensed; **ABRUPT:** curt, inconsiderate, rude, testy; **DEFICIENT:** inadequate substandard

shortage *n.* lack, deficiency, failure, dearth, shortfall

shortcoming *n.* fault, defect, flaw, drawback

shoulder *v.* bear, support; shove, crowd

shove *v.* push, nudge, jostle, press

show *v.* display, explain, indicate, reveal, demonstrate

show *n.* **PRODUCTION:** play, ceremony; **DISPLAY:** appearance, plausibility, pretext

showy *adj.* conspicuous, flamboyant, pretentious

shower *n.* rainfall, sprinkle, drizzle, mist

shred *n.* strip, fragment, splinter, rag

shred *v.* cut, mince, grate, tear

shrew *n.* scold, nag, harridan

shrewd *adj.* cunning, sharp, keen, intelligent, perceptive, sly, canny, crafty, cagey

shriek *v.* scream, yell, shout, howl, squawk

shrill *adj.* piercing, sharp, harsh

shrine *n.* temple, altar, church, sanctuary
shrink *v.* **CONTRACT:** shrivel, constrict, lessen; **RECOIL:** cringe , wince, retreat, withdraw
shrivel *v.* wither, shrink, decrease
shroud *v.* hide, cover, conceal, obscure, veil, screen
shudder *v.* tremble, shake, shiver, quiver
shun *v.* avoid, ignore, eschew, evade
shut *v.* close, bar, secure, fasten, enclose
shy *adj.* timid, reserved, distrustful, suspicious
sick *adj.* ill, diseased, infected, afflicted, queasy, nauseous, feeble, unhealthy
side *n.* **EDGE:** border; **FACTION:** team, party
siege *n.* attack, assault, onslaught, blockade
sieve *v.* strain, purify, filter
sift *v.* separate, strain, filter, screen
sigh *n.* moan, groan, gasp, cry
sight *n.* view, spectacle, scene, display, show, vision
sign *n.* **SYMPTOM:** indication, hint, clue, suggestion; **EMBLEM:** badge
sign *v.* **GESTURE:** indicate, signal; **ENDORSE:** confirm, acknowledge, initial, autograph
signal *v.* signify, motion, gesture, wave
significant *adj.* important, notable, momentous, symbolic, meaningful
signify *v.* mean, indicate, communicate, denote, imply, intimate, portend
silence *n.* serenity, hush, tranquillity, quiet
silence *v.* hush, still, quiet, muzzle, stifle, suppress
silent *adj.* quiet, hushed, still, reserved, dormant
silly *adj.* foolish, imprudent, ridiculous, absurd, inane, frivolous
similar *adj.* resembling, like, comparable, related

similitude *n.* resemblance, likeness
simple *adj.* unaffected plain clear, unadorned, un-complicated, bare, innocent, artless
simplify *v.* clarify, explain, elucidate, interpret
simulate *v.* feign, fake, pretend, disguise, fabricate
simultaneous *adj.* concurrent, coexisting
sin *v.* transgress, misbehave, offend, trespass
sincere *adj.* honest, genuine, earnest, faithful
singe *v.* scorch, burn, sear, char
single *adj.* individual, lone
singular *adj.* unique, unusual, remarkable, individual
sinister *adj.* ominous, menacing, base, bad, evil
sink *v.* submerge, depress, fall, slump, lower, droop
sip *v.* drink, imbibe, taste, sample, savor
sit *v.* PERCH: seat, squat; MEET convene, assemble
site *n.* location, place, spot, position
situation *n.* circumstances, predicament, state, job, profession, trade, status, station, rank
size *n.* bulk, magnitude, extent, mass, dimensions
skeleton *n.* bones, framework, outline, structure
skeptic *n.* doubter, cynic, unbeliever, agnostic
skeptical *adj.* doubtful, cynical, incredulous
sketch *v.* draw, outline, design, plan, draft, picture
skid *v.* slip, slide, swerve, veer, glide
skill *n.* DEXTERITY: ability, expertise, competence, tal-ent; OCCUPATION: craft, vocation, trade, job
skillful *adj.* adept, adroit, proficient, accomplished
skin *v.* strip, peel, husk, scale, scalp
skinny *adj.* thin, lean, bony, gaunt, emaciated
skirmish *n.* scuffle, scrimmage, engagement, combat
skirt *v.* circumvent, bypass, detour, sidestep
skittish *adj.* jumpy, nervous, fidgety, timid, bashful

skulk *v.* sneak, lurk, prowl
slab *n.* hunk, block, chunk
slack *adj.* lax, loose, lazy, indolent, sluggish, slow
slacken *v.* decrease, abate, diminish
slander *n.* gossip, libel, scandal, misrepresentation
slander *v.* malign, vilify, besmirch, disparage
slang *n.* jargon, lingo, dialect, colloquialism
slant *n.* slope, incline, grade, inclination, bent
slant *v.* **LEAN:** angle, tilt; **DISTORT:** misrepresent, color
slap *v.* smack, strike, hit, spank, cuff, buffet
slash *v.* cut gash, slice, slit, wound
slaughter *n.* slaying, bloodshed, carnage, massacre
slay *v.* kill, murder, butcher, destroy, annihilate
sleazy *adj.* flimsy, shoddy, cheap, trashy, run–down
sleek *adj.* smooth, glossy, glassy, shiny, neat
sleep *v.* slumber, rest, doze, snooze, nod, nap
sleepy *adj.* drowsy, tired, sluggish
slender *adj.* thin, slim, slight, spare, fragile, flimsy
slight *adj.* **TRIVIAL:** trifling, insignificant, petty, unimportant, superficial; **DELICATE**, dainty, flimsy, slender, fragile, frail, insubstantial
slight *v.* disregard, insult, snub, neglect, overlook
slim *adj.* slender slight trifling, dainty, slender
slime *n.* mire, muck, mud, ooze
sling *v.* hurl, throw, chuck, pitch, launch
slink *v.* skulk, cower, creep, lurk, sneak, steal, prowl
slip *n.* error, mistake, blunder, indiscretion
slip *v.* slide, totter, stumble, fall
slipshod *adj.* slovenly, careless, sloppy, untidy
slit *v.* cut, gash, slash, rip, slice, split, tear, pierce
sloppy *adj.* careless, lax, untidy, messy, disorderly
slope *n.* incline, hill, grade, slant, inclination

slouch v. slump, droop, bend, stoop, loll

slovenly adj. messy, careless, sloppy, disorderly, disheveled, bedraggled, untidy, slipshod

slow adj. **LEISURELY:** gradual, deliberate, lethargic; **DENSE:** dull, stupid

sluggish adj. languid, lethargic, indolent, slothful

slumber v. sleep, rest, nap, doze, snooze

slump n. decrease, drop, depression, setback, decline

slur n. insult, innuendo, slight, affront, blemish

sly adj. cunning, wily, deceitful, deceptive, tricky, artful, shifty, evasive, elusive, shrewd, clever, calculating, treacherous, shady, slick, smooth, slippery

small adj. **INCONSEQUENTIAL:** little, insignificant, trivial, unimportant; **SELFISH:** stingy, mean, petty

smart adj. **CLEVER:** intelligent, keen, penetrating, alert, bright; **STYLISH:** sharp, dashing, neat, elegant

smash v. break, shatter, crush, pound, destroy, demolish, wreck, ruin

smear v. **SLANDER:** libel, , sully, slur; **SMUDGE:** daub, plaster, spread, apply

smell n. odor, aroma, fragrance, scent, stench, stink

smile v. grin, smirk, beam, laugh

smirk n. sneer, leer, grimace

smoky adj. hazy, foggy, smoggy, dingy, frosted, filmy

smooth adj. **EVEN:** level, flat, flush, polished, sleek, uniform; **SUAVE:** glib, polite, courteous

smother v. suffocate, stifle, asphyxiate, strangle, subdue, suppress

smudge n. smear, blot, blur, stain, blemish, streak

smug adj. conceited, egotistical, satisfied

smutty adj. pornographic, lewd, indecent, obscene, vulgar, suggestive, raunchy

snag *n.* hindrance, impediment, obstacle, impasse
snare *v.* catch, entangle, trap, trick, lure
snatch *n.* fragment, scrap, shred, snippet, tatter
snatch *v.* grab, pluck, seize, steal, filch, swipe, take
sneak *v.* lurk, prowl, creep, slink, steal, skulk
sneer *v.* criticize, deride, ridicule, scoff, gibe, taunt
snicker *v.* giggle, laugh, chortle, chuckle, titter
snide *adj.* underhanded, sarcastic, derogatory, insinuating, vicious, nasty, mean, malicious
snip *v.* clip, pare, cut, lop, nip, slice, slit
snivel *v.* weep, whine, bawl, bemoan, blubber
snobbery *n.* contempt, arrogance, insolence
snobbish *adj.* snooty, condescending, patronizing
snub *n.* insult, affront, slight, slur, rebuke
snug *adj.* comfortable, cozy, secure, safe
snuggle *v.* cuddle, nestle, nuzzle, burrow, hug
soak *v.* steep, saturate, douse, permeate, infuse
sob *v.* cry, moan, weep, wail, lament, whimper, bewail
sober *adj.* serious, solemn, subdued, restrained, sedate, composed, rational, reasonable, sound, somber
social *adj.* genial, pleasant, polite, civil, pleasant
society *n.* **ORGANIZATION:** fellowship, association, brotherhood, fraternity, club; **CULTURE:** community, civilization, people, nation
soft *adj.* malleable, pliant, yielding, fluffy
soggy *adj.* saturated, damp, wet, soaked, sodden
sojourn *n.* stay, visit, stopover, vacation, abide
solace *v.* comfort, console, soothe, cheer, relieve, alleviate, assuage, allay, soften, mitigate
sole *adj.* one, single, lone, exclusive, individual, unique, unshared
solemn *adj.* sacred, grave, serious, grim, imposing,

thoughtful, dignified, formal, somber, austere

solemnize *v.* commemorate, honor, celebrate, hallow

solicit *v.* supplicate, beg, implore, urge, request, ask, inquire, question, proposition

solicitation *n.* request, petition, suit, claim, appeal

solicitor *n.* attorney, petitioner, supplicant

solicitous *adj.* concerned, anxious, heedful, kind, devoted, tender, loving, thoughtful

solid *adj.* whole, regular, unbroken, firm, substantial, sound, hard, stable, dense, stout

solidify *v.* harden, crystallize, set, coagulate, congeal

solitary *adj.* single, sole, individual, singular, isolated, lonely, remote, separate

solitude *n.* isolation, seclusion, privacy

solution *n.* answer, resolution, conclusion, explanation, settlement

solve *v.* answer, resolve, explain, decipher, decode

somber *adj.* dull, gloomy, dark, dim, drab, dismal, depressing, dreary, melancholy

sonorous *adj.* resonant, reverberating, vibrant

sooty *adj.* blackened, dirty, grimy, dingy, filthy

soothe *v.* calm, comfort, ease, quiet, refresh, soften, alleviate, assuage, mitigate, pacify

soothsayer *n.* prognosticator, diviner, oracle, prophet, astrologer, seer, mystic

sophisticated *adj.* worldly, refined, cultured

sorcery *n.* magic, witchcraft, alchemy, enchantment

sordid *adj.* vile, dirty, squalid, foul, low, base, abject

sore *adj.* sensitive, raw, tender, painful, inflamed

sorrow *n.* grief, affliction, anguish, remorse, misery, sadness, woe, trouble, affliction

sorrow *v.* grieve, mourn, weep, lament, deplore

sorry *adj.* regretful, repentant, apologetic
sort *v.* order, arrange, classify, distribute, assort
sot *n.* drunkard, lush, drunk, alcoholic, wino
soul *n.* spirit, essence, ghost, being
sound *adj.* safe, whole, healthy, strong, complete, vigorous, stable, sensible, rational, sane, hale
sound *n.* tone, noise, vibration, resonance, intonation
source *n.* origin, beginning, inception, cause, root
souvenir *n.* keepsake, token, memento, relic, trophy
sow *v.* scatter, disseminate, disperse, plant
space *n.* room, area, gap, expanse, distance, interval
spacious *adj.* roomy, capacious, large, ample, commodious, vast, huge, voluminous, extensive
span *n.* distance, measure, length, extent, stretch
span *v.* cross, traverse, reach, connect, link, bridge
spare *adj.* LEAN: thin, gaunt, slight, emaciated; EXTRA: excess, additional
sparkle *v.* glitter, gleam, twinkle, glisten, shine
sparse *adj.* meager, inadequate, scanty, thin, spare
spasm *n.* convulsion, fit, contortion, seizure
spatter *v.* splash, slosh, spray, shower, speckle
speak *v* talk, articulate, say, utter, lecture, address
special *adj.* specific, certain, particular, designated, unique, distinctive, uncommon, unusual
specialist *n.* expert, professional, authority
specie *n.* coin, money, currency
species *n.* type, kind, class, breed, variety, category
specific *adj.* precise, particular, distinct, explicit
specify *v.* stipulate, designate, cite, name, define
specimen *n.* sample, example, model, type, pattern
specious *adj.* deceptive, misleading, false
speck *n.* bit, particle, trace, grain, iota

speckle *n.* spot, speck, dot, mote, fleck
spectacle *n.* sight, show, demonstration, wonder
spectacular *adj.* amazing, marvelous, impressive, sensational, dramatic, splendid, striking, fabulous
spectator *n.* onlooker, observer, witness, bystander
specter *n.* ghost, spook, phantom, spirit, apparition
spectrum *n.* range, scale, sweep, extent
speculate *v.* **CONSIDER:** theorize, contemplate, consider, infer; **RISK:** gamble, venture, chance
speech *n.* language, oration, communication
speed *v.* hasten, hurry, expedite, precipitate
speedy *adj.* quick, fast, hasty, brisk, swift, hurried
spend *v.* give, waste, disburse, dissipate, deplete
sphere *n.* **GLOBE:**, orb, shell, planet; **DOMAIN:** province realm, environment
spill *v.* slop, splash, drop, flow
spin *v.* turn, rotate, twirl, whirl, gyrate
spindle *n.* shaft, beam, axle, arbor
spirit *n.* **GHOST:** apparition, phantom, specter; **VITALITY:** vivacity, vigor, zeal, ardor; **SIGNIFICANCE:** intent, meaning, sense
spite *n.* malice, malevolence, rancor, grudge
spiteful *adj.* vindictive, malicious, cruel, malevolent
splash *v.* spatter, douse, spray, swash
spleen *n.* anger, petulance, wrath, rancor
splendid *adj.* grand, magnificent, impressive, dazzling
splendor *n.* glory, magnificence, grandeur
splice *v.* join, implant, unite, graft
splinter *n.* sliver, shaving, fragment, chip, piece
splinter *v.* crumble, shatter, fracture, break, smash
split *v.* divide, sever, break, separate, cleave
spoil *v.* decay, ruin, damage, decompose, putrefy

sponsor *n.* patron, mentor, supporter, backer
spontaneous *adj.* impromptu, impulsive, natural
sporadic *adj.* occasional, infrequent, scattered
spot *n.* **STAIN:** blot, blemish; **LOCATION:** locale, site
spout *v.* pour, discharge, emit, flow, spill, gush
sprawl *v.* recline, lounge, relax, slouch
sprightly *adj.* lively, frisky, nimble, animated, agile
spring *v.* bound, leap, issue, jump, hop, vault
sprinkle *v.* disperse, distribute, scatter, spatter
sprint *v.* run, race, zip, dash, tear
sprout *v.* germinate, bud, burgeon, grow, develop
spry *adj.* nimble, agile, active, vigorous, animated, brisk, lively, quick, energetic
spunk *n.* pluck, mettle, courage, daring, nerve, spirit
spur *v.* urge, incite, induce, provoke, goad, press
spurious *adj.* false, fake, deceptive, phony, feigned
spurn *v.* reject, shun, slight, snub, scorn, disdain
spurt *v.* burst, gush, spout, issue, spring
spy *v.* see, discover, glimpse
squabble *v.* wrangle, quarrel, bicker, argue, feud
squalid *adj.* filthy, foul, dirty, unclean, seedy
squalor *n.* filth, poverty, misery
squander *v.* waste, dissipate, expend, lavish, misuse
square *adj.* fair, just, honest, straight, level, true
squeamish *adj.* queasy, modest, prudish, finicky
squeeze *v.* compress, crush, squash, press, pinch
squelch *v.* subdue, crush, squash, thwart, suppress
squirm *v.* wriggle, writhe, fidget, twist, shift
stab *n.* wound, cut, puncture, thrust
stabilize *v.* steady, secure, brace, poise
stable *adj.* fixed, firm, steady, sturdy, enduring, perpetual, steadfast, sound, reliable, solid

staff *n.* personnel, employees, crew, cast
stage *n.* platform, dais, scaffold
stagger *v.* WEAVE: falter, waver; ASTONISH: astound, amaze, dumbfound, shock, surprise
stagnant *adj.* inert, stale, dirty, filthy, fetid
stagnate *v.* decay, rot, decompose, taint
staid *adj.* steady, sober, sedate, quiet, solemn
stake *v.* wager, risk, imperil, hazard, venture, bet
stale *adj.* dry, trite, common, dull, humdrum
stalk *v.* hunt, track, chase, pursue
stall *v.* delay, obstruct, hamper, hinder, impede
stalwart *adj.* stout, sturdy, strong, rugged, robust, vigorous, bold, gallant, steadfast, formidable
stamina *n.* endurance, strength, vigor, vitality, power
stammer *v.* sputter, falter, stumble, hesitate, stutter
stand *n.* position, attitude, belief, opinion
stand *v.* endure, resist, oppose, confront, withstand
standard *n.* MODEL: measure, gauge, example; BANNER: symbol, flag, pennant
staple *adj.* basic, necessary, essential, fundamental
stare *v.* gaze, gawk, gape, glare, look, watch
stark *adj.* simple, desolate, dreary, grim, harsh
start *n.* beginning, origin, onset, outset, initiation
start *v.* initiate, begin, commence, establish
startle *v.* surprise, alarm, scare, frighten, disturb
state *n.* condition, situation, circumstances, status, position, standing, station
state *v.* recite, declare, pronounce, assert, affirm
statement *n.* declaration, allegation, assertion, remark, report, account
stately *adj.* majestic, dignified, regal, grand, elegant
static *adj.* immobile, stationary, fixed, rigid

station *n.* rank, standing, position
stationary *adj.* fixed, static, permanent, rooted, stable
statue *n.* sculpture, bust, image, icon, figurine
stature *n.* height, bulk, build, status, standing
status *n.* state, condition, position, rank, standing
statute *n.* law, decree, act, bill, rule, ordinance, edict
stay *n.* prop, support, brace, prop
stay *v.* remain, continue, wait, linger, pause, detain, hinder, suspend, curb
steadfast *adj.* resolute, unwavering, constant, faithful, dependable, firm
steal *v.* rob, thieve, filch, pilfer, swindle, embezzle
steep *adj.* precipitous, sheer, abrupt
steeple *n.* spire, tower, minaret
steer *v.* guide, direct, pilot, conduct, lead, navigate
stellar *adj.* remarkable, phenomenal, outstanding
stem *v.* stop, check, curb, halt
stereotype *v.* classify, categorize, typecast, label
sterling *adj.* genuine, flawless, noble, perfect, excellent, superior, exceptional
stern *adj.* severe, rigid, hard, strict, austere, rigorous
stiff *adj.* rigid, formal, inflexible, firm, stubborn, obstinate, unyielding, formal, uncompromising, severe
stiffen *v.* harden, congeal, thicken, coagulate
stifle *v.* suppress, repress, restrain, stop
stigma *n.* disgrace, shame, infamy, blemish, blot, stain, taint
stigmatize *v.* disgrace, discredit, dishonor, defame, shame, brand, humiliate
still *adj.* silent, motionless, inert, stationary, hushed, calm, serene, tranquil
still *v.* silence, hush, calm, soothe, stop, stall, arrest

stilted *adj.* awkward, affected, unnatural, strained, contrived, artificial, labored, stiff

stimulate *v.* excite, arouse, activate, rouse, provoke

stingy *adj.* niggardly, miserly, tight, closefisted

stint *v.* limit, confine, restrict, restrain

stipulate *v.* specify, determine, designate, indicate

stipulation *n.* prerequisite, condition, qualification, term, requirement, clause

stir *n.* tumult, bustle, excitement, commotion, disorder, uproar, furor, agitation, fuss

stir *v.* agitate, rouse, excite, incite, provoke, stimulate

stock *v.* store, supply, hoard, equip, fill, furnish

stockpile *n.* reserve, supply, deposit, hoard, store

stoic *n.* impassive, apathetic, indifferent, nonchalant, composed, poised

stolid *adj.* impassive, unemotional, dispassionate, indifferent, imperturbable

stomach *n.* belly, paunch, abdomen

stoop *v.* bend, bow, crouch

stop *v.* halt, end, terminate, discontinue, arrest, restrain, hinder, impede, prevent, thwart

store *v.* hoard, gather, collect, stash, stockpile

storm *n.* tempest, blizzard, gale, squall, commotion, turmoil, outbreak, disturbance

stormy *adj.* tempestuous, wild, blustering, tumultuous, raging, turbulent, boisterous

story *n.* TALE: anecdote, yarn, parable, fable, legend, report, account; LEVEL: floor, landing

stout *adj.* PLUMP: portly, heavy, bulky, corpulent; RESOLUTE: brave, courageous, bold, fearless, dauntless, indomitable, firm, strong, robust, hardy

straggler *n.* dawdler, lingerer, laggard, slowpoke

straight

straight *adj.* direct, honest, fair, just, virtuous, open
straighten *v.* adjust, align, rectify, correct
strain *n.* effort, exertion, force, pressure, anxiety, tension, stress
strait *n.* difficulty, distress, predicament, plight
strange *adj.* unusual, abnormal, bizarre, peculiar, extraordinary, outlandish, unfamiliar, unknown
stranger *n.* foreigner, alien, outsider
stratagem *n.* trick, deception, ruse, wile, scheme, plan, contrivance, device
strategy *n.* tactics, scheme, system, approach
stray *v.* wander, drift, roam, deviate, digress
stream *n.* flow, emit, issue, pour, run
streamer *n.* flag, banner, pennant, standard, ensign
strength *n.* power, force, might
strengthen *v.* fortify, reinforce, restore, invigorate
strenuous *adj.* vigorous, spirited, laborious
stress *n.* EMPHASIS: weight, significance, accent; APPREHENSION: trepidation, misgiving
stretch *n.* expanse, range, reach, extent
strew *v.* scatter, spread, disseminate, broadcast
strict *adj.* demanding, exacting, rigid, inflexible
strident *adj.* raucous, shrill, harsh, piercing, grating
strife *n.* conflict, fight, discord, clash
strike *v.* HIT: slap, cuff; UNEARTH: find, uncover
stringent *adj.* strict, harsh, severe
stripling *n.* youth, child, lad, lass, youngster
strive *v.* endeavor, attempt, compete, contend
stroll *v.* walk, saunter, meander, wander, roam
strong *adj.* muscular, potent, solid, impregnable
struggle *n.* battle, clash, conflict, exertion, endeavor
struggle *v.* grapple, contend, strive, toil, labor

strut *n.* support, brace, prop, mainstay

stubborn *adj.* obstinate, headstrong, stiff, resolute, inflexible, intractable

student *n.* pupil, scholar, disciple, apprentice

study *v.* investigate, analyze, scrutinize, examine, ponder, consider, reflect

stump *v.* perplex, confuse, confound, baffle, mystify

stun *v.* shock, confound, amaze, astonish, astound, bewilder, overwhelm, stupefy

stupendous *adj.* amazing, astounding, marvelous, extraordinary, incredible, spectacular, wondrous

stupid *adj.* dull, boring, tedious, vapid, tiresome, foolish, absurd, inane, senseless

stupor *n.* daze, trance, numbness, lethargy

sturdy *adj.* robust, rugged, stalwart, strong, strapping, muscular, firm, indomitable, stout

stutter *v.* stammer, stumble, falter

stylish *adj.* fashionable, chic, smart, modish

suave *adj.* sophisticated, smooth, cultured, worldly

subdue *v.* defeat, conquer, overpower, tame

subjective *adj.* biased, prejudiced, individual

subjugate *v.* conquer, enslave, subdue, defeat

sublime *adj.* lofty, inspiring, imposing, majestic

submerge *v.* immerse, engulf, plunge, sink

submission *n.* surrender, resignation, compliance

submit *v.* ACCEDE: comply, obey; SUGGEST: volunteer, propose, present, tender

subordinate *adj.* inferior, lower, junior, subservient

subscribe *v.* support, donate, authorize, sanction

subsequent *adj.* following, ensuing, succeeding, later

subservient *adj.* subordinate, servile, deferential

subside *v.* decline, dwindle, diminish, lessen, wane

subsidize *v.* support, sponsor, fund, back, assist
subsidy *n.* endowment, allowance, grant, bequest
substance *n.* object, element, essence, basis, meaning, import, gist, significance
substantial *adj.* plentiful, abundant, ample, considerable, wealthy affluent, influential, valuable
substantiate *v.* authenticate, confirm, validate, prove, verify, corroborate, attest, document
substitute *adj.* alternative, surrogate, tentative
subterfuge *n.* ploy, scheme, stratagem, device, expedient, deceit, deception
subtle *adj.* delicate, understated, refined, elusive, deceptive, inferred, insinuated, artful, insidious
subtract *v.* deduct, decrease, diminish, lessen, lower
succeed *v.* FLOURISH: thrive, prevail, triumph; REPLACE: supersede
success *n.* achievement, mastery, victory, attainment
successful *adj.* triumphant, flourishing, thriving
succession *n.* sequence, order, continuation
succinct *adj.* brief, concise, terse, abbreviated
succor *n.* aid, help, sustenance, assistance
succumb *v.* submit, concede, relent, capitulate, die, collapse, fail
sudden *adj.* abrupt, quick, unexpected, impromptu
suffer *v.* endure, tolerate, bear, undergo, agonize
sufficient *adj.* plenty, ample, enough
suffuse *v.* saturate, pervade, soak, impregnate
suggest *v.* propose, submit, imply, insinuate
suit *v.* satisfy, please, gratify, shape, accommodate
suitor *n.* wooer, admirer, gallant, beau
sulk *v.* pout, scowl, frown, glower
sullen *adj.* moody, morose, gloomy, somber

sully *v.* shame, dishonor, stain, taint, tarnish, blemish, defile, corrupt, besmirch

sultry *adj.* sweltering, muggy, humid, sticky

sum *n.* quantity, value, aggregate, total, tally

summary *n.* condensation, digest, abridgment, brief

summit *n.* peak, pinnacle, apex, crown, culmination

summon *v.* call, invite, invoke, request, petition

sumptuous *adj.* luxurious, elegant, lavish, opulent

sundry *adj.* various, several, divers

superb *adj.* outstanding, exquisite, grand, magnificent, luxurious

supersede *v.* replace, supplant, succeed

supervise *v.* superintend, chaperon, manage, control

supervision *n.* management, guidance, surveillance

supplant *v.* replace, displace, succeed, supersede

supple *adj.* elastic, pliable, compliant, limber

supplement *n.* addition, subsidiary, extension

supplement *v.* augment, enhance, fortify

supplicate *v.* implore, beseech, beg, entreat

supply *v.* equip, stock, replenish

support *n.* **AID:** assistance, help, relief, succor; **BRACE:** prop, column, buttress, strut

suppose *v.* assume, infer, presume, believe, think

suppress *v.* **OVERPOWER:** repress, curb, quell, crush; **CONCEAL:** bury, cover

supreme *adj.* preeminent, superior, greatest

supremacy *n.* dominion, dominance, preeminence

surcharge *n.* tax, duty, surtax, tariff, levy, toll

sure *adj.* trusty, reliable, infallible, certain, safe, solid, precise, accurate, unerring, inevitable

surface *n.* rise, appear, emerge

surge *v.* gush, rush, pour, rise, heave, oscillate

surly *adj.* cantankerous, rude, irritable, sullen, hostile
surmise *v.* speculate, guess, infer, imagine, suppose
surmount *v.* conquer, transcend, hurdle, overcome
surpass *v.* exceed, transcend, excel
surplus *n.* excess, abundance, remainder, residue
surprise *n.* astonishment, amazement, shock, wonder
surprise *n.* astound, bewilder, dumbfound, startle
surrender *v.* submit, abandon, capitulate, yield
surreptitious *adj.* furtive, clandestine, stealthy
surrogate *adj.* substitute, backup, alternative
surround *v.* encompass, enclose, circle
survey *n.* poll, study, review, outline, critique
survey *v.* scrutinize, scan, examine, inspect, observe
survive *v.* endure, persist, remain, continue
survival *n.* subsistence, continuation, durability
susceptible *adj.* receptive, impressionable, responsive, vulnerable
suspect *v.* **DISTRUST:** mistrust, doubt; **BELIEVE:** suppose, imagine, conjecture
suspend *v.* postpone, delay, defer, interrupt
suspense *n.* apprehension, indecision, anxiety
suspension *n.* delay, deferment, postponement
suspicion *n.* skepticism, misgiving, mistrust, cynicism, notion, impression
suspicious *adj.* **DUBIOUS:** shady, untrustworthy, doubtful; **WARY:** skeptical
sustenance *n.* food, nourishment, provisions
swagger *v.* strut, prance, boast, brag, gloat
swallow *v.* drink, eat, gulp, consume, devour
swamp *n.* bayou, marsh, mire, morass, slough
swarm *n.* horde, mass, flock, multitude, host
sway *n.* dominion, dominance, control, influence

swear *v.* **PROMISE:** declare, testify, affirm; **BLASPHEME:** damn, curse

sweet *adj.* luscious, aromatic, fragrant, clean, fresh, melodious, harmonious, mellow

swell *v.* increase, inflate, bloat, bulge, grow

swift *adj.* fast, rapid, expeditious, fleet, prompt, quick

swig *v.* drink, swallow, quaff, gulp, guzzle

swindle *v.* trick, deceive, dupe, defraud, victimize

swing *v.* hang, dangle, flap, oscillate, wave

switch *v.* swap, trade, exchange, replace, substitute

sycophant *n.* flatterer, flunky, parasite, toady

sylvan *adj.* picturesque, pastoral, idyllic, bucolic

symbol *n.* character, letter, numeral, representation

symbolize *v.* signify, connote, mean, represent

sympathetic *adj.* considerate, compassionate

sympathize *v.* commiserate, console, pity

sympathy *n.* compassion, understanding, warmth, consolation, solace, comfort

symptom *n.* clue, trait, characteristic, feature, sign

synchronize *v.* accommodate, adjust, attune

syndicate *n.* coalition, alliance, company, association

syndicate *v.* affiliate, connect, consolidate, merge

synopsis *n.* summary, abridgment, condensation

synthesis *n.* combination, integration, formation

system *n.* strategy, plan, scheme, method,

systematic *adj.* methodical, orderly, precise, regular

table *v.* postpone, delay, defer, shelve

tabloid *n.* newspaper, periodical, publication

taboo *adj.* forbidden, banned, prohibited

tacit *adj.* implied, understood, assumed, inferred

taciturn *adj.* reserved, quiet

tact *n.* subtlety, discretion, finesse, style

tactics *n.* scheme, stratagem, procedure, system
tag *v.* label, ticket, designate, identify
tailor *v.* customize, adapt, adjust, conform
taint *v.* corrupt, infect, defile, contaminate
take *v.* obtain, get, procure, seize, grasp, capture, adopt, select, accept, choose, pick
tale *n.* YARN: narrative, account; FALSEHOOD: fib, lie
talent *n.* aptitude, genius, gift
talisman *n.* amulet, charm
talk *n.* conversation, dialogue, discourse, speech
talk *v.* converse, speak, discuss, chatter, gossip
talkative *adj.* loquacious, garrulous, chatty, gabby
tall *adj.* towering, high, big, rangy, lanky
tally *n.* count, reckoning, sum, calculation
tame *adj.* docile, gentle, obedient
tamper *v.* alter, change, meddle, damage
tangible *adj.* material, corporeal, tactile, discernible, evident, actual, real, genuine
tantalize *v.* tease, provoke, torment, frustrate, vex
tantamount *adj.* equivalent, parallel, identical
tape *n.* bind, wrap, seal, mend
tarnish *n.* blemish, blot, stain, taint
tarnish *v.* defame, disgrace embarrass
tarry *v.* stall, linger, loiter, dally, dawdle, stay
task *n.* job, labor, assignment, duty, chore
taste *n.* partiality, liking, bias, preference
taste *v.* sample, try, sip, savor, relish, enjoy
taunt *v.* insult, jeer, mock, provoke
tavern *n.* bar, saloon, pub, cafe, inn, lodge, hostelry
tawdry *adj.* cheap, sleazy, flashy, ostentatious
tax *n.* levy, assessment, tariff, toll, duty, obligation
teach *v.* instruct, inform, train, enlighten, guide

tear *v.* rip, split, sever, cleave, rend

tease *v.* annoy, taunt, torment, harass, irritate, vex

technique *n.* **METHOD:** procedure, system, approach, methodology; **ABILITY:** skill, aptitude, knack

tedious *adj.* monotonous, tiresome, dull, boring

tell *v.* recount, describe, report, speak, mention, explain, reveal, declare, divulge

temper *n.* disposition, temperament, humor, composure, poise

temper *v.* calm, soothe, pacify, mollify

temperament *n.* disposition, attitude, mood, emotion

temperance *n.* restraint, sobriety, abstinence

temperate *adj.* calm, composed, cool, reasonable

tempestuous *adj.* stormy, raging, tumultuous

temporary *adj.* transitory, fleeting, interim

tenable *adj.* defensible, justifiable, maintainable

tenacious *adj.* resolute, persistent, obstinate

tenant *n.* renter, leaseholder, inhabitant

tend *v.* guard, protect, keep, manage

tendency *n.* inclination, partiality, bias, penchant

tender *adj.* **DELICATE:** fragile, frail; **COMPASSIONATE:** sympathetic, kindhearted considerate

tenet *n.* belief, conviction, dogma, creed, doctrine

tenor *n.* drift, trend, tone, course

tense *adj.* taut, nervous, agitated, strained, drawn

tension *n.* pressure, strain, stress, unease

tentative *adj.* provisional, probationary, experimental, indefinite

tenuous *adj.* fine, narrow, insubstantial, flimsy, feeble

tepid *adj.* lukewarm, indifferent, halfhearted, languid

terminal *adj.* boundary, limit, extremity

terminate *v.* complete, conclude, eliminate, cancel

termination *n.* close, finish, cessation, completion
terminology *n.* vocabulary, language, jargon
terminus *n.* extremity, objective, conclusion
terrible *adj.* frightful, appalling, dreadful, horrible, horrendous, disastrous, disturbing, extreme
terrific *adj.* splendid, marvelous, wonderful, outstanding, super
terrify *v.* terrorize, appall, paralyze, horrify, frighten
territory *n.* area, region, dominion
terror *n.* fright, horror, alarm, dismay, consternation
terse *adj.* brief, succinct, concise, precise, curt
test *n.* inspection, experiment, examination, quiz
testify *v.* swear, certify, demonstrate, indicate, argue
testimony *n.* statement, declaration, confirmation, testament, affidavit
testy *adj.* irritable, cranky, grouchy, edgy, short–tempered, touchy, peevish
thank *v.* acknowledge, appreciate, recognize, credit
thaw *v.* warm, melt, dissolve, liquefy, loosen
theft *n.* burglary, robbery, thievery, looting
theology *n.* religion, faith, belief, scripture, dogma, convictions, creed
theorem *n.* principle, hypothesis, postulate, premise
theory *n.* conjecture, speculation, rationale, explanation, view, conception, outlook
theoretical *adj.* abstract, academic, hypothetical
theorize *v.* speculate, postulate, presume, suppose
therapeutic *adj.* restorative, curative, recuperative, remedial, corrective
thesis *n.* opinion, contention, argument, assumption, assertion, hypothesis
thick *adj.* abundant, dense, packed, crowded

thicken *v.* jell, congeal, stiffen, harden, intensify

thin *adj.* lean, gaunt, scanty, meager, scarce

thin *v.* dilute, weaken, reduce

think *v.* contemplate meditate, consider, remember, recall, recollect, believe, suppose

thirst *n.* longing, desire, yearning, eagerness

thorough *adj.* total, meticulous, precise, painstaking

thoroughfare *n.* artery, highway, expressway, boulevard, concourse, freeway

thought *v.* concept, conviction, notion, opinion, theory, hypothesis, supposition

thoughtful *adj.* considerate, caring, attentive, concerned, discreet, tender

threadbare *adj.* worn, shabby, tattered, frayed, seedy

threat *n.* risk, hazard, danger, jeopardy, menace

threaten *v.* endanger, menace, terrorize, scare

threshold *n.* start, beginning, outset, commencement

thrift *n.* economy, husbandry, conservation

thrifty *adj.* frugal, sparing, provident

thrill *n.* excitement, stimulation

thrill *v.* delight, electrify, rouse

thrive *v.* flourish, succeed, increase, grow

throb *v.* pulse, pound, thump, pulsate

throng *n.* mass, multitude, horde, swarm, host, assemblage, crowd

through *adj.* completed, done, finished

throw *v.* fling, hurl, pitch, heave, toss

thrust *v.* shove, plunge, jab, push

thug *n.* hoodlum, goon, heavy, gangster, criminal

tiara *n.* crown, diadem, coronet

tidings *n.* news, information, gossip, lowdown

tidy *adj.* neat, orderly, spruce, trim

tie

tie *n.* **ROPE:** band, strap, cord, **NECKTIE:** bow, scarf, cravat, choker, **CONNECTION:** relation, bond, link, knot, **STANDOFF:** draw, deadlock, stalemate
tie *v.* fasten, secure attach, connect, join, link
tier *n.* line, row, array, bank
tiff *n.* quarrel, dispute, disagreement, scrap, spat
tighten *v.* squeeze, compress, constrict, clench
tilt *n.* tip, list, slant, incline, slope, angle, pitch
time *n.* **AGE:** epoch, generation, cycle; **INTERVAL:** duration, span; **RHYTHM:** tempo, beat, cadence
timely *adj.* auspicious, propitious, favorable, prompt
timetable *n.* schedule, program, calendar, agenda
timid *adj.* shy, retiring, fearful, withdrawn, reticent, indecisive, vacillating
timorous *adj.* timid, fearful, apprehensive, anxious, scared, afraid
tinge *n.* trace, hint, trifle, dab, nuance
tinker *v.* dabble, putter, potter, trifle
tint *v.* stain, color, tinge
tiny *adj.* small, diminutive, minute, microscopic
tip *n.* **PEAK:** pinnacle, summit; **GRATUITY:** compensation, consideration; **ADVICE:** pointer, hint, clue
tirade *n.* harangue, denunciation, outburst
tire *v.* exhaust, fatigue, drain, irk, bore
title *n.* **DESIGNATION:** name, appellation, epithet; **CLAIM:** interest, holding, ownership
titter *v.* laugh, giggle, snicker, chuckle
toil *v.* labor, work, strive, slave, sweat
token *adj.* nominal, superficial, minimal
token *n.* sign, emblem, mark
tolerable *adj.* **ENDURABLE:** sufferable, bearable; **ADEQUATE:** decent, average

tolerance *n.* **STAMINA:** forbearance, toleration; **IM-PARTIALITY:** magnanimity, compassion

tolerant *adj.* unprejudiced, moderate, merciful

tolerate *v.* **ALLOW:** oblige, indulge; **SUFFER:** abide, accept, bear

tomb *n.* grave, vault, crypt, sepulcher, mausoleum

tonic *adj.* refresher, restorative, stimulant

tool *n.* implement, appliance, utensil, gadget

top *n.* pinnacle, crest, summit, zenith, crown

topical *adj.* local, isolated, provincial, regional

topple *v.* fall, tumble, collapse, overturn, upset

torment *n.* anguish, suffering, distress, misery

torment *v.* distress, vex, afflict, annoy, tease, harass, irritate, pester, provoke, needle

torpid *adj.* inactive, inert, lethargic, sluggish, motionless, dormant, hibernating

torpor *n.* idleness, inactivity, indolence, sluggishness

torrent *n.* cloudburst, deluge, flood

tortuous *adj.* winding serpentine, twisted, snaky, crooked, bent

toss *v.* throw, fling, pitch, cast, hurl, chuck

total *adj.* entire, utter, whole, gross

totter *v.* stumble, falter, weave, reel, lurch

touchy *adj.* irritable, peevish, grouchy, testy

tough *adj.* rugged, hardy, durable, sturdy, hardy, unyielding, incorrigible

tourist *n.* visitor, sightseer, wayfarer

tournament *n.* competition, rivalry, contest, match

tousle *v.* dishevel, disarray, ruffle, muss

tout *v.* vaunt, plug, promote, herald, extol

town *n.* community, municipality, village, hamlet

toxic *adj.* poisonous, deadly, lethal, virulent

trace *n.* vestige, indication, hint, suggestion
track *v.* hunt, trail, pursue, trace
tractable *adj.* docile, compliant, pliable, flexible
trade *n.* vocation, profession, livelihood, craft
trade *v.* exchange, swap, barter, buy, sell
tragedy *n.* disaster, calamity, catastrophe, affliction, suffering, tribulation
tragic *adj.* disastrous, dreadful, distressing
train *v.* tutor, teach, enlighten, educate, inform, instruct, guide
trait *n.* characteristic, quality, property, attribute, mannerism, habit
tramp *n.* hobo, vagabond, vagrant, gypsy
tramp *v.* roam, rove, hike, tromp, march
tranquil *adj.* peaceful, serene, placid, still, pleasant
tranquillity *n.* quiet, calm, serenity
transform *v.* alter, transfigure, convert, commute
transgress *n.* overstep, infringe, violate, trespass
transient *adj.* brief, transitory, passing, fleeting
translate *v.* reword, explain, interpret, decipher
translucent *adj.* transparent, clear
transmit *v.* send, transfer, convey, dispatch
transparent *adj.* translucent, diaphanous, lucid, clear, thin, sheer
transpire *v.* happen, occur, ensue, result
transpose *v.* switch, swap, exchange, transfer
trap *n.* snare, trick, stratagem, maneuver, artifice
traumatic *adj.* alarming, upsetting, frightful
travel *v.* journey, tour, roam, expedition, excursion
travesty *n.* parody, satire, spoof burlesque, lampoon, caricature, farce
treacherous *adj.* unfaithful, deceitful, deceptive,

insidious, disloyal, treasonous, difficult, unstable
treatise *n.* dissertation, thesis, essay, discourse
treaty *n.* agreement, settlement, covenant, pact
tremble *v.* shiver, quiver, shake
tremendous *adj.* colossal, huge, immense
tribulation *n.* distress, suffering, hardship
tribute *n.* accolade, homage, recognition, applause
trick *n.* deception, artifice, ruse
trim *adj.* neat, orderly, tidy, groomed, natty
trinket *n.* bauble, adornment, decoration, ornament
trip *n.* voyage, excursion, jaunt, pilgrimage
trite *adj.* ordinary, commonplace, hackneyed, stale
triumph *v.* prevail, conquer, overwhelm, overpower
trivial *adj.* insignificant, inconsequential, unimportant, irrelevant, frivolous
troll *v.* goblin, gremlin, hobgoblin, demon
trophy *n.* award, citation, medal
trot *v.* canter, jog, lope, amble
trouble *n.* calamity, distress, misfortune, tribulation
trouble *v.* distress, harass, harry, irritate, pester
troublesome *adj.* pesky, bothersome, trying, perplexing, galling, burdensome, disturbing
trough *n.* channel, furrow, rut, crater, ditch
truce *n.* armistice, reprieve, amnesty, cease–fire
truculent *adj.* fierce, mean, malevolent, pugnacious, belligerent, contentious, hostile
true *adj.* real, genuine, truthful, undistorted, authentic, just, honest, faithful, reliable
trunk *n.* chest, strongbox, coffer, case
trust *n.* confidence, dependence, reliance, faith,
try *v.* endeavor, strive, test, examine
tryst *n.* meeting, rendezvous, assignation

tumble *v.* fall, slip, descend, decline, totter, drop

tumor *n.* growth, cyst, polyp, sarcoma, melanoma

tumult *n.* disorder, commotion, turmoil, melee, agitation, ferment

tumultuous *adj.* riotous, violent, restive, uneasy, boisterous, disorderly, obstreperous

turbulent *adj.* violent, blustery, disorderly

turbulence *n.* commotion, excitement, uproar, tumult, disturbance

turmoil *n.* chaos, commotion, disorder, tumult, turbulence, uproar

turn *v.* **ROTATE:** spin, gyrate; **CONVERT:** transform, change, alter, transmute,

turnout *n.* attendance, audience, crowd, spectators

turpitude *n.* depravity, baseness, perversion, vileness, evil, sinfulness, corruption

tussle *v.* scuffle, grapple, struggle, fracas, brawl

tutor *n.* instructor, trainer, coach, teacher

tweak *v.* nip, pinch, grasp, squeeze, pull, twist

twine *n.* rope, cord, strand, string, braid

twinge *n.* twitch, tingle, spasm, crick, stitch, throb

twinkle *v.* shimmer, glitter, flicker, glint, glimmer

twirl *v.* twist, gyrate, turn, rotate, pivot

type *n.* kind, class, breed, group, family, genus

typical *adj.* characteristic, representative, ideal

typify *v.* represent, personify, epitomize, exemplify

tyrannical *adj.* oppressive, despotic, arbitrary, domineering, unjust, cruel

tyro *n.* amateur, novice, apprentice, neophyte

ubiquity *n.* prevalence, pervasiveness, commonness, omnipresence, universality

ugly *adj.* homely, unsightly, displeasing, monstrous,

objectionable, nasty

ulcer *n.* abscess, infection, boil

ulterior *adj.* concealed, shrouded, obscured

ultimate *adj.* extreme, final, decisive, concluding, eventual, maximum, utmost, preeminent

ultimatum *n.* warning, mandate, demand, order

umpire *v.* mediate, arbitrate, judge, decide, settle

unaffected *adj.* **NATURAL:** simple, sincere, genuine, real, artless; **UNMOVED:** indifferent, unemotional, unresponsive, disinterested

unassuming *adj.* modest, unpretentious, humble, simple, plain, diffident

unauthorized *adj.* unsanctioned, prohibited, illicit, forbidden, banned

unbalanced *adj.* unstable, maladjusted, biased, untrustworthy, treacherous

unbearable *adj.* intolerable, insufferable, obnoxious

unbecoming *adj.* inappropriate, unsuitable, indecent, unseemly, rough, improper, unfit

unbend *v.* relax, rest, soften, ease, relent

unbiased *adj.* impartial, objective, neutral, unprejudiced, tolerant, disinterested

unbounded *adj.* **IMMENSE:** endless, vast, boundless; **UNCONFINED:** free, unbridled, unfettered

uncanny *adj.* strange, odd, weird, mysterious, eerie

unceasing *adj.* continual, incessant, chronic, perpetual, persistent

uncivilized *adj.* primitive, barbarous, crude, uncouth

unclean *adj.* dirty, grimy, soiled, squalid, foul, vile, impure, defiled, adulterated, profaned

uncommon *adj.* exceptional, extraordinary, unique, remarkable, rare, scarce

uncompromising *adj.* obstinate, inflexible, unyielding, immovable, steadfast,

unconditional *adj.* absolute, certain, unrestricted

unconscionable *adj.* unscrupulous, unprincipled, wicked, wanton, dishonest, unholy

unconscious *adj.* senseless, oblivious, benumbed

uncouth *adj.* rude, ill-mannered, vulgar, crass

uncover *v.* reveal, expose, disclose, unearth

undaunted *adj.* fearless, courageous, valiant, intrepid, audacious

underestimate *v.* misjudge, miscalculate, slight

undergo *v.* endure, tolerate, suffer, bear, abide

underhanded *adj.* sly, furtive, deceitful, dishonest, traitorous, unscrupulous

undermine *v.* weaken, erode, corrode, decay, threaten

underrate *v.* devaluate, lessen, downgrade, depreciate

underscore *v.* emphasize, accentuate, accent

understand *v.* comprehend, grasp, perceive, discern, interpret, hear, accept, conclude

understanding *adj.* sympathetic, accepting, tolerant

understanding *n.* comprehension, grasp, awareness

undervalue *v.* minimize, cheapen, misjudge, belittle, discredit, underrate

underwrite *v.* guarantee, support, endorse

undetermined *adj.* dubious, obscure, enigmatic, doubtful, unsettled

undo *v.* cancel, efface, erase, expunge, obliterate

undress *n.* disrobe, undrape, shed, peel

undulate *v.* wave, surge, heave, flap, pulsate, billow

unduly *adj.* excessively, inordinately, exceedingly

undying *adj.* eternal, permanent, everlasting, unending, unceasing, persistent

uneasy *adj.* restless, perplexed, troubled, apprehensive, fidgety, nervous, jittery, uncomfortable

unencumbered *adj.* free, unobstructed, unhampered, unhindered, unfettered

unequal *adj.* disparate, unlike, uneven, odd

unequaled *adj.* matchless, incomparable, unparalleled, distinct, peerless, dissimilar, special

unequivocal *adj.* definite, unmistakable, incontestable, evident, absolute, explicit, clear, plain

unerring *adj.* accurate, exact, precise, perfect, correct, definite, unfailing, infallible

uneven *adj.* jagged, coarse, rugged, lumpy, serrated, intermittent, spasmodic, irregular, rough

unfailing *adj.* certain, absolute, sure, reliable, surefire, dependable

unfair *adj.* unjust, prejudiced, discriminatory, biased, inequitable, despotic, wrongful, arbitrary

unfaltering *adj.* steadfast, resolute, untiring, unfailing, unflagging, tireless, persistent, firm, constant

unfasten *v.* uncouple, detach, free, separate, undo

unfathomable *adj.* incomprehensible, enigmatic, mysterious, inscrutable, profound, baffling, puzzling

unfeeling *adj.* callous, merciless, cold-hearted, unsympathetic, hard, brutal, cruel

unfeigned *adj.* genuine, real, natural, unaffected, truthful, candid, sincere

unflagging *adj.* tireless, unrelenting, persisting, assiduous, devoted, consistent

unfold *v.* evolve, reveal, show, unravel, unearth, resolve, open, extend, expand

unfortunate *adj.* unlucky, hapless, doomed, ill–fated, inept, cursed, condemned

unfounded *adj.* groundless, baseless, unsupported, unsound, idle, vain, erroneous, untrue

unfurl *v.* unfold, open, uncoil, extend, expand

ungainly *adj.* clumsy, awkward, ungraceful, lumbering, maladroit, inept, ponderous, bulky

ungovernable *adj.* uncontrollable, headstrong, unruly

unguarded *adj.* open, undefended, unprotected, imprudent, incautious

unguent *n.* ointment, salve, lotion, balm, dressing, poultice, dressing

uniform *adj.* regular, routine, normal, unwavering, invariable, consistent, steady

uniformity *n.* regularity, similarity, accord, steadiness, order, concord

unify *v.* combine, integrate, consolidate, compact, concentrate, arrange, blend, integrate, synthesize

unimpeachable *adj.* irrefutable, obvious, conclusive, unassailable, adequate, satisfactory

unintentional *adj.* involuntary, accidental, inadvertent, unplanned, unconscious

union *n.* coalition, merger, melding, alliance, confederacy, association, order, league, brotherhood, society, matrimony, juncture, connection

unique *adj.* singular, particular, peerless, unrivaled, unequaled, matchless, unusual, uncommon, odd, peculiar, rare

unison *n.* coincidence, agreement, concord

unit *n.* element, constituent, component, part, section, piece, member

unite *v.* combine, join, link, couple, connect, associate, incorporate, blend, consolidate, compound, fuse, weld, marry, join, couple

unity *n.* union, harmony, agreement, concert, unison, concord, rapport, congruity

universal *adj.* general, widespread, extensive, entire, whole, sweeping

universe *n.* creation, cosmos, world, totality

unjust *adj.* unfair, partial, prejudiced, biased, inequitable, shabby, undeserved, unjustified, unmerited

unkempt *adj.* disorderly, disheveled, messy, tousled, untidy, crude, vulgar

unkind *adj.* cruel, harsh, unfeeling, callous, coldhearted, hard, brutal, heartless

unlettered *adj.* untaught, ignorant, uneducated, illiterate, unenlightened, untutored

unlike *adj.* different, dissimilar, incompatible, mismatched, disparate, divergent, diverse

unlimited *adj.* boundless, infinite, immense, vast, extensive, endless, unconstrained, unrestricted, total, complete, totalitarian

unmanageable *adj.* difficult, unruly, ungovernable, uncooperative, stubborn, obstinate, balky, rebellious, uncontrollable, wild, irrepressible

unmoved *adj.* determined, decided, solid, unshaken, unaffected, collected, firm, steadfast, indifferent, resolute, unemotional

unnerve *v.* upset, unsettle, disarm, aggravate, fluster, discourage, disconcert

unparalleled *adj.* uncommon, rare, singular, unequaled, unrivaled, unique, peerless, matchless

unprecedented *adj.* unparalleled, unique, unequal, unusual, uncommon, untoward

unprepared *adj.* surprised, unaware, dumfounded, unguarded, careless, imprudent, unwary

unprincipled *adj.* amoral, corrupt, wanton, unscrupulous, unethical, dishonest

unqualified *adj.* incompetent, unable, inept, unskilled, untrained, unsatisfactory, unsuitable, incapable, unfit, ineligible,

unravel *v.* explain, elucidate, clarify, justify, resolve, interpret, solve, untangle, unwind, disengage

unremitting *n.* constant, ceaseless, endless, incessant, constant, perpetual, unending, continuous,

unrest *n.* agitation, disquiet, trouble, disturbance, bickering, confusion, crisis, quarrel, turbulence

unscathed *adj.* unharmed, safe, unimpaired, sound, uninjured

unseemly *adj.* indecent, improper, unbecoming, inappropriate, wrong, incorrect,

unsettle *v.* confuse, disturb, disrupt, perturb, bother, trouble, upset, fluster, ruffle, rattle

unsightly *adj.* unattractive, homely, plain, disagreeable, repulsive, hideous

unsophisticated *adj.* naive, provincial, callow, unrefined, simple, coarse, crude, harsh, vulgar, artless, guileless, ingenuous, pure, natural, genuine

unspeakable *adj.* unutterable, indescribable, astonishing, incredible, offensive, abusive, nasty, coarse, repulsive, odious, ineffable

untiring *adj.* inexhaustible, constant, powerful, resolute, strong, unflagging

unveil *v.* reveal, show, expose, divulge, announce

upbraid *v.* censure, scold, admonish, chide, reproach, reprove, berate, condemn,

upheaval *n.* eruption, earthquake, volcano, blowup, outbreak, explosion, outburst

uphold v. maintain, support, champion, sustain, endorse, sanction, bolster, help

uppermost adj. topmost, foremost, highest, predominant, supreme, loftiest

upright adj. upstanding, honest, good, outstanding, moral, ethical, principled, just, righteous, pure, true

uprising n. revolt, insurrection, rebellion, revolution, demonstration, skirmish

uproar n. clamor, commotion, disturbance, fracas, furor, hubbub, melee

uproarious adj. hilarious, funny, noisy, tumultuous, turbulent, frenzied, confused, disorderly

uproot v. remove, transport, liquidate, excavate, extirpate, eradicate, eliminate, dislodge

upset adj. irritated, worried, uneasy, shaky, troubled, unsettled, disturbed, aggravated, concerned, perturbed, disconcerted

upset v. capsize, overturn, topple, founder, upend, invert, flip

upshot n. outcome, consequence, conclusion, result

upstart n. opportunist, pretender, snob, phony, fraud, rogue, impostor

urban adj. city, metropolitan, municipal, civic

urbane adj. suave, poised, polished, refined, smooth, elegant, gracious, courteous

urchin n. waif, stray, foundling, orphan, ragamuffin, child, infant

urge n. drive, desire, impulse, craving, passion, push, influence, stimulus, impulse

urge v. drive, impel, press, spur, incite, goad, stimulate, implore, beg, beseech, entreat, persuade, induce, advise, advocate, recommend

urgent *adj.* pressing, compelling, demanding, driving, forcing, imperative, anxious, insistent, earnest

urgency *n.* seriousness, need, insistence, gravity, exigency, emergency, crisis, necessity

usable *adj.* useful, employable, applicable, functional

usage *n.* custom, practice, acceptance, habit, convention, fashion, form

use *n.* application, help, habit, custom, way

use *v.* employ, utilize, operated, apply, exploit

useful *adj.* beneficial, helpful, serviceable, effective, practical, functional, handy

usual *adj.* common, customary, ordinary, familiar

usurp *v.* capture, commandeer, appropriate, assume

usury *n.* greed, avarice, rapacity, loansharking

utensil *n.* instrument, device, implement, gadget

utility *n.* usefulness, value, advantage

utilize *v.* use, employ, exploit, operate

utmost *adj.* ultimate, maximum, maximal, entire, greatest, undiminished, unlimited

utopian *adj.* idealistic, ideological, visionary, perfect, ideal, fanciful, theoretical

utter *adj.* complete, entire, total, unconditional, unqualified, thorough

utter *v.* speak, articulate, vocalize, voice, say, remark, express, announce, proclaim, state,

utterance *n.* assertion, declaration, enunciation, proclamation, pronouncement

vacant *adj.* empty, uninhabited, abandoned, deserted, expressionless, vacuous, vapid

vacate *v.* leave, abandon, depart, quit

vacation *n.* holiday, furlough, respite, sabbatical

vaccinate *v.* immunize, inoculate, inject

vacillate *v.* waver, hesitate, fluctuate, alternate, sway

vacuum *n.* void, emptiness, vacuity, nothingness

vagary *n.* caprice, whim, urge, notion, impulse, fancy, quirk, eccentricity

vagrant *n.* beggar, tramp, hobo, idler, loafer, rascal

vague *adj.* obscure, indistinct, indefinite, imprecise, unspecified, uncertain, loose, unclear

vain *adj.* **FUTILE:** unavailing, fruitless, ineffective, inefficient, hollow; **CONCEITED:** egotistical, smug, arrogant, proud, narcissistic

valet *n.* manservant, attendant, butler, steward

valiant *adj.* valorous, brave, bold, courageous, intrepid, stouthearted, fearless, chivalrous

valid *adj.* logical, well–founded, sensible, sound, convincing, authoritative, legal, lawful

valley *n.* glen, dale, hollow, basin, lowland, vale

valor *n.* bravery, courage, boldness, spirit

valorous *adj.* brave, valiant, courageous, fearless

valuable *adj.* expensive, precious, rare, priceless, useful, beneficial, profitable, serviceable

value *n.* worth, importance, cost, price, significance

value *v.* appraise, assess, estimate, evaluate, rate, judge, weigh, consider, reckon

vandalism *n.* defacement, damage, mutilation, disfiguration, marring, spoiling

vanguard *n.* forefront, leaders, precursors, spearhead

vanish *v.* disappear, depart, evaporate, fade, dissolve

vanity *n.* conceit, pretension, self–esteem, pride, folly

vanquish *v.* conquer, overwhelm, overpower, defeat, quell, quash, subdue, suppress, subjugate, crush

vapid *adj.* dull, lifeless, insipid, uninteresting, tiresome, spiritless, vacuous, prosaic, mundane

vapor *n.* fog, haze, mist, gas, smog, condensation
vaporize *v.* evaporate, vanish, dissolve, disappear
variable *adj.* fluctuating, inconstant, wavering
variance *n.* difference, divergence, discrepancy, incongruity, disagreement, discord
variation *n.* alteration, modification, deviation, difference, discrepancy, diversity, dissimilarity, irregularity, inequality, aberration, departure
variety *n.* category, group, classification, division
various *adj.* miscellaneous, assorted, divers, diverse, diversified, varied, sundry
varnish *v.* embellish, disguise, mask, veil, falsify
vary *v.* change, alter, modify, diversify, deviate, differ, fluctuate, alternate
vast *adj.* boundless, large, limitless, unbounded, extensive, immense, widespread
vat *n.* container, keg, barrel, cask, tub
vault *n.* crypt, tomb, mausoleum, sepulcher
vault *v.* jump, hurdle, bound, leap, spring
vaunt *v.* boast, gloat, brag, strut, swagger, flaunt
veer *v.* swerve, deviate, diverge, curve, deflect, bend
vehement *adj.* fervent, energetic, impassioned
vehemence *n.* ardor, eagerness, energy, enthusiasm, passion, zeal, spirit, determination
vehicle *n.* conveyance, transportation, medium, means, agency, instrumentality
veil *v.* conceal, mask, cover, shroud, cloud, obscure
velocity *n.* speed, swiftness, dispatch, quickness
venal *adj.* corrupt, unscrupulous, treacherous, dishonorable, mercenary, corruptible
vend *v.* sell, merchandise, market, retail
veneer *n.* facing, cover, coating, surfacing, facade,

front, pretension, display

venerable *adj.* esteemed, revered, distinguished, honorable, ancient, respected

venerate *v.* admire, worship, revere, esteem, respect

vengeance *n.* revenge, retaliation, retribution

vengeful *adj.* vindictive, unforgiving, unrelenting, spiteful, rancorous, intractable, malicious

venial *adj.* excusable, justifiable, forgivable

venom *n.* bitterness, virulence, malice anger, contempt, spitefulness, malevolence, hate

vent *v.* express, air, assert, verbalize, articulate, expound, release, unleash, discharge

venture *n.* undertaking, enterprise, adventure, investment, speculation, endeavor attempt

venture *v.* chance, wager, risk, gamble, hazard, dare, plunge, imperil, jeopardize, endanger, hazard

veracious *adj.* truthful, accurate, precise, honest, sincere, trustworthy, righteous

veracity *n.* truth honesty, sincerity, accuracy, precision, exactness, correctness

verandah *n.* terrace, porch, deck, patio, courtyard

verbal *adj.* oral, spoken, stated

verbose *adj.* wordy, windy, loquacious, tedious, garrulous, talkative, chatty

verdant *adj.* green, flourishing, thriving, dense, lush

verdict *n.* decision, judgment, ruling, finding, adjudication, decree, determination, sentence

verge *n.* edge, brink, border, limit, margin, rim, brim

verify *v.* confirm, prove, authenticate, corroborate, substantiate, validate

verification *n.* evidence, proof, validation, documentation, support, confirmation

veritable *adj.* real, genuine, actual, positive, true, virtual, authentic

vernacular *adj.* native, indigenous, regional, informal, colloquial, everyday, ordinary, familiar

vernacular *n.* dialect, argot, jargon, idiom

versatile *adj.* flexible, pliable, adaptable, tractable, docile, pliant, yielding

versatility *n.* flexibility, pliancy, agility, compliance, adaptability, amenity, amiability

versed *adj.* experienced, seasoned, competent, adept, capable, skilled, practiced, trained

version *n.* rendition, interpretation, rendition

vertical *adj.* erect, upright, perpendicular, plumb

vestibule *n.* foyer, hallway, entry, lobby

vestige *n.* trace, indication, shred, fragment, remainder, hint, suggestion

veteran *adj.* experienced, seasoned, skilled, versed

veto *v.* reject, discard, eliminate, refuse, void, nullify, invalidate, forbid, dismiss

vex *v.* annoy, harass, irk, bother, disturb, irritate, plague, torment, agitate

viaduct *n.* bridge, overpass, trestle, scaffold, catwalk

vibrate *v.* shake, flutter, tremble, quiver, undulate, fluctuate, oscillate, reverberate

vicarious *adj.* substituted, delegated, sympathetic

vice *n.* wickedness, corruption, evil, depravity, immorality, depravity, iniquity, malignancy

vicinity *n* area, locality, neighborhood, environment, proximity, nearness

vicious *adj.* immoral, corrupt, base, degenerate, vile, depraved, reprehensible, wrong, malicious, malevolent, spiteful, malignant, unruly

victim *n.* casualty, dupe, gull, prey, sucker, fool

victor *n.* winner, champion, vanquisher, conqueror

victory *n.* triumph, conquest, success, achievement

victorious *adj.* triumphant, successful

vie *v.* compete, oppose, contend, clash, rival, strive

view *n.* scene, sight, spectacle, vision, glimpse, aspect, object, purpose, intention, description, notion, opinion, judgment, assessment

view *v.* observe, regard, behold, survey, witness, inspect, examine, study, scrutinize

vigil *n.* watchfulness, wakefulness, surveillance

vigilant *adj.* watchful, alert, observant, attentive, careful, wary

vigor *n.* strength power, potency, stamina, energy, endurance, vitality, soundness

vile *adj.* evil depraved, wretched, repulsive, contemptible, revolting, disgusting, offensive, vulgar

vilify *v.* malign, slander, slur, defame

village *n.* town, community, hamlet, municipality

villain *n.* miscreant, cad, rascal, rogue, scoundrel

vindicate *v.* exonerate, acquit, absolve, clear, defend, justify, support, uphold, corroborate, assert

vindictive *adj.* vengeful, unforgiving, spiteful

vintage *adj.* classic, choice, old, excellent

violate *v.* breach, infringe, transgress, trespass

violation *n.* transgression infringement, breach, defilement, debasement, assault, outrage

violent *adj.* intense, fierce, furious, rough, vicious, brutal, barbarous, savage, fierce

virgin *n.* pure, undefiled, unsullied, unadulterated, unmixed, fresh, unspoiled

virile *adj.* vibrant, strong, forceful, vigorous, robust

virtue *n.* integrity, justice, temperance, purity, decency, merit, distinction, excellence

virtuous *adj.* moral, ethical, honest, noble, right, pure, good, chaste

virulent *adj.* **LETHAL:** malignant, venomous, poisonous; **HATEFUL:** bitter, malicious, antagonistic

virus *n.* infection, disease, germ, microbe

visa *n.* endorsement, permit, authorization

visage *n.* countenance, appearance, aspect

viscous *adj.* sticky, thick, sticky, gummy

visible *adj.* discernible, perceptible, perceivable, obvious, apparent, clear, evident, conspicuous

visibility *n.* distinctness, perceptibility, prominence

vision *n.* **PERCEPTION:** sight, understanding, discernment, intuition; **CONCEPT:** image, imagination, view, **HALLUCINATION:** apparition, ghost, phantom

visit *n.* call, appointment, interview, talk, sojourn

visitor *n.* guest, caller, company

visor *n.* shield, sunshade, bill, peak

vista *n.* view, perspective, prospect, outlook

visual *adj.* visible, perceptible, obvious; ocular

vital *adj.* **ESSENTIAL:** necessary, important, critical, requisite; **VIGOROUS:** lively, energetic, active

vivacious *adj.* lively, animated, brisk, spirited, sprightly, energetic, spry

vivid *adj.* **BRIGHT:** shining, intense, lucid, lively, spirited, energetic, vivacious, realistic, picturesque, distinct, graphic, striking, clear, discernible

vocabulary *n.* lexicon, glossary, dictionary

vocal *adj.* **UTTERED:** spoken, oral, expressed, articulated, verbalized; **OUTSPOKEN:** open, honest, assertive, candid, blunt, frank

vocation *n.* occupation, profession, trade, business, pursuit, calling

vociferous *adj.* noisy, boisterous, uproarious, blatant

vogue *n.* fashion, style, custom, trend, fad, popularity, acceptance, rage

voice *n.* expression, utterance, assertion, declaration, preference, opinion, say, vote, view

void *adj.* useless, empty, barren, destitute, vacant, abandoned, unoccupied

void *n.* nothingness, emptiness, space, vacuum

volatile *adj.* explosive, unstable, fickle, erratic, frivolous, passing, transient, ephemeral

volition *n.* will, choosing, choice, preference, election, discretion, determination

voluble *adj.* talkative, loquacious, fluent, articulate, verbose, wordy, garrulous

volume *n.* EDITION: book, manuscript; MASS: size, magnitude, bulk; LOUDNESS: intensity, strength

voluntary *adj.* willing, disposed, inclined, prone, deliberate, intended, intentional, planned, willful

volunteer *v.* offer, extend, render, submit, proffer, tender, propose, suggest, recommend

voluptuous *adj.* sensual, indulgent, carnal, erotic, lustful, licentious

voracious *adj.* greedy, insatiable, ravenous, hungry, rapacious, grasping

vote *v.* elect, choose, enact, legislate, select, decide

vouch *v.* certify, attest, swear, state, assure

vow *n.* promise, pledge, covenant, contract

vow *v.* swear, promise, assure, attest, certify, affirm

voyage *n.* journey, excursion, trip, tour

vulgar *adj.* coarse tasteless, gross, crude, unrefined

vulgarity *n* obscenity, rudeness, indelicacy, coarseness, crassness, impropriety, immodesty

vulnerable *adj.* unprotected, unguarded, defenseless, exposed, susceptible, unsafe

waft *v.* float, hover, drift, skim flit flutter

wage *v.* conduct, undertake, pursue, execute

wages *n.* pay, compensation, stipend, remuneration

wager *v.* bet, stake, risk, gamble, speculate, hazard

waif *n.* stray, foundling, orphan, urchin, ragamuffin

wail *v.* lament, bemoan, sob, whine, mourn

wait *v.* abide, delay, linger, remain, tarry, stay

waive *v.* forgo, sacrifice, relinquish, renounce, resign, postpone, defer, shelve, table

wake *v.* arouse, rise, awaken, stir, rouse, call, prod, activate, provoke, stimulate, motivate, kindle

walk *n.* path, lane, passageway, promenade

wan *adj.* pallid, sickly, pale, pasty, ashen, blanched

wand *n.* baton, staff, stick, scepter

wander *v.* roam, drift, ramble, meander, rove, range, stroll, saunter, digress, stray, shift, veer

wane *v.* diminish, subside, abate, decline, weaken, dwindle, decrease, fade, sink, fail

want *n.* **NECESSITY:** requirement, demand, lack, deficiency, inadequacy, **POVERTY:** impoverishment, indigence, privation, need

want *v.* desire, crave, long, covet, wish, fancy

wanton *adj.* **MALICIOUS:** hateful, spiteful, reckless, willful, unruly; **LEWD:** lascivious, lustful, dissolute

ward *n.* **DEPENDENT:** child, minor, orphan; **DISTRICT:** territory, precinct, parish

warden *n.* guard, jailer, guardian, caretaker, custodian, watchman

wariness *n.* caution, alertness, vigilance

warm *adj.* gracious, amiable, pleasant, kind, intimate, amicable, sympathetic, close

warn *v.* caution, advise, admonish, counsel, forewarn, alert inform, apprise

warrant *n.* guarantee insurance, assurance, pledge, certificate, authorization commission, license, permit, order, writ

warrant *v.* certify, approve, authorize, sanction

wary *adj.* alert, attentive, wary, cautious, circumspect, vigilant, watchful

wash *v.* clean, cleanse, scrub, swab, lave, bathe

waste *adj.* superfluous, excess, useless, extra, unused

waste *n.* **DEVASTATION:** ruin, blight, destruction; **TRASH:** garbage, debris, refuse, rubbish; **SQUANDER:** consume, expend, misuse, dissipate

watch *v.* observe, view, see, regard, scrutinize, inspect, guard, patrol, protect

watchful *adj.* vigilant, alert, careful, mindful, attentive, observant, wary

water *v.* irrigate, sprinkle, douse, drench, wet, soak, flood, shower, rain

waterlogged *adj.* soaked, sodden, sopping, saturated

waver *v.* fluctuate, vacillate, hesitate

wax *v.* increase, grow, enlarge, expand, flourish

way *n.* method, style, custom, technique, system

waylay *v.* ambush, assail, lurk, trap

weak *adj.* delicate, dainty, feeble, puny, infirm, powerless, flimsy, slight, wobbly

wealth *n.* riches, affluence, assets, abundance

wear *n.* deterioration, erosion, fraying, fatigue

weary *adj.* tired, exhausted, drained, fatigued, spent

weary *v.* harass, annoy, bother, badger, pester, irk, vex, distress, harry, torment

weep *v.* cry, sob, whimper, bawl, moan, wail, lament

weigh *v.* consider, contemplate, ponder, study

weight *n.* **SIGNIFICANCE:** import, importance, gravity, consequence, influence; **MASS:** density, heft, heaviness, tonnage

weird *adj.* mysterious, eerie, spooky, uncanny, unnatural, ghostly, puzzling, arcane

welcome *adj.* appreciated, desirable, delightful

welcome *v.* greet, salute, hail, embrace

weld *v.* join, connect, bind, bond

well *adj.* healthy, strong, hardy, robust, fit, sound

wet *v.* soak, drench, saturate, douse, dampen

wheedle *v.* coax, wangle, entreat, appeal, beg, cajole

whereabouts *n.* location, position, situation, locale, place, spot, site

whet *v.* sharpen, hone, strop, file, grind, taper

whim *n.* impulse, inclination, urge, impulse, desire, craving, caprice, whimsy, notion, fancy, quirk

whimper *v.* cry, whine, sniffle, snivel, weep

whimsical *adj.* capricious, fanciful, playful, impulsive

whine *v.* cry, complain, grumble, snivel, whimper

whip *v.* beat, lash, flog, scourge, switch, punish

whirl *n.* revolve, rotate, spin, gyrate

whittle *v.* form, fashion, sculpt, carve, chisel, shape

whole *adj.* entire, unbroken, undivided, complete

wholesome *adj.* nourishing, healthy, nutritious, beneficial, advantageous, good

whoop *v.* holler, howl, shout, cheer, scream, yell

wicked *adj.* evil, depraved, immoral, nefarious

wide *adj.* extensive, comprehensive, universal

widen v. broaden, increase, expand, extend, spread, extend, enlarge, augment, stretch

width n. breadth, expanse, amplitude, scope

wield v. handle, utilize, operate, use, control, manage

wild adj. untamed, uncivilized, unrestrained

wile n. trickery, deception, deceit, artifice, ruse

will n. **COMMAND:** decree, order, bidding, **DECISION:** choice, determination, **DESIRE:** purpose, fancy, pleasure, wish

will v. **COMMAND:** order, decree, proclaim, direct; **BEQUEATH:** grant, give, leave

willful adj. **DELIBERATE:** intended, meant, voluntary, willed; **STUBBORN:** obstinate, headstrong, inflexible, adamant, resolute

wilt v. droop, wither, shrivel, decay, slump

wily adj. deceitful, artful, cunning, skillful, crafty, sly, treacherous, tricky

win v. **TRIUMPH:** prevail; **ACHIEVE:** secure, persuade, influence, convert

wince v. flinch, recoil, cringe, falter, twitch

wind v. curve, twist, swerve, snake, meander, curl, twist, twine, encircle

windfall n. blessing, godsend, boon, bonanza

winning adj. **ENGAGING:** captivating, charming, pleasant, likable, dazzling, winsome; **VICTORIOUS:** triumphant, conquering, successful

winnings n. accumulation, profits, gain

winnow v. sift, separate, sieve, extract, eliminate

winsome adj. winning, beautiful, charming, captivating, lovely, cute, engaging, comely, delightful

wisdom n. sagacity, understanding, discretion, insight, tact, diplomacy, intelligence, knowledge

315

wise *adj.* intelligent, scholarly, learned, educated, sagacious, rational, sensible, prudent, insightful, discerning, smart

wish *n.* desire, craving, inclination, ambition, aspiration, goal, promise

wish *v.* **CRAVE:** yearn, want, need; **DIRECT:** order, bid, instruct; **REQUEST:** beg, , entreat, solicit

wisp *n.* tuft, clump, shred, shock

wistful *adj.* melancholy, longing, yearning, sentimental, nostalgic, wishful, plaintive

wit *n.* intellect, reason, sagacity, sense, wisdom

witch *n.* sorceress, enchantress, hag, crone, hex

witchcraft *n.* sorcery, wizardry, divination, magic

withdraw *v.* retract, revoke, recant, abrogate

wither *v.* shrivel, wilt, shrink, atrophy, languish

withhold *v.* repress, restrain, check, retain

withstand *v.* oppose, defy, confront, resist, endure

witness *n.* spectator, bystander, onlooker, eyewitness

witness *v.* observe, see, watch, perceive, notice

witticism *n.* quip, jest, pun, gag, joke, wisecrack

witty *adj.* humorous, amusing, bright, keen, droll

wizard *n.* magician, conjurer, soothsayer, sorcerer

wizened *adj.* withered, shriveled, dry, dehydrated

woe *n.* sorrow, anguish, grief, misery, agony

woeful *adj.* mournful, sad, sorrowful, doleful

wonder *n.* amazement, astonishment, shock, awe

wonder *v.* **QUESTION:** ponder, doubt, speculate; **MARVEL:** gape, stare

wonderful *adj.* extraordinary, marvelous, astounding, awesome, remarkable, startling, excellent, superb

wondrous *adj.* amazing, astonishing, striking, astounding, extraordinary, miraculous

woo *v.* court, charm, pursue, cultivate, entice, entreat, petition, supplicate

word *n.* pledge, promise, guarantee, assurance

work *n.* labor, enterprise, undertaking, profession, business, occupation, achievement

work *v.* labor, toil, accomplish, perform, produce

world *n.* earth, globe, planet, realm, sphere, domain, kingdom, province, environment

worldly *adj.* sophisticated, urbane, suave

worry *n.* anxiety, apprehension, fear, disquiet, uneasiness, misgiving

worry *v.* **FRET:** care, fuss; **IRRITATE:** bother, disturb, harass, pester, plague, torment, trouble

worship *n.* adoration, devotion, reverence, veneration

worship *v.* esteem, revere, venerate, glorify, respect

worst *adj.* poorest, lowest

worth *n.* value, importance, quality, excellence

worthy *adj.* deserving, commendable, estimable, noble, excellent, exemplary

wound *v.* injure, harm, hurt, lacerate

wrangle *v.* dispute, bicker, quarrel, squabble

wrap *v.* enfold, envelop, swathe, bandage, swaddle

wrath *n.* anger, fury, ire, irritation, resentment

wreak *v.* perpetrate, do, perform, commit

wreath *n.* garland, bouquet, decoration

wreathe *v.* curl, entwine, encircle

wreck *v.* destroy, demolish, ruin, shatter, spoil, raze

wreckage *n.* remains, debris, wreck, flotsam

wrest *v.* extort, extract, exact, take

wretch *n.* miscreant, rogue, villain, rascal, brute

wretched *adj.* miserable, woeful, dejected, depressed, forlorn, unhappy, contemptible, pitiful, sorry, vile

wriggle *v.* wiggle, squirm, writhe, worm, twist
wrinkle *n.* fold, crease, pucker, furrow, ridge
writ *n.* law, decree, order, edict
write *v.* inscribe, scrawl, sign, compose, record
writing *n.* penmanship, hand, lettering, calligraphy
writhe *v.* squirm, contort, agonize, thrash, flail
wrong *adj.* immoral, evil, false, inaccurate, improper
wrong *v.* harm, abuse, oppress, maltreat, dishonor
wrongful *adj.* unlawful, criminal, illegal, illicit
yard *n.* tract, area, enclosure, patch, courtyard, lot, plot, square
yardstick *n.* measure, standard, scale, guide, gauge, model, norm
yarn *n.* tale, anecdote, alibi, fabrication
yearning *n.* longing, craving, desire, want, wish
yell *v.* cheer, root, shout, call, holler, scream
yellow *adj.* cowardly, timid, timorous, scared, craven
yen *n.* longing, yearning, desire, urge, craving
yield *v.* surrender, abdicate, cede, concede, resign, grant, acquiesce, give
yoke *n.* couple, harness, join, link, attach, connect
young *adj.* immature, juvenile, adolescent, youthful, inexperienced, green
youth *n.* immaturity, adolescence, minority
zany *adj.* crazy, funny, silly, nonsensical, wacky
zeal *n.* enthusiasm, fervor, passion, spirit, ardor
zealot *n.* fanatic, devotee, partisan
zealous *adj.* enthusiastic, eager, fervent, passionate, spirited, ardent, earnest
zenith *n.* top, peak, crest, elevation
zephyr *n.* breeze, draft, wind
zest *n.* relish, enthusiasm, gusto, enjoyment, delight